CHINA ASCENDANT

CHINA ASCENDANT

ITS RISE AND IMPLICATIONS

Edited by

Harsh V. Pant

HarperCollins *Publishers* India

ORF

First published in India by
HarperCollins *Publishers* in 2019
A-75, Sector 57, Noida, Uttar Pradesh 201301, India
www.harpercollins.co.in

2 4 6 8 10 9 7 5 3 1

P-ISBN: 978-93-5357-063-7
E-ISBN: 978-93-5357-064-4

Typeset in 11/14 Adobe Caslon Pro at
Manipal Digital Systems, Manipal

Printed and bound at
Thomson Press (India) Ltd.

MIX
Paper
FSC FSC® C010615

This book is produced from independently certified FSC® paper to ensure responsible forest management.

Contents

PART 3: CHINA AND THE WORLD

Introduction

The China Challenge

HARSH V. PANT

China's rise is debated extensively these days and its causes and consequences are dissected and analysed in great detail. For some, China is an emerging global superpower. For others, it has already arrived. But few can deny the impact that China is having on the international order. China is everywhere nowadays, simultaneously challenging and trying to be the guarantor of the global economic order in the age of Donald Trump.

With a population of 1.3 billion and prevailing as the world's second largest economy, China seems ready to play an even more influential role internationally. Since the global financial crisis of 2008, China's political leadership has been more vocal than ever about its key role in world affairs.

China faces a range of challenges: from its per capita income still being a fraction of that of the developed world to its rising inequality, to its environmental degradation and an ageing population. Most significantly, it has an archaic political system that wants to bring in economic development in a controlled manner and the very survival of that political system seems to be dependent on continuing economic growth.

The Xi Era

These challenges are not precluding Chinese political leadership from proclaiming an ambitious global agenda. Whereas previous Chinese leaders would prefer to talk of their nation as 'developing' or 'poor', President Xi Jinping is unabashed in declaring China a 'great power'.[1] Xi Jinping is now officially the most powerful Chinese leader since Mao Zedong, who died more than forty years ago, after the National People's Congress voted overwhelmingly in favour of a constitutional amendment (to remove a constitutional clause limiting presidential service to just two terms in office) – giving Xi the right to remain in office indefinitely. Not that there was any doubt about it, but when it finally happened it seemed to mark another red line in China's evolution as a pre-eminent global power of our times. This has been one of the most significant developments in global politics, given China's growing heft in the current global order.

Xi began his second term as head of the party and military in October 2016 at the end of a once-every-five-years' party congress. His real source of authority emanates from him being the Communist Party of China (CPC) general secretary – a post that has no term limit – as well as being the head of the powerful Central Military Commission (CMC). His political doctrine, 'Xi Jinping Thought on Socialism with Chinese Characteristics for a New Era', is now part of the amended constitution.[2] This takes China back to the good old days of Mao, when he was the supreme leader deciding the fate of millions based on his whims and fancies. Recognizing the dangers of one-man rule, Deng Xiaoping got the limit of two five-year presidential terms written into China's constitution in 1982, six years after Mao's death.

Xi's rise has challenged most of the assumptions about China. He wants to make China the pre-eminent global power and he is convinced of his own destined role in making that a reality. He has already removed most of his political opponents through an aggressive anti-corruption drive and has sought a fuller control of the military. For the rest of the world and India, a more aggressive China is now a given. Beijing under Xi has moved with greater confidence towards asserting its interests. He has pursued an ambitious foreign policy agenda – active militarization of islands in the South China Sea and the setting up of China's first overseas military base in Djibouti to his ambitious Belt and Road Initiative (BRI).

There have been some isolated critical voices in China, mostly on social media, who have compared their changing political system to that of North Korea or underlined the dangers of a Mao-type cult personality. But mostly there has been support for the move in the name of protecting the country's long-term stability. Some have argued that since Xi's anti-graft movement and his key BRI are still in their infancy, such a stratagem was necessary. But let there be no doubt that this is all about Xi's ambition.

In his marathon address to the nineteenth party congress in October 2017, Xi had unveiled his vision of China's future of achieving 'moderate' prosperity in the next four years, and emerging as an advanced socialist nation by 2050.[3] Underlining that China would pursue its own path of developing 'socialism with Chinese characteristics' and inviting 'peoples of all countries to join China's effort to build a common destiny for mankind and enduring peace and stability',[4] he was building a case for the 'Beijing Consensus' as an alternative to the so-called Washington Consensus. Xi's address was one of the most resounding of Chinese articulations about its growing weight in global politics and its intent of acquiring a central position therein, after years of keeping a low profile.

At a time when the US under the Trump administration is looking more and more inwards, Xi has tried to position China as a defender of the extant global order. In his address to the World Economic Forum in 2017, Xi delivered a strong defence of globalization, underlining Beijing's credentials to usurp America's traditional role as the champion of free trade and open markets. But it should have been clear to anyone who has observed China closely that its credentials as an exemplar of market economy remain very weak for a nation that has benefitted enormously from the American-led international economic system. China's history of currency manipulation, closed capital markets, and subtle non-tariff barriers leading to trade imbalances weaken it as an economic leader.

Nevertheless, the world was willing to buy this with a certain degree of credulity because of the attractiveness of a rising power. It wanted to believe in China's rhetoric because it was very reassuring, leaving all the difficult questions for another day. It wanted to believe that as long as China is rising it needs the rest of the world, and therefore it would like to preserve the extant order.

India's China Conundrum

Indian policymakers have also been part of this vacuous thinking for the past two decades. They got carried away by the propaganda that often managed to put China and India in the same league, assuming that being peers would somehow preclude any overt hostility. They also got carried away when their Chinese interlocutors assured them of their benign intentions and how there was enough space for both China and India to rise. Then came the biggest charade of all – BRICS, an association of five major emerging national economies: Brazil, Russia, India, China, South Africa. From an investment banker's catchy acronym phrase for his clients, it was converted into a geopolitical grouping. New Delhi entered it with its eyes closed, only to be bamboozled by the Chinese attempt to convert the grouping into an extension of its own economic superiority.

Chinese power has grown over the last two decades. Concomitantly, its interests have continued to expand. As it ventured into South Asia and the larger Indian Ocean region, India looked on without any sense of purpose. Reassured by our Sinologists that the Chinese have no expansionist designs, we continued to neglect our military and logistical preparedness, not even bothering about our border infrastructure. After all, if the Chinese don't intend to encroach into our terrain, what would be the point in building up our defences?

As China continued to move towards the Indian doorstep, Indian policymakers were only focused on assuaging Chinese sensitivities. We would not meet the Dalai Lama publicly for fear of offending Beijing. We would not have joint exercises with like-minded countries in the region lest China think ill of us. We would not sign foundational agreements with the US as this would make us America's followers – never mind if that hampers our ability to track Chinese submarines in the Indian Ocean. And, of course, we would keep talking of non-alignment because that's the best way to guarantee our interests in a world shaped by Chinese power.

However, China's increasing assertiveness has been a function of its power and emphasis on its own interests. It has very little to do with India's behaviour. We have misunderstood China in the past and there is a danger that we will continue to misunderstand China in the future if we don't comprehend the underpinnings of Chinese behaviour today.

Power, by its very nature, is expansionist. China's growing economic and diplomatic footprint around the world is now being followed by its military footprint. That's the reality of great power politics. Understanding that is not being belligerent but preparing oneself adequately. This was the lesson from the Doklam crisis in 2017.

The Doklam Lesson

On 28 August 2017, disengagement started at the Doklam plateau on the Sikkim border where Indian and Chinese forces have been at a standoff since June 2017. According to a statement issued by the Ministry of External Affairs (MEA), 'expeditious disengagement of border personnel at the face-off site at Doklam has been agreed to and is on-going'.[5] The Chinese foreign ministry, for its part, suggested that 'Indian forces have already withdrawn to the Indian side of the border' and that 'Chinese forces will continue to patrol in Doklam region'. It has also said that its forces 'will remain in the region' and continue to exercise their 'sovereignty over the region'.[6] The fact that

China was trying to put a spin on the issue to suggest the outcome was border patrolling by them was never really an issue.

The standoff had begun immediately after the Chinese troops began constructing a concrete road in Doklam inside Bhutanese territory. The Indian troops promptly halted the construction work, forming a human chain, calling it a change in 'status quo' with serious security implications for India – as the Doklam plateau overlooks the strategic Chumbi Valley.

For more than two months, Beijing continued to harangue and wage its psychological warfare, sometimes by reminding India of 1962 and sometimes by suggesting that countermeasures from Beijing would be unavoidable if the Narendra Modi-led Indian government continues to ignore Chinese warnings. China also provoked India by asking what New Delhi would do if it 'enters' the Kalapani region in Uttarakhand or Kashmir. This was the first time that the issue of Kashmir was raked up by China at the official level.

Indian diplomacy, by contrast, was mature and the government did not lose its nerve. Sushma Swaraj, the minister of external affairs, asserted in Parliament that war was not a solution and that India would resolve the border standoff with China through dialogue. But she also made it clear that India's reasonableness should not be mistaken for weakness. 'Just because we want to have friendly relations with our neighbours, they shouldn't cross the line. India always wanted smooth relations with China. But the alignment of boundaries involving India, China and Bhutan has to always be finalised in consultation with all three countries,'[7] Swaraj said, underscoring New Delhi's resolve not to be cowed down by Beijing's relentless high-pitched campaign.

This crisis between China and India was different from other such episodes in the past but what made it unique in recent memory was New Delhi's determination not to concede the standoff on China's terms. Beijing tried everything: it used its media to bully India; it threatened India officially; it used colonial era records selectively; it tried to rally global public opinion; it even tried to childishly ridicule

India, with its media using racist videos. Beijing also tried to corner India in other parts of the border with Chinese troops entering the Indian border near Pangong lake in Ladakh on 15 August 2017 and pelting stones at Indian soldiers. But India did not budge.

And that, in essence, foreshadows the future of the global order. Underlying all this petulance about boundaries and territories, behind all this façade of sovereignty, the Sino–India standoff in Doklam has been about whether the future of Asia will be one where China will be the dominant actor and dictate the terms of behaviour to other nations or whether the future of Asia will be a multipolar one in the real sense of the term. India decided to stand its ground because there was far too much at stake if it did not respond to Chinese bullying.

China talks of a multipolar world order but, in reality, it wants a unipolar Asia. Its assertiveness in staking maritime territorial claims in recent years might have convinced it that there is no real opposition in this region and beyond. The West is too preoccupied with its own internal challenges to pose any serious problems in China's way and the regional states are too weak to do anything about Chinese belligerence. The Association of Southeast Asian Nations (ASEAN) has turned out to be a paper tiger when it came to the crunch. China's divide-and-rule policy has fractured any sense of unity in Southeast Asia. A rather weak and ineffective negotiating framework for a code of conduct in the South China Sea has been adopted by the ASEAN under Chinese pressure, reflecting the challenges being faced by the Indo-Pacific nations at a time when the US remains distracted and lacks a clear Asia policy under Donald Trump.

Thus, India remains the last nation standing, a stumbling block in China's drive for domination of the Indo-Pacific. Already, the ambitious BRI has made China central to the evolving global economic structure. Even when nations realize the folly of their joining this mega connectivity initiative, they see no real alternative. New Delhi is the sole major power that has decided to publicly oppose Xi Jinping's vanity project. The other major power centres remain constrained in their policy responses to China. Japan has domestic, political and legal constraints despite Prime Minister Shinzo Abe's proactive foreign policy. Australia's economic future is so deeply intertwined with China's that its elites are today having to debate the choice between the US and China.

The Narendra Modi government, in contrast, has been robust in its response to China's rise. When it came into power, it quickly realized that China remains determined to pursue a unilateral foreign policy and Indian interests will suffer if India does not make a change in its foreign policy behaviour. While a section of Indian elites continues to believe that India can shape Chinese behaviour by its policies, policymakers have been confronting the consequences of China's growing capabilities in multiple ways. Although a tad late, New Delhi has been focusing on building its border infrastructure while trying to reach out to other like-minded powers such as Japan, Australia, Indonesia and Vietnam to shape a favourable balance of power in the region.

Ahead of the BRICS Summit in China and the nineteenth congress of the CPC, the standoff with India could have been really damaging for the Chinese president, who stood to lose the most if a quick resolution to the crisis was not found. But the Doklam episode marks an inflection point in India's relations with China. India seems to have recognized that standing up to China to protect its core interests is its only available option. Otherwise, it will have to acquiesce in shaping a China-centric Indo-Pacific – and for most Indians that option is clearly not even worth considering. Despite the informal Wuhan Summit between the Indian prime minister and the Chinese president in May 2018, the structural factors shaping the Sino–Indian divergence remain far too powerful in the trajectory of this bilateral relationship.

Understanding China

Despite China being the most important factor in shaping our foreign policy imperatives, our understanding of the country remains sketchy at best. At Observer Research Foundation (ORF), we have devoted considerable attention to the implications of China's rise for India in various domains, from foreign and security policies to economic, social and environmental policies. Based on the research conducted by ORF researchers over the last few years, this collection of essays, written from early 2017 to the end of 2018, is intended to generate a healthy debate in India on China's rise and its consequences for India. Only if we understand China better can we have a foreign policy discourse in India which does justice to the nation's rising global aspirations. We present these essays hoping to engender a more fruitful and productive conversation not only about China but also about evolving Indian foreign policy priorities.

PART 1

China's Strategic Posture

1

In Search of China's Grand Strategy

ABHIJNAN REJ

No other country in recent history has so systematically pursued its national objectives as China. Its single-minded pursuit of grand strategic objectives invokes respect even among analysts not usually predisposed to optimism about China's strategic intent. In particular, Deng Xiaoping's public call in 1984 to quadruple Chinese gross domestic product (GDP) by the end of the twentieth century – and meeting the target ahead of time – is often taken to be a leading exhibit of the single-minded devotion of national resources to meet Chinese core objectives.[1] Similarly, today when Xi Jinping talks about his vision of China's 'Two Centenaries' – 1921–2021, the centenary of the establishment of the Communist Party of China, and 1949–2049, the centenary of the creation of the People's Republic of China – analysts read Chinese resoluteness.

But grand strategy is more than just setting national goals and meeting them by deploying adequate resources. It is, as diplomatic historian Hal Brands states in the book *What Good Is Grand Strategy?*, an act of matching power and purpose. Grand strategy is, Brands writes, 'the intellectual architecture that gives form and structure to foreign policy'.[2] It is in this sense that detailed analyses of China's grand strategy by Chinese authorities in English (as opposed to Western experts) are hard to come by. Two works stand out in being exceptions to this rule. The first one is a 2003 book by Peking University professor Ye Zicheng, translated to English in 2011. The second is a 2011 article by another professor from the same university, Wang Jisi. Both works are remarkably candid about China's vision of its role in the world.

Ye Zicheng describes China's core grand-strategic goal as becoming a 'world power' through 'peaceful development'.[3] Economic development will be, for Ye, what makes China a world power. On the face of it, this is innocuous enough. After all, almost every emerging state would aspire to be a world power, preferably through non-conflicting means of strengthening its economy. But the interesting thing about Ye's characterization is that, in his schema, there are two other kinds of powers: a 'global superpower' and a 'super power'. An international system with a 'global superpower' would be, by definition, unipolar; a world of 'super powers' multipolar. Ye therefore makes China's preference for a multipolar world of 'world powers' known. He writes (of the Russia–China relationship): 'The rise of only China or only Russia would not lead to a stable *multipolar* world [emphasis mine].'[4] Indeed for Ye, the mutual quest for multipolarity is what results in both Russia and China pursuing cooperation over competition. Ye also states that China and India need to manage their differences to establish a 'multipolar world'.[5]

Ye points to a pervasive theme in the writings of other Chinese experts – within the People's Liberation Army (PLA) and elsewhere – that 'China pursue a national defence policy that calls for the construction of national defence to serve overall economic development'.[6] This is consistent with the Chinese pursuit of dual-use technology and the possibility of military Keynesianism adopted to Chinese needs.[7] But there is another subtle point in Ye's argument. If China were to arm itself to the point that the hegemon is worried, that may imperil China's sustained economic growth through the possibility of war – a security dilemma. By emphasizing economic development priorities over national defence ones, China is willing to seek 'relative' as opposed to 'absolute' security, Ye contends.[8]

But Ye is no dove, seeking the cause of world peace alone. The most striking parts of his book are his descriptions of the vulnerabilities of the United States even in the face of 'their overwhelming power [that] enables them to pursue and achieve absolute security'.[9] Ye reminds the readers of the story of David and Goliath and notes: 'The United States is so strong that none of its enemies will confront it directly. Rather, *they will adopt asymmetrical methods to oppose it* [emphasis mine].' In a way that should give pause to American policymakers, Ye lists, 'nuclear power plants, electronic communications centres, and hydroelectric power plants', as additional examples of American vulnerabilities.[10] In fact, in 1999, two PLA colonels had written a book on what they termed 'unrestricted warfare' – a menu of asymmetric means, including terrorist attacks, to defeat the United States in the event of a conflict.[11]

The David-versus-Goliath story also finds a re-expression in the works of another PLA colonel and National Defence University scholar, Liu Mingfu, who wrote a book called *The China Dream* in 2009. Liu described the competition between the US and China as a marathon of endurance – sustained by dollops of cunning – in contrast to a duel or boxing match between equals.[12] And Liu is not on the fringe. For example, many analysts (most notably, former American intelligence official, Michael Pillsbury) have speculated that when Xi Jinping talks about the 'Chinese Dream',[13] he is taking a cue from Liu. But the crucial difference between Liu and Ye is that Liu's grand strategic goal is China emerging as a worldwide hegemon by 2049 (the end of the 'Hundred-Year Marathon') after deposing the United States from that position. Ye, on the other hand, wants a multipolar world that keeps American power and unilateralism in check in tandem with other powers.

Peking University professor Wang Jisi's 2011 *Foreign Affairs* article is on every reading list about China's grand strategy.[14] It is also striking in the lengths it goes to, to suggest 'it is almost impossible to devise a straightforward organising principle for Chinese foreign policy' – a grand strategy for China, in other words. But the fact that economic growth will remain the key objective of Chinese strategy is clear from Wang's remarks. He notes the 2006 Communist Party of China Central Committee announcement that China's foreign policy 'must maintain economic construction as its centrepiece, be closely integrated into domestic work, and be advanced by coordinating domestic and international situations'.[15] More broadly, Wang notes three core interests of the People's Republic according to a former state councillor for external relations: political stability, in that the Communist Party leadership is perpetuated; 'sovereign security, territorial integrity and national unification' (that is maintaining China's territorial integrity as well as its long-standing policy to eventually reunite Taiwan with mainland China); and economic development and growth that can be sustained over the long run.[16] Wang does note that these 'three prongs, which are sometimes in tension',[17] are the reasons why China may be forced to *not* have a coherent grand strategy.

Without calling it as such, Wang is alluding to China's persistent grand-strategic trilemma. If China were to choose economic growth and sovereign security, it would have to crack down on dissidents that could – unintentionally, perhaps – imperil the latter, much like the 1989 Tiananmen Square episode. That, in turn, could ultimately lead to the collapse of the Communist Party rule. If China were to choose political stability and assert its strong sovereignty posture (including more assertive claims toward Taiwan, for example), it could possibly lose access to Western capital and technology needed for its sustained economic growth. Finally, if China were to choose continued Communist Party rule as well as sustained economic growth, it would have to keep its larger geostrategic goals – including reunification with Taiwan – in check because that could imperil both.

Until now it is evident that China's grand strategic priorities are tilted towards the continued economic growth of China under the Communist Party's watch – and thus keeping its geopolitical ambitions (such as favourable resolutions of its border disputes) in rein. But recent Chinese assertiveness suggests that China's grand strategic trilemma may be a chimera after all. In any case, by the time the second of Xi's 'Two Centenaries' – the hundredth anniversary of communist China – rolls around, Chinese economic, military, and diplomatic might, put together, may lead to a situation where this trilemma no longer applies.

2

China's Military Modernization and Its Implications

MANOJ JOSHI

China's current phase of military modernization began in the 1990s. But from 1990, when the People's Liberation Army (PLA) was overwhelmingly equipped with reverse engineered Soviet-era weapons, until the beginning of this decade (2010–20) the focus was on enhancing the quality of the PLA's weapons and systems. We are now witnessing the latest phase, as of 2015, with China launching a comprehensive reform of its military organization.

The goal is to provide China with the ability to fight high-intensity, short duration 'informationized' regional wars with an emphasis on 'maritime military struggle', which means the ability to fight 'in a complex electromagnetic environment' at greater distances from the mainland than the PLA had planned for in the past. At the same time, the Chinese are looking to reduce third-party – most prominently the United States' – ability to intervene against China in regional crises, which means developing anti-access/area denial (A2/AD) capabilities, as well as capabilities for cyber- and space-based operations.[1]

The goals of the organization are domestic-political, as well as external and military. So, at one level, the reform has led to a tightening of the role of the Communist Party of China (CPC) and its chairman over the military high command, the Central Military Commission (CMC). From the military point of view, they seek to enhance: a) the ability to conduct joint operations, b) to be able to do so in what the Chinese call 'informationized' conditions and c) to do so far away from its mainland. All three objectives segue into the China Dream of a strong military 'with Chinese characteristics' that will give it a great power status by 2049, which can provide China diplomatic payoff, enhance its regional pre-eminence and protect its interests across the globe.

The focus of the Chinese military remains a possible conflict over the Taiwan Strait and newer contingencies in the South China Sea and the seas of Japan and Korea. China is seeking to create a buffer zone of friendly states along land borders in Central Asia, aimed at shoring up its rule in Xinjiang even while pushing to control the waters up to the first island chain. As China's global footprint grows with its growing economic interests, China is also creating a global infrastructure to support these interests with bases in Djibouti and Gwadar and port call rights in Sri Lanka and Maldives.

Hardware

Nuclear: The principal goal of China's modernization efforts in the nuclear field is to achieve assured second-strike capability against the US. In 2016, the PLA Second Artillery Force was renamed as the PLA Rocket Force and upgraded to a full service. Until the 1980s, it dealt with only nuclear missiles but since the mid-1990s it also got conventional missiles. The force is directly under the CMC and is around 1,30,000 strong, the equivalent of PLA Group Armies, operating from six main missile bases. The Chinese nuclear arsenal was estimated at 260 weapons in 2015 by the Stockholm International Peace Research Institute (SIPRI),[2] double of what it was in 2006;

clearly, it is a growing arsenal. The People's Liberation Army Rocket Forces (PLARF) has continued to deploy the TEL-based Dong Feng (DF)-31, the DF-31A and the DF-5B&C MIRV (Multiple Independently Targetable Re-entry Vehicles) nuclear-tipped missiles and to develop the DF-41.

The Science of Military Strategy 2015[3] suggests that the conventional and nuclear interface in the PLARF is a deliberate strategy. China also fields a variety of conventional Intermediate Range Ballistic Missiles (IRBMs) and Land Attack Cruise Missiles (LACMs). The DF-26 or the 'Guam Killer' is both a conventional and nuclear capable ballistic missile, while the DF-21D is an anti-ship ballistic missile. China deploys four or five Jin (094) class SSBN submarines and is set to deploy JL-2 missiles on them to get assured second strike capability. In the future, China aims to field an advanced (096) SSBN and one capable of launching cruise missiles.

The People's Liberation Army Navy (PLAN) has evolved from coastal or in-shore defence which focused on preventing infiltration from sea and supporting land engagements in the 1950s and 1960s. In the 1980s, China began to look at the defence of its crucial offshore waters of the Yellow Sea, East China Sea and the South China Sea in terms of Lines of Communications (LoC) defence, possible Taiwan contingency, as well as preventing an invasion and protecting maritime rights and interests.[4]

In this millennium, the shift has moved from offshore defence to open waters protection. This means strengthening offshore defence, even while having the ability to protect Chinese Sea Lines of Communication (SLOCs).[5] China's goal is to be the premier navy within the first island chain in the short term and to develop similar capabilities for the Indian Ocean in, say, twenty years from now.

The goals of Chinese naval modernization can be discerned from its various, increasingly sophisticated, naval exercises. These feature action beyond the second island chain and island recapture exercises focused on the South China Sea. There has been a sharp accretion in the strength of the PLAN with the acquisition of the Luhu (052), Luhai (051B), Sovremenny, Luyang (052) and Luzhou

(051C) class destroyers, Jiangwei (053) and Jiangkai (054) class frigates, the Song, Yuan and Kilo class subs, the Jin and Shang nuclear-powered attack subs, Liaoning and a hundred fourth-generation fighters which include J-10, J-11, Su 30s and thirty H-6 bombers with air to ship missiles.[6] China commissioned eighteen ships in 2016, and in January 2017 it commissioned an electronic reconnaissance vessel.

The modernization of the PLA Air Force (PLAAF) has been encouraged by Revolution in Military Affairs (RMA) issues as well as the balance of power with Taiwan and greater PLA presence in the sea. The first Gulf War brought out the value of long-range precision strikes using integrated intelligence, surveillance and a reconnaissance network.

The PLAAF emphasizes integrated aerospace operations with simultaneous offensive and defensive operations. This means an air force marrying the information technology (IT) component of China's space satellite system with the PLAAF and developing command and control systems for integrated aerospace operations for an air offensive campaign, air and missile defence and strategic force projection.[7]

Currently, the PLAAF is developing the J-10B follow-up on to its indigenous fourth-generation fighter and acquiring 24 Su-35 fighter planes with advanced radar. By the end of the decade we may see the first Chinese fifth-generation fighters like the J-20 entering service. In 2015, it tested the fifth and sixth prototypes of the fighter. In addition, China is modernizing its bomber fleet by upgrading the H-6K bomber to be able to carry six LACMs each.

Organizational Modernization of the PLA

The CPC's third plenum called for optimizing the size and structure of the army, adjusting the inter-service balance and reducing non-combat institutions and personnel. At present the personnel distribution is the following – PLA Artillery (PLAA) has 73 per cent, PLAAF has 17 per cent and PLAN has 10 per cent. Also announced at the plenum was a 'joint operation command authority under the CMC and a theatre joint operation command system'.

In September 2015, Xi called for a reduction of 3,00,000 personnel to bring the force down to two million.[8] In the ensuing months China announced a series of major changes in the way the PLA would be organized and led. In November 2015, Xi declared that the current Military Area Commands (MACs) would be regrouped into new battle zone commands, supervised by the CMC. A three-tier system would be created, and a separate administrative chain of command would link the four service headquarters to units. These would be responsible for organization, manning and equipping units. All of this was expected to take place in the following five years.

In January 2016, the four General Departments that had hitherto led the PLA – the General Staff, the General Political Department, the General Logistics Department and the General Armament Department – were replaced by fifteen functional units. The powerful General Staff Department has been replaced by a Joint Staff Department, but has lost oversight over training and education, mobilization, strategic planning and possibly cyberwar and electronic warfare (EW) units.[9]

In this way, Xi has flattened the higher command structure and enhanced the authority of the CMC. The new system is called the 'CMC Chairman responsibility system', which has developed two clear lines of authority under the CMC – the various services manage their respective forces, while the theatre commands fight the wars. Both report to the CMC and in that sense, the Communist Party. The organizational reforms that began in 2015 are scheduled to be fully operationalized by 2020 – in time to be presented as an achievement of the first centenary of the founding of the CPC, in 2021.

China is reforming its military at a rapid pace and its firepower is growing faster than many had anticipated even a few years ago. The implications of these changes for China's rise as a credible global military force, however, remains far from clear now.

3

Can India Counter Emerging Chinese Capabilities like Stealth Aircraft?

PUSHAN DAS

As the Chinese People's Liberation Army (PLA) continues to undertake significant organizational and modernization reforms to build a military that is 'built to fight' in line with President Xi Jinping's ambitions, the PLA Air Force (PLAAF) is beginning to make a transformative shift in its war-fighting capabilities with the commissioning of its first fifth-generation fighter aircraft – the Chengdu J-20A.

The induction of the J-20A will present a greater and fundamentally different threat for militaries in the Asia Pacific compared to the Russian Su-30/35 Flanker family derivatives that currently form the mainstay of Chinese air power.[1] The J-20A represents a fast-emerging capability to launch low-observable strikes within Indian airspace by China. And for an Indian Air Force (IAF) struggling to achieve requisite combat numbers on any given day, the latest developments in Chinese airpower require imaginative and cost-effective counter-capabilities, given the limitations of the defence budget.

Stealth technology is a core component in the transformation of the PLAAF from a predominantly territorial air force to one capable of conducting both offensive and defensive operations.[2] The twin-engine J-20A, built by Chengdu Aerospace Corporation, is a single-seat stealth fighter designed for long-range fighter missions which can pose a significant threat to forward bases in the opening phase of any conflict due to its radar evading properties, long range and ability to carry significant amounts of munitions.

The J-20 contains three weapons bays for air-to-air missiles and a variety of air-to-ground missiles and surface attack weapons. It also features an active electronically scanned array (AESA) radar, nose-mounted infrared search and tracking sensors, and fuselage-mounted cameras to give its pilot 360-degree imaging. These capabilities are set to grow as the platform matures in the coming years, saddling China's rival air forces with a formidable challenge.

Additionally, recent Chinese organizational military reforms also give the PLAAF an edge over the IAF. One rather simple reform undertaken by the PLA at the 2015 Central Military Commission Reform Work Conference was to reduce the number of theatre command air forces in line with the establishment of five theatre commands overall for the PLA.[3] Due to this reorganization, the PLA would control all operations, including air operations, through the newly-created Western Theatre Command in the event of hostilities with India over the land boundary.[4]

The IAF's current fleet of ageing combat aircraft, including the numerically dominant fleet of Sukhoi-30 MKI, has few answers to an aircraft like the J-20A. Stealth aircraft will always have the capability to detect the Su-30 MKI from very long ranges, and can take positions to either avoid it or engage under the best possible attack parameters.

The IAF will soon have to contend with the task of defending Indian airspace from any potential Chinese aerial challenges or intrusions, given the proliferation of stealth aircraft in the region.

Currently, the IAF is on course to fall seriously short in both the quality and the quantity of its fighter force to pose a counter with its approved procurement plans till 2032, by when it hopes to achieve its elusive strength of 42 fighter squadrons, which it considers the benchmark to effectively take on China and Pakistan.[5]

The IAF needs to adopt a more flexible approach to countering emerging Chinese capabilities like stealth combat in air. One solution could be to pursue the acquisition of modern Airborne Warning and Control System (AWACS) aircraft, which can improve the situational awareness of the IAF and help better utilize its limited fourth generation combat aircraft with an idea of where to look for low-observable aircraft. Second, developing a modern and potent ground-based integrated air defence system (IADS) with long-wavelength frequency, agile ground radars focused on counter-stealth capabilities for defence against China, paired with a smaller number of fourth and 4.5th generation multirole fighters to provide flexible air defence. This combination, far more than any aircraft which the IAF has in its procurement or development pipeline at present, is more likely to be a serious threat to any low-observable, would-be intruders into Indian airspace.[6] The acquisition of long-range S-400 air defence systems from Russia in adequate quantities could prove the first step for the second option.

While analysts have pointed out that it is comparatively simple to develop flying prototypes that look like fifth-generation fighters, a case in point being the J-20A or the Russian Sukhoi T-50 – which India plans to acquire at some point in the future – it is exceedingly difficult to produce an aircraft that performs like a fifth-generation fighter, both in low-observability and sensor fusion-enabled situational awareness, in large enough quantities.

While Western fifth-generation aircraft may still have significant advantages in low-observable technologies or situational awareness capabilities, once the Chinese J-20A enters the PLAAF in significant numbers in the coming years, it will represent a transformative capability jump in any conflict over less capable militaries in Asia, including India.[7]

4

Sea Drones: Implications of the Great Underwater Wall of China

SYLVIA MISHRA

On 15 December 2016, the People's Liberation Army Navy (PLAN) seized a United States Navy Unmanned Underwater Vehicle (UUV) in international waters, 50 to 100 nautical miles off Port of Subic Bay in the Philippines, turning the international code of conduct between navies at sea on its head.[1] Although the Chinese Navy returned the US UUV, which it had unlawfully captured, the incident displayed yet another example of China's attempt to reassert its power and willingness to intercept naval assets and challenge US maritime operations.[2] More importantly, the incident underscored the growing strategic and tactical significance of UUVs, the use of such vehicles in contested waters and lack of a globally accepted code of conduct to govern the use of underwater drones. This article argues that Indian security planners must pay attention to China's efforts at ramping up disruptive technologies like UUVs, which has both civilian and military applications.[3] As Beijing moves towards active deployment of underwater drones for forward operations, there will be implications for regional stability in the Indo-Pacific. India along with its strategic partners – the United States, Japan, Australia and Vietnam – should strengthen maritime security, focus on anti-submarine warfare (ASW) and urgently work towards developing a global code of conduct for using underwater drones.

China's Drones and UUVs Ecosystem

In the last two decades, rapid advancements in drone technologies, especially the development of swarming platforms, whereupon large numbers of drones coordinate together in formation, has been considered transformative to the future of warfare. More substantive technological advancements have taken place in unmanned aerial vehicle (UAVs) technologies and China has emerged as a key military drone exporter, selling drones with capabilities of carrying bigger weapons payload as noted by a Stockholm International Peace Research Institute (SIPRI) report.[4] On the other hand, underwater drones are also emerging as a key area of emphasis for China. Steady improvements in UUVs' technologies and advancements in robotics, including communications and navigation, have enhanced UUVs' ability to guide themselves on their missions – at further distances and in harsher environments.[5] Advancements in UUVs present far-reaching consequences affecting strategic stability through their capacity to detect and track submarines. This ability of UUVs to detect and hunt submarines, thereby rendering oceans transparent, potentially changes the ways of warfare. This is precisely why Beijing has been investing in a burgeoning underwater drones industry that enjoys considerable national-level funding and support.[6] A Rand Report from 2016 highlighted that Beijing is currently funding fifteen different university research programmes for UUV projects.[7] At the Shenyang Institute of Automation in the Chinese Academy of Sciences in Liaoning province, Chinese researchers have developed an underwater glider, Sea Wing, and have conducted several successful missions in the Western Pacific.[8] After China developed the autonomous Haiyan/Petrel, the Chinese state media said that while their country is presently using UUVs for scientific research, these UUVs would potentially undergo upgradations for underwater combat, patrol, minesweeping and submarine detection operations.[9] These developments indicate that in the near future, Beijing will continue to make advancements in UUV technologies and it is likely that the PLAN will utilize UUVs for military purposes.

It is reported that the Shenyang Institute's Qianlong III will be tasked with a variety of combat ready missions, like identifying enemy submarines, mines, and other UUVs. Simultaneously, Chinese firms are also preparing for unmanned drone swarms in the seas and in the air. For instance, defence contractors in China are pitching for multi-hulled robot warships to transform the way naval warfare is conducted.[10]

Implications for India and Stability in the Indo-Pacific

The Indo-Pacific plays a significant role in geopolitics and tactical manoeuvres and is largely becoming a theatre for security competition. There are genuine concerns about the increase of strategic arsenals in the Indo-Pacific and the addition of disruptive naval technology – UUVs – will significantly contribute to the destabilization of the maritime security environment and escalate nuclear tensions. China is increasingly following the lead of countries like the United States and Russia to develop and deploy UUVs to bolster its blue-water navy. The deployment of Chinese UUVs in the waters of the Indo-Pacific can cause major disruptions to the status quo. China's growing presence in the Indian Ocean and assertiveness in maritime territorial disputes in the East and South China Sea has alarmed Indian security analysts and the international community. An Observer Research Foundation (ORF) report authored by Abhijit Singh argued that China would develop and deploy underwater vehicles for forward operations.[11] If China begins deploying UUVs in the Indian Ocean Region (IOR) to detect Indian submarines, it would greatly accelerate instability in the region. Other analyses indicate that UUVs will improve

Chinese long-distance targeting and bolster Beijing's surveillance and reconnaissance capabilities. Experts argue that China could utilize UUVs for 'hold-at-risk' missions, as UUVs could be effective in blockading choke points.[12] These trends demonstrate that by heavily investing in emerging technologies, China is poised to alter the traditional way of fighting wars. In such a scenario, India must seek to strengthen its maritime security ties with the United States, Japan and Australia. India's defence planners also need to intensify the process of upgrading their own ASW capabilities and indigenously designing and developing UUVs to meet India's security needs for subsurface naval operations.

Disruptive Technologies: Need for a Global Code of Conduct and the Way Forward

Several emerging trends, like the rise in congestion of the global commons – especially in the maritime domain – and the rapid development of disruptive technologies highlight that over the next few decades, countries are likely to reconfigure their military forces to fight protracted conflicts at distant places. However, one of the more dangerous trends is that technology is advancing at a faster pace than the ability of the international arms control community to agree upon a globally accepted code of conduct to govern new technologies. The United States' Defense Advanced Research Projects Agency (DARPA) is exploring new ways for UUVs to use active sonar to detect and track enemy vessels and transmit their location back to the host submarine.[13]

In 2018, DARPA awarded BAE Systems (British Aerospace) a contract to build the first phase of its Mobile Offboard Clandestine Communications and Approach (MOCCA) programme, which is aimed at combining the advantages of active and passive sonar detection and enhanced levels of coordination between submarines and UUVs to achieve stand-off detection and to track the ranges of enemy subs.[14] If in the future, UUVs are able to make the oceans transparent and degrade the stealth factor of submarines, it would seriously damage strategic stability and the insurance of nuclear second-strike capabilities of countries. While there are several technological challenges that lie ahead for UUVs to effectively detect and hunt submarines, ignoring technological surprises and advancements would be folly. Therefore, the international arms control community needs to find ways to formulate and adhere to a global code of conduct to govern and use UUVs to preserve stability and prevent adventurism by any one state in particular.

5

The Dragon Challenge: The Necessity for an Indian Space Deterrent Posture

KARTIK BOMMAKANTI

Most Indian analyses address the importance of the country's space programme for military purposes. Yet, they fail to establish what exactly should constitute a space military strategy for India vis-à-vis China. Should Indian space military capabilities serve as instruments of coercion or should they be aimed at fighting wars? Why and how should the available and potential Indian military power in space be disciplined to meet objectives likely to arise during disputes? Should military power in space be used either as a deterrent or as an offensive capability to wage wars, or both? If both, how should one be balanced against the other?

India's space strategy vis-à-vis China, if it has any, requires Indian strategic planners and policymakers to clearly delineate whether they see space as a *medium* or a *domain* for conducting terrestrial military operations. This would mean developing and deploying militarily applicable technological capacities and assets to conduct defensive, as well as offensive, space-based military operations.

At one level, space as a medium and as a domain for the conduct of military operations are interrelated – corresponding roughly with the tensions between deterrence and active combat in conventional warfare. Interests determine objectives. India's interests across its disputed frontier with China give it a ready and immediate rationale for space military capabilities vis-à-vis its neighbour. Indian space military strategy, and the capabilities that will be a part of it, should be directed towards those goals.

India's military capabilities in space can play a significant part in a Sino–Indian land war as well. Political and military objectives align in a contest for territory and therefore, Indian political decision-makers ought to invest in military capabilities related to space not just because they are critical for successful operations but also because China could potentially use exactly these capabilities in a land war against India.

Relative vs. Absolute Capabilities

Henry Kissinger rightly said: 'Power has no absolute measurement; it is always relative.'[1] Most force planning for any range of contingencies is predicated generally on *relative* capabilities.[2] India faces a massive if not an absolute asymmetry in space military technological capabilities. However, decades of investments it has already made in space technologies can help redress some of the present imbalance between India and China.

India cannot match China pound for pound on every dimension of space military power, simply because it faces a relative gap in resources (but not in terms of abilities in space-related or missile-related technologies). S. Chandrashekhar captured this dilemma well:

> India may have to make some hard choices on the trade-offs between the efforts required to put a man in space and the

> associated benefits in building a robust, space-based network-centric war-deterring capability. Doing both simultaneously may not be possible, given the resources that are currently available in the country.[3]

While absolute parity with China is almost unattainable, the costs of not pursuing a space military strategy are equally high due to the adversarial postures of China vis-à-vis India. From an Indian perspective, the worst is possible and preparing at least a limited retaliatory capability is a critical requirement. India need not destroy *all* of China's space assets in the event of war, but only a strategic fraction of its space assets in order to force it to cease armed hostilities.

Two recommendations are in order for Indian policymakers and strategic planners. Neither of the options listed can avoid political or financial trade-offs but if India's territorial interests are to be protected, the choice is unavoidable. It is possible to come up with a choice that combines the two options in some manner.

Firstly, it is important to recognize that space-based operations are heavily dependent on land-based infrastructure. India's retaliatory capabilities can be directed towards targeting the ground segments of China's extensive space surveillance network. For this, India needs long-range land attack cruise missile forces that can strike deeply and accurately at the ground nodes of China's space segment. The advantage of this option is that land attack cruise missiles have low radar signature and are hard to intercept. The downside to this option is that India's current land attack cruise missile capability lacks range and will necessitate investment.

The second option involves passive measures that several experts have already identified. These include building redundancy by launching numerous satellites into space. Numerically, China has substantially more satellites than India and to get anywhere close, India will need to increase launch rates significantly. However, Chinese launch rates dwarf India's, so parity is perhaps out of the question. In addition, India will need to build and launch more dual-use satellites so that, in the event China destroys Indian military satellites following the outbreak of a land war and during the course of a land war, India can migrate to the dual-use satellites as a backup. This measure can be accompanied by cyberspace warfare capabilities that target the electrical grid of the ground stations of China's space-based infrastructure.

6

Should BRICS Rally Around China's Call for Cyber Sovereignty?

MADHULIKA SRIKUMAR

For a few years now, Beijing has been steadily pushing for the idea of cyber sovereignty – the idea that every state has the right to govern not just the infrastructure of the internet within its borders, but also the content that flows through it. President Xi Jinping and Lu Wei, the former head of Cyberspace Administration of China (CAC), have shared China's vision for information sovereignty with the world, warning against US dominance in the cyberspace. With the enactment of the national cybersecurity law[1] and the release of a position paper[2] on global cyber norms in 2017 – both firsts for China – Beijing is looking both inwards and outwards to enforce its agenda in cyberspace. After the 2018 BRICS (Brazil, Russia, India, China, South Africa) summit in Xiamen – India, Brazil and South Africa (IBSA) have the option of acceding to the Sino -Russian agenda to enforce state control over the digital domain. Domestic developments within China that signal a softer position on cyber sovereignty have brought IBSA to a crossroads. The grouping must strongly consider the opportunity of reaching a consensus with their partners to make a play for the creation of global norms in cyberspace.

While the UN Group of Governmental Experts (GGE)[3] is currently at the forefront of setting the rules of the road for responsible state behaviour in cyberspace, a BRICS consensus on cyber norms can be formidable in the global discourse. This is true for two reasons. First, the number of internet users across BRICS economies, despite only two countries boasting an internet penetration rate over 50 per cent (Brazil and Russia), is still enormous. An agreement and a potential plan of action between these economies – be it on reform in internet governance institutions or combating cyber-crimes and terrorism or protecting user-privacy – can be meaningful. Second, all the BRICS countries had a pivotal role to play in the successful Internet Assigned Numbers Authority (IANA) transition last year that resulted in the US government forfeiting control over the Internet Corporation for Assigned Names and Numbers (ICANN) – the body responsible for running the infrastructure layer of the internet. The IANA transition was proof that BRICS states can play a defining role in cyber diplomacy.

With China hosting some of the biggest internet companies and becoming a leading provider for hardware around the world, the US is no longer the only dominant player in the market. Western countries such as the UK are enforcing laws[4] to increase government control over the internet to preserve national security while China softens its stance, even recognizing the role of different stakeholders in administering the internet. Beijing is likely willing to concede its position on primacy of the state over cyberspace to support Chinese companies, increase their user base and welcome foreign investment. With an intention to appease foreign companies, an official of the Chinese administration during the release of its position paper, 'International Strategy of Cooperation on Cyberspace', in 2017, noted that the Chinese internet is 'fully open'[5] as long as companies comply with the law and do not undermine national interests. As China looks to prioritize individual rights through enforcement of the national cybersecurity law by requiring foreign service providers to store sensitive data domestically, countries such as India or Brazil could find China's new cyber sovereignty outlook more agreeable than before.

China's earlier approach to cyber sovereignty was guided by two predominant interests: first, that its citizens must not be exposed to opinions online that the state would deem harmful or against national interest; second, that US and other Western powers must cease to influence the governance of the internet. BRICS states should ideally stay clear of the first requirement and not agree to impose any form of excessive censorship like China's Great Firewall.[6] BRICS economies must weigh their interest in maintaining national security against the economic necessity to keep their digital markets open. As for countering US dominance over the internet, it is likely that BRICS states would be willing to commit to principles requiring increased participation from emerging economies in ICANN and other standards-setting bodies.

China's new vision for cyber sovereignty as expressed in their position paper is couched in different terms. China is keen on encouraging cooperation between states to ensure the security and stability of cyberspace. This is a welcome change. Beijing's biggest concern is to prevent outside interference in any form – be it espionage or surveillance, or by undermining the integrity of supply chains. Considering recent events such as the alleged Democratic National Committee (DNC) hack and the spread of the WannaCry ransomware, these concerns may not be unfounded. Increased militarization of cyberspace has put many countries on the edge, with many experts[7] calling for the US National Security Agency to take responsibility for the proliferation of the WannaCry malware that was based on the EternalBlue exploit developed by the spy agency. In this backdrop, it would be prudent for the BRICS countries to assert agency over the information and communication technology (ICT) infrastructure while not straying from the democratic principles of an open internet. This is the right time for the BRICS countries to arrive at a middle ground in their internet governance norms with the intent of influencing global cyber norms.

7

Strategic Technology Might Disrupt India–China Status Quo

ARUN MOHAN SUKUMAR

Ant Financial's (the fintech arm of the Alibaba Group) effort to acquire MoneyGram, one of the world's leading money transfer companies, reflects China's naked ambition to control the technology ecosystems of the twenty-first century.

The range of products and services that Chinese behemoths have eyed (and in many cases, acquired) is astonishing. At the time of writing, this author found that Tencent, the Shenzhen-based messaging platform, has bought a 5 per cent stake in Tesla, leading many to speculate on its plans for the self-driving car market. Last year, Chinese appliance manufacturer, Midea, announced its takeover of Kuka, a German robotics company that the European Commissioner for Digital Economy and Society saw as 'important for the digital future of [the] European industry'. Brazil's most successful 'online-discount' company – also known as a deal-a-day website – Peixe Urbano, was bought by Chinese search engine giant Baidu as early as 2014. And finally, in 2015, India's own Paytm ceded a 40 per cent stake to Alibaba, China's biggest e-commerce company.

These instances – a fraction of the global mergers and acquisitions (M&A) deals that Chinese companies have driven in the last five years – reveal a trend of strategic acquisitions of technologies. They are attempts at vertical convergence and control of digital platforms. For example, by owning or being the dominant stakeholder in an e-commerce company (Alibaba), a payment gateway (AliPay, Paytm) and a money transfer platform (MoneyGram), Ant Financial aims to create an interoperable system that starts with a consumer receiving money in their e-wallet and ends with them spending it on products anywhere in the world. Its investment in a leading robotics company (Kuka) suggests Midea is betting on an intelligent, Internet of Things–driven environment, where 'traditional' appliances are seamlessly connected by sensors responding to the needs of their owners. If consumer needs can be gauged without human input or intervention, they can also be addressed by robots who automate daily tasks like cleaning or cooking. These M&As were likely given green signals by the political leadership in Beijing, given the close ties between China's internet giants and the Communist Party of China (CPC).

What does the quest by Chinese companies for 'top-to-bottom' domination of digital platforms mean for India? In an extreme scenario, Chinese applications and devices could not only become the custodians of Indian users' data, but also the gatekeepers of security while shaping consumer behaviour. To an extent, this is already the case with four of the top Chinese smartphone models (by market share) in India. The pervasive influence of Chinese technologies is an eventuality of enormous geopolitical significance for New Delhi. Should China gain levers over digital markets, it will mark the second phase of the economic relationship between both countries, heralding a shift from a demand-driven market for Chinese products to being necessity-driven. Needless to say, this scenario will curtail the strategic and military options of India's foreign policy planners.

A second and more probable outcome is that New Delhi and Beijing will collaborate to tailor products and services for the Indian market. Current developments reflect the desire on both sides to pursue such efforts. The fourth India–China Strategic Economic Dialogue in October 2016 sought to strengthen cooperation 'to take advantage of digitisation in all areas of economy; [...] jointly promote manufacturing technology, [promote] cooperation through the partnership of enterprises between the two countries in the area of high performance computing, smart cities [etc.].'[1]

The communique also suggests: '[T]he complementary strengths of India and China in ICT sector, specially computer hardware of China and computer software of India should be leveraged for competitive and economic advantage.'

The goal of producing Indian technological solutions for Chinese platforms is many years away, but there is no doubt that Beijing will have to work with Delhi if it wants to further service India's platform economy. Security testing of Chinese telecom equipment as well as applications, for instance, will be a sticking point for both sides to resolve at an early stage of talks.

No matter which scenario is realized, technology cooperation will cast away closely held beliefs that currently dictate India's approach to China.

The political relationship will be subsumed by economic factors, prompting Indian regulators to work with their Chinese counterparts to secure the digital economy. As a result, big-ticket, intractable issues like Nuclear Suppliers Group membership or United Nations Security Council reform may be pushed to the back-burner. That is not to say such issues will matter less to India's foreign policy moorings, but their potential to act as a spoiler in India–China ties may consequently diminish.

The Chinese private sector will emerge as an influential factor in bilateral ties. While it is true that Chinese businesses are connected to the political establishment in Beijing, they are also driven by bottom lines and market shares. As their India operations expand, Chinese companies will exert considerable influence over the CPC, and perhaps even steer the trajectory of the relationship.

India and China will likely work together to develop technical standards and protocols for the interoperability of devices and digital platforms in Asia. Asian digital ecosystems are currently fragmented, given that no one company has a monopoly over its infrastructure. As Chinese devices and applications continue to penetrate the Indian market, they will also have to design technologies that address security concerns indigenous to India: vulnerabilities in handheld devices, the linking of mobile phone numbers to India's Aadhaar database, encryption standards for communication platforms, etc. Technology-based cooperation may also spill over into regional cooperation for standard-setting, given that digital economies in Southeast and Central Asia are booming.

Beyond technology standards, New Delhi and Beijing may also be prompted to coordinate national policies on data protection (or at a minimum, compare notes on how best to harmonize them) given the inextricable linkages between Chinese platforms and data from India contained in them. Policy questions addressed may include: What data should remain within Indian borders? What safeguards will apply to the data of Indian citizens stored abroad? How can both sides create information sharing channels between Indian and Chinese law enforcement agencies to tackle cybercrimes? Policy coordination is an inherently political exercise, which will require high-level representation, making up for its deficit in current bilateral discussions.

Wary of expanding Chinese influence, American and European technology manufacturers and platforms will court the Indian market, offering New Delhi a bargaining chip that could be used for political ends. Currently, Chinese apps do not compete with their Western counterparts in many markets, but that is set to change as they turn towards developing English language platforms.

As digital platforms converge, it would be ill-advised for India to cede space to its eastern neighbour to determine the rules of governance in cyberspace. At the same time, economic and business imperatives driving Chinese companies to India offer an opportunity for New Delhi to bring China to the negotiating table. While China is able to pump money and resources into developing new technologies, their utility and interoperability will be determined by consumers in emerging markets like India. Regulatory norms or technology standards designed to exclude Chinese players can seriously hurt Beijing's economic prospects, which is a card India should not hesitate to deploy. The negotiation process that follows may ultimately break the political stalemate to which the relationship is currently hostage.

8

China: A Threat to the Liberal Democratic Order?

NIRANJAN SAHOO

Unlike the United States and the former Soviet Union, China has never tried to instal regimes of its preference in foreign countries. For a long time, the Communist Party of China (CPC) never claimed its system of government had any universal appeal. Lately, this seems to be changing. Since its embrace of market capitalism in the late 1970s and the unprecedented economic growth that followed, making it the second largest economy in less than four decades, the Middle Kingdom is steadily employing hard and soft tools (some call it Sharp Power)[1] to alter 'self-imposed' restraints. Apart from spreading its 'soft power' among the wider regions of Asia, Africa, and Europe, the country is using its economic might particularly through the Belt and Road Initiative (BRI) to promote its geopolitical interests in distant regions. What is worrisome, however, is the fact that China under Xi Jinping has little regard for democracy, human rights and universal liberal values. At a time when America and the West are 'withdrawing' from their global commitment to democratic values, Xi and the CPC are having an easy time to laugh at the liberal order and the values that it stands for.

Hard-selling the Chinese Model

According to Andrew Nathan, a well-known China expert, 'China encourages authoritarian regimes elsewhere by the power of example. By demonstrating that advanced modernisation can be combined with authoritarian rule, the Chinese regime has given hope to authoritarian rulers everywhere.'[2] Further, China's ability to execute major infrastructure projects such as high-speed rail networks in the shortest possible time without political hurdles has created many admirers as most Western democracies are gridlocked. The recent government shutdown in the US is a reminder.

The super efficiency of the Chinese state in executing big ticket projects and its ability to take swift decisions persuaded influential columnist Thomas Friedman to famously remark that the US 'could be China for a day' simply to get things done.[3] The American political scientist Daniel Bell has written an effusive book, *The China Model: Political Meritocracy and the Limits of Democracy*, praising the 'meritocratic' advantages of the Chinese political system. In short, while the Western liberal order is facing backlash and a crisis of legitimacy as citizens increasingly question its ability to deliver, the Chinese model is gaining popularity across many regions of the world including America's own backyard. More and more countries are embracing Chinese authoritarianism to increase growth and development.[4] From Turkey and Poland to Hungary, there is a growing list of democracies that have developed a fascination for China's 'authoritarian capitalism'. For instance, Rodrigo Duterte, Philippines's strongman, has openly praised the Chinese model. Similarly, the Hungarian leader Viktor Orbán has been making fun of liberal democracy while seeking solace in the Chinese style of governance. In other words, the Chinese model is gaining traction in many regions including Africa and Latin America.

Installing Friendly Regimes?

The popularity of the Chinese model has its own standing and is promoted without any regard for an individual country's democratic process and rule of law. In the past few years, there are alarming trends of the Chinese state and its agencies influencing and managing internal policies, including the change of governments in a few cases. The most widely reported incident in recent times is the alleged role of China in the fall of the Robert Mugabe regime in Zimbabwe. *Reuters* revealed that Mugabe, a long-time friend of China, had become a liability for Beijing because of his indigenization law debarring Chinese companies from getting majority ownership of State Owned Enterprises (SOEs). Beyond Zimbabwe, China has made deep inroads into other African democracies. Both Angola and Ethiopia have come under heavy Chinese influence including 'regime change'.[5]

Closer home, China has been working relentlessly to dislodge democracies in Taiwan and Macau. Beijing's record of honouring democratic principles on its own territory of Hong Kong has come under a heavy cloud with the rise of the Umbrella Movement in this former British colony. Activists and dissidents demanding better democratic rule in Hong Kong have been repressed and jailed by Beijing. As regards Taiwan, apart from frequent threats of forcible reunification with the mainland, the Chinese government is using its huge trade and the Chinese diaspora to check anti-Chinese and pro-democracy activities in this small island nation. For example, in January 2017, pro-China groups attacked leaders of the Umbrella Movement, Nathan Law and Joshua Wong, in Taiwan.[6]

Beyond its own region, China's interference has spread to its extended neighbourhood, particularly in Southeast Asia. Over the years, China has spread its influence into the Association of Southeast Asian Nations (ASEAN) largely in the form of business and investment. Most ASEAN countries that earlier shared a strong relationship with the US and its Western allies have found it more profitable to do business with China, with no pressure to adhere to democratic principles. Cambodia, Thailand and even Malaysia have been throwing away their 'whatever democratic credentials' and drawing greater inspiration from China.[7] Promoted and supported by China, Cambodia's strongman Hun Sen has been clamping down on democracy and basic freedoms by restricting the media and jailing opponents. Again, China is the only big country in the region which has gone on to defend Myanmar in the United Nations Security Council (UNSC) and the Human Rights Council (HRC) on the Rohingya issue. The list gets even bigger especially if one includes the South Asian region.

For instance, China has a long shadow over the affairs of Pakistan and with the mega China–Pakistan Economic Corridor (CPEC) initiative: literally no area of Pakistan's politics, economy and society is out of China's influence. China has made deep inroads into Nepal's internal politics and democratic processes. Recently, in an unprecedented interference in the country's domestic politics, China went on to fund the local elections in Nepal. Other smaller nations in South Asia, particularly Sri Lanka and Maldives, are coming under growing Chinese pressure – and politicians in these countries often consult Beijing for major decisions.[8] In short, China has used its huge economic and strategic resources, including infrastructural and technical expertise, to influence and often 'manage' political regimes to the great disadvantage of India – the region's democracy powerhouse.

Meddle Kingdom

In June 2017, the *Economist* sarcastically referred to China as 'Meddle Kingdom'. The magazine's categorization was in response to a Fairfax Media and Australian Broadcasting Corporation (ABC) investigation revealing the role of the CPC in monitoring 14,000 Chinese students in Australia and its alleged role in trying to buy influence through political donations. In 2017, Sam Dastyari, an influential Labour Party MP had to resign from his position after it was revealed that a Chinese donor had paid for his bills, including a settlement of his personal debt. Mr Dastyari was lobbying peers to 'respect' China's claims in the South China Sea apart from persuading his party's foreign affairs spokesperson to avoid meeting a pro-democracy activist in Hong Kong.

While the focus of press attention has been on Australia, China's attempts to buy political influence abroad extends to other countries. For instance, the CPC meddling in the internal politics of New Zealand recently rocked the country's parliament. As extensively reported by *Financial Times*, a Chinese-born member of New Zealand's parliament serving on the country's key parliamentary select committee on foreign policy, defence and trade had evidently spent fifteen years in Chinese military intelligence.

Even the United States is not insulated from Chinese meddling. The US media and influential members of the Congress have been debating the growing influence of hundreds of Confucius Institutes and overseas Chinese students and business. For instance, over the last one decade, China has set up some 1,000 Confucius Institutes in 120 countries and hundreds of them are in the US. They are directly funded by the Chinese government's outreach arm. Complaining about growing Chinese interference in the US, the Congressional Executive Commission on China chaired by Senator Marco Rubio hosted a public hearing titled 'The Long Arm of China: Exporting Authoritarianism with Chinese Characteristics'.

Attack on Human Rights

The Chinese regime is known to be utterly contemptuous of human rights and it displayed this tendency vividly when it defended the Burmese regime's 'brutal and systematic attempt to cleanse an entire ethnic minority' at the UNSC meet. In another clear display of its rising profile and contempt for human rights, China used its influence to prevent hundreds of non-governmental organizations (NGOs) from attending President Xi Jinping's speech at the United Nations in January 2019. Similarly, China used its influence to eject

Dolkun Isa, well-known Uyghur minority activist, from speaking at the United Nations.[9]

As has been extensively documented by Human Rights Watch (HRW), in a growing number of instances Chinese officials have been harassing activists, primarily those from China, by photographing and filming them on UN premises in violation of rules and restricting their travel to Geneva. According to HRW, China in good measure has used its membership in the Economic and Social Council's NGO Committee to block civil society organizations from getting UN accreditation. The country has sought to blacklist accredited human rights activists and deprive funding for the UN's rights officers.

Beyond the UN, the Chinese state has launched an all-out war against democracy and human rights activists in Taiwan, Hong Kong and even Cambodia. Recently, a Chinese court jailed Lee Ming-Che, a visiting Taiwanese democracy activist, for five years for discussing democracy on social media.[10] Similarly, since 2012, several democracy activists from Hong Kong have been jailed for demanding greater freedom. In January 2018, it incarcerated democracy icon, Joshua Wong, a second time for three months.

The above analysis illustrates a growing Chinese challenge to the liberal democratic order and universal values. While there is no need to panic, the liberal democracies cannot simply wish away the growing threats emerging from the illiberal behemoth. China's carefully camouflaged soft power, supported by a massive financial muscle and its growing appeal as an alternative model through the 'power of example', has many admirers among new democracies and authoritarian regimes. With the United States, the biggest promoter of democracy and human rights, in retreat and the European Union experiencing an existential battle, it is uncertain how the liberal order can check the rise of the Chinese authoritarian model. The quadrilateral alliance between four major democracies – India, the US, Japan and Australia – could be a potential check on China's disruptive influence over democracies and universal values.

9

China's Naval Power and National Prestige

TUNEER MUKHERJEE

China's assertive stance in regard to its territorial disputes in the South China Sea (Figure 1.1) and the East China Sea (Figure 1.2) has considerably strained its relations with its neighbouring nations and regional naval powers.[1] The growing prospect of a naval compact in the Indo-Pacific verifies the impression that China's impact as a rising naval power of Asia has been inhibitive for the region.[2] The main concern behind the rapid development of Chinese naval forces – the People's Liberation Army Navy (PLAN) and the Chinese Coast Guard (CCG) is its implication on the freedom of navigation in international waters and its accompanying economic prosperity, peacefulness as well as ideational stability or legitimacy. These concerns become vocalized when certain Chinese actions restrict maritime rights and access to common resources. The combination of all these facets place China's maritime ambitions at the heart of both theoretical and more practical discourses of Asian security. While classic security dilemma theorists will allude the naval build-up to the substantial presence of the United States Navy in the area, the real motivation behind the rise in Chinese naval activity can be attributed to Chinese nationalism.[3]

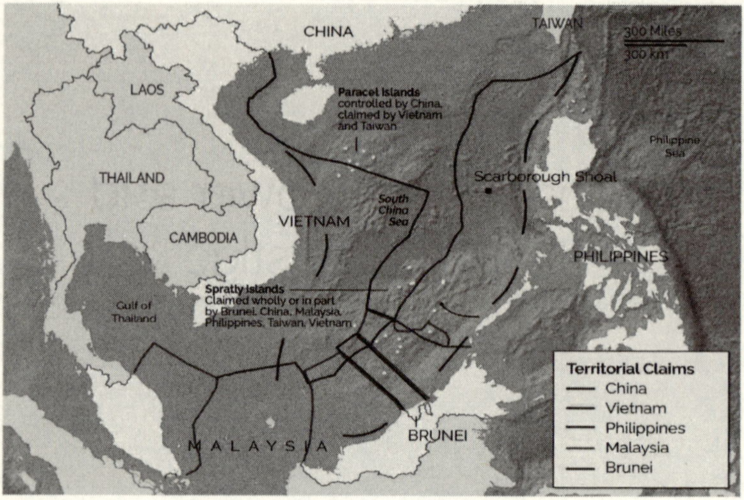

Figure 1.1 – Territorial Claims between China and other Southeast Asian nations in the South China Sea[4]

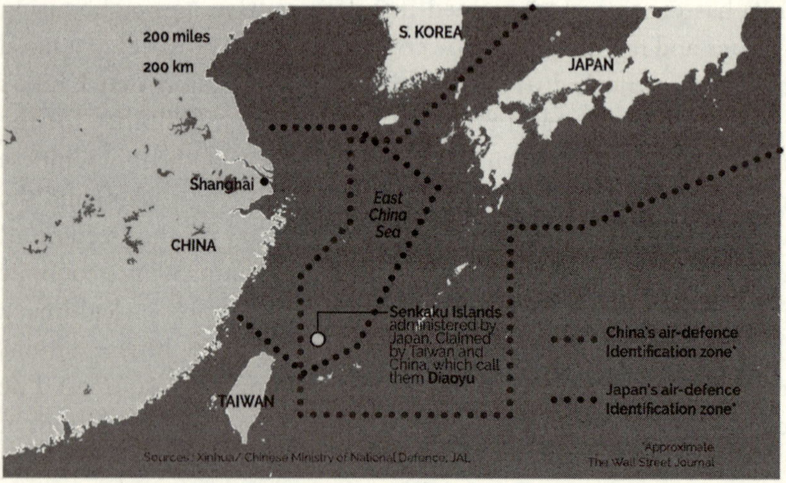

Figure 1.2 – Territorial Dispute over the Senkaku Islands in the East China Sea[5]

Since the mid-1860s, Chinese political discourse and its accompanying foreign policy has gone through a series of transformations. A Chinese nation that was once considered the leader of the Orient was severely weakened by continuous disruptions like the Opium Wars, the Boxer Rebellion and the Sino–Japanese Wars. Consequently, these incidents also dented the nationalist pride of the Chinese people as they suffered various atrocities during this period. Recently, the rejuvenation of the Chinese economy has helped the Chinese nation regain that missing prestige. The Communist Party of China (CPC) has taken advantage of this rising nationalist sentiment to unite a disenfranchised and fragmented Chinese society as this supplies the state the requisite authority to pursue prestige and legitimacy in the international arena. A key component of this prestige, one fuelled by China's nationalistic ambitions, is a wide-ranging naval force. Naval power lies at the centre of Chinese aspirations and coalesces energy security, maritime strategy, territorial integrity, naval nationalism, foreign policy, power projection and regional leadership.[6] The China of today doesn't fit the definition of an actual communist state; rather it has transformed into an authoritarian oligarchic state with mixed economic principles where nationalist sentiment weighs heavy on the administration.

China's naval capabilities may have come to bear fruit in the present, and the acceleration might have happened in the past few years, but China's nationalistic ambition to be a 'blue water navy' and to regain its 'lost territories' has been a core policy objective of the CPC for some time now. China's journey to naval power has been paved by successive administrations that have repeatedly harped on the 'aggrieved power' narrative to justify their actions. Chinese nationalists demand the development of a 'blue water navy' spearheaded by aircraft carrier groups because it would serve the dual purpose of reuniting Taiwan with the Chinese mainland and of defending Chinese sovereignty in the above-mentioned territorial disputes. China's actions in its near waters – reclaiming islands, imposing unilateral fishing bans, employing its maritime militia to harass other countries' fishermen, using coast guard vessels for grey zone coercion – all form a part of this nationalistic principle to secure territories that it considers to be its own. China's claim in the South China Sea outlined by the nine-dash line (NDL), often drummed up by state-sponsored outlets, displays this sense of historical entitlement. The NDL that was first formulated by the Kuomintang administration in 1947 covers a majority of the South China Sea and it infringes upon the sovereignty and maritime boundaries of multiple Southeast Asian nations – and China makes these claims in the face of international law and seeks to benefit from the economic exploitation of the region's resources.[7] The East China Sea is another example. Figure 1.3 demonstrates how China's maritime presence in the contiguous zone surrounding the Senkaku Islands has increased over the last few years. These forays in the East China Sea seek to establish control over natural gas fields present in the territorial sea surrounding the Senkakus, and these state actions have unsurprisingly been accompanied by a feverous anti-Japanese sentiment on the Chinese mainland.

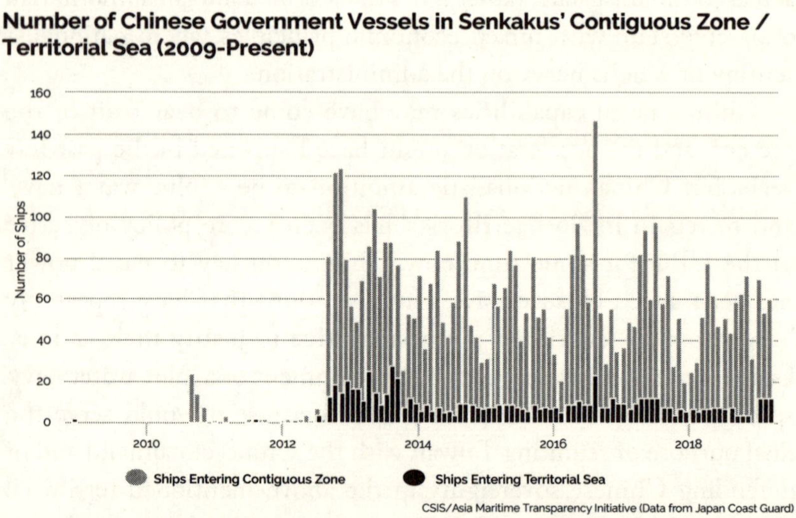

Figure 1.3 – Tracking Chinese Government Vessels in Senkakus' Contiguous Zone[8]

China fits into Robert Ross's definition of naval nationalism as the manifestation of nationalist 'prestige strategies' pursued by governments seeking domestic legitimacy.[9] According to Ross, 'China's nationalists seek the prestige and power enjoyed by great powers throughout history, including by dynastic China.'[10] The sudden splurge in China's naval spending is not something that has developed overnight. China's increased expenditure on its maritime capabilities is a combination of nationalist sentiment, defensive security strategy and growing economic clout. A core concept of Chinese nationalism – recovery of 'lost territories', further justifies this evolving naval acquisition program. Naval power has become the crux of domestic legitimacy and this is well reflected in the intentions of naval planners in Beijing to build a robust navy by 2020, centred around three aircraft carrier groups. As a growing circle of Chinese netizens regularly attach nationalist sentiments to Chinese naval power, the amplification of construction activities in the Spratly Islands further underscores this 'pressure from Chinese society'.[11] A powerful PLAN along with a dominant CCG encapsulates the evolving power of the Chinese nation in the minds of its people. Meanwhile, publicly, China masks its national sentiments by depicting a classic case of security dilemma. It alludes to the build-up in naval forces and militarization of its reclaimed islands to the US Navy's Freedom of Navigation Operations (FONOP) in the South China Sea.[12] This process is repeated by Chinese state agencies, state-controlled media outlets and nationalist netizens every time the US Navy challenges China's territorial claims.

An 8.1 per cent rise in Chinese defence spending in 2018, and a subsequent 7.5 per cent increase in 2019, demonstrates that China's naval expansion is moving at a steady pace.[13] A majority of this funding will be devoted to finance its swift acquisition programme and to develop capabilities for anti-access/area denial (A2/AD) operations to deter any ambitious US naval action beyond the routine FONOP. China has devoted a considerable amount of resources over the past decade to bring itself at par with US capabilities. The tactful movements of the US Navy dominate Chinese naval strategy, and its naval force structures are designed keeping US force deployments in the Western Pacific in mind. Furthermore, the construction of surface-to-air missile (SAM) sites and runways on reclaimed islands in the South China Sea convert them into reliable bases from where Chinese forces can be deployed. The declaration of an Air Defense Identification Zone (ADIZ) over these disputed territories further consolidates this position. All of these tie into China's strategy to secure the first island chain of the Western Pacific as an extension of its national power. Figure 1.4 shows the growth in the number of Chinese warships and what it aims to achieve in the near future. This bridging of the gap between Chinese and American conventional naval forces is the realization of Chinese naval nationalism. Moreover, increased force deployments in the Indian Ocean suggest the presence of a larger strategy beyond China's immediate littorals. Anti-piracy task force deployments in the Gulf of Aden, submarine patrols in the Indian Ocean and offshore naval bases as far as Eastern Africa, all add to the rising profile of Chinese naval power as China expands its horizon to the high seas.

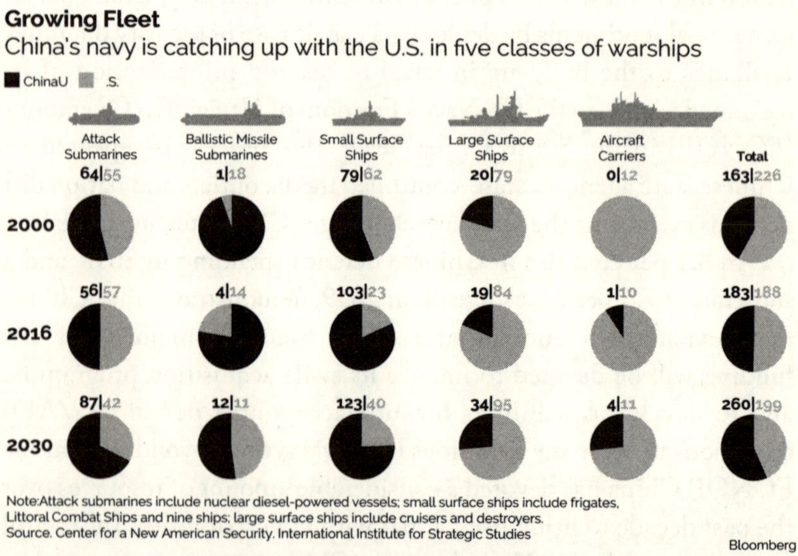

Figure 1.4 – Growth in Chinese naval capabilities in comparison to US naval forces[14]

China under President Xi Jinping has shed its 'Brand China' image and shown its true ambitions to the world. Every great power has secured its status on the geopolitical stage by using a robust naval force, and China is no different. When national ambitions are frequently stirred by the state administration for popular support, the result is a civil society gripped with imagination and fervent nationalism. This, in turn, influences policy decisions of the state. The key difference in Chinese ambitions is its sense of privilege in the region and its rhetorical duplicity that assuages nations with tools like the Belt and Road Initiative (BRI) and negotiations for a binding code of conduct, while transgressing upon their exclusive economic zones (EEZs). In the quest to rejuvenate its great power status, it has injected every section of its naval force – the navy, the coast guard and the maritime militia – with a sense of unabashed autonomy that heeds no one, not even international law. When these forces harass fishermen from other nations and restrict their access to traditional fishing areas, their actions antagonize the population of other nations and feeds their nationalist sentiments. These actions put to doubt the sovereignty of neighbouring nations, their capabilities and their access to resources, threatening the saliency of norms that have dominated Asian political discourse since the end of the Cold War. Chinese naval power and state prestige go hand in hand – in creating a new security dynamic in Eastern Asia and beyond. Nations have employed a variety of strategies ranging from bandwagoning to balancing to hedging, for them to address an increasingly bellicose China, and are still in the process of positioning themselves to the idea of a Chinese hierarchy in the region. The Chinese state needs to rethink its attitude towards its neighbouring maritime space before their quest for naval power actualizes a naval alliance against them.

10

From Silk Threads to Fiber Optics: The Rise of China's Digital Silk Road

KESHAV KELKAR

The Silk Road calls to mind an image of the distant past, where traders traversed the vast expanse of Eurasia in pursuit of silk, spices and various other commodities. Today, China is attempting to revive these once forgotten routes as part of President Xi Jinping's signature Belt and Road Initiative (BRI). However, while much ink has been spilled about China's growing network of port, pipeline, rail and road infrastructure projects, there is one overlooked component of the BRI that deserves greater attention: the digital Silk Road.

This essay examines the origins of this lesser known road, its gradual inclusion into the mainstream belt-and-road discourse, and the underlying forces pushing Beijing to promote greater digital connectivity.

The broad policy outline for the digital Silk Road can be traced to a joint white paper released in 2015 by China's National Development and Reform Commission (NDRC), the ministry of foreign affairs and the ministry of commerce. The white paper notes:

> [China] should jointly advance the construction of cross-border optical cables and other communications trunk line networks, improve international communications connectivity, and create an information Silk Road. We should build bilateral cross-border optical cable networks at a quicker pace, plan transcontinental submarine optical cable projects, and improve spatial (satellite) information passageways to expand information exchanges and cooperation.[1]

Moreover, in 2016, China's State Council issued the 13th Five-Year Plan, which dedicates a specific section on improving internet and telecommunications links across BRI countries. The five-year plan emphasizes the creation of land and sea cable infrastructure, an internet Silk Road between China and the Arab states, and the creation of a China–ASEAN information harbour.[2]

The concept soon became part of China's mainstream discourse and has been promoted at key international gatherings such as the first Belt and Road Forum, the Fourth World Internet Conference at Wuzhen, and more recently, during the Eighth Ministerial meeting of China–Arab States Cooperation Forum (CASCF), where Xi Jinping extended the scope of the BRI to outer space when he called for the creation of a 'Space and Information Corridor'.[3]

All these monikers for greater digital connectivity have become what is known today as the Digital Silk Road. The rise of this new third road, however, begs a simple question: what are the forces that are pushing China to expand its digital footprint?

Confronted with slower growth rates, industrial overcapacity, and an ageing society, China is placing its bets on the future of the digital economy to sustain stable levels of growth.[4] By investing financial resources into ambitious national initiatives such as 'Made in China 2025' and Internet Plus, China not only wants to technologically upgrade and digitize its economic base, but also deploy 'national players' in telecommunications, e-commerce and information technology to secure access to untapped markets abroad – and there is no better way to achieve this objective than to marry state-led infrastructure development projects with digital connectivity.

Furthermore, as China's digital economy matures, domestic firms are not only facing stiffer competition, but also witnessing a decline in local demand. As such, these companies have a strong interest in pushing the digital Silk Road agenda not only because it provides them with an expedient means to venture out to new markets but also because they see themselves as the largest beneficiaries. As Hong Shen points out:

> Given that many BRI projects are directly funded by Beijing-backed financial institutions that often explicitly or implicitly require receiving countries to outsource projects to Chinese companies, China-based internet firms see the digital Silk Road as an opportunity to seek state largesse and political support for their own decapacity needs. For example, in 2015, China Development Bank and Industrial and Commercial Bank of China issued a $2.5 billion credit line to Bharti Airtel, the largest telecom operator in India, for its domestic infrastructure projects. Bharti Airtel then outsourced part of its network equipment to Huawei and ZTE, boosting the external markets of the two Chinese equipment makers.[5]

Lastly, there is a strategic dimension to the digital Silk Road. The lifelines of the modern digital economy are undersea fiber optic cables, which according to estimates carry more than 98 per cent of international internet, data and telephone traffic.[6] However, the bulk of these cables are both geographically concentrated and largely dominated by US power, which has raised concerns in Beijing about data security. Therefore, Beijing's push to build cross border and undersea cables, such as the Pakistan–China Fiber Optic Project, is motivated by a desire to circumvent heavily used choke points such as the Straits of Malacca, and to shield its communications from foreign intelligence agencies.[7]

Another illustrative example is China's promotion of its indigenous global navigation satellite system (GNSS), the BeiDou Navigation System (BDS). BeiDou is one of four major global navigation satellite systems in the world, along with the US Global Positioning System (GPS), European Union's Galileo and Russia's Global Navigation Satellite System (GLONASS). As part of the Digital Silk Road, China aims to extend coverage of its home-grown satellite-navigation system to the sixty-plus countries along the BRI and beyond.[8] BeiDou has already commenced basic global coverage ahead of its 2020 target and will add more satellites to the constellation in the coming years[9] – allowing China to end its reliance on US-based GPS; increase its diplomatic clout in regional and international forums on Position, Navigation and Timing (PNT)–related affairs; and provide the People's Liberation Army's sensor-equipped platforms and missiles with enhanced guidance capabilities.[10]

In sum, while the advent of the digital Silk Road presents opportunities and challenges for China and BRI countries, its ongoing development will undoubtedly raise important questions about the future of the global digital order.

PART 2
China in South Asia

1

India, China and the BRI

ASHOK MALIK

India's decision to boycott the Belt and Road Forum – China's showpiece international conference on its most ambitious economic and political initiative – in 2017 made news and provoked strong and divergent opinions, not least within India.

Prime Minister Narendra Modi's critics saw it as a mistake and a needless rejection of a Chinese investment and connectivity project that India could benefit from. The mainstream view, however, was that the Indian government had been left with no real option. As Modi's foreign policy team considered it, he had made strenuous efforts to offer market access to the Chinese and gone out of his way to make them comfortable. President Xi Jinping had misinterpreted these gestures and had snubbed India on a variety of issues, from refusing to open up the Chinese market to Indian pharmaceutical products and even to Indian concerns on terrorism.

The Belt and Road Initiative (BRI) was the final straw. One part of it, the China–Pakistan Economic Corridor (CPEC), challenged Indian sovereignty as it passed through territory that India legally claimed. Moreover, individual BRI projects in South Asia and the Indian Ocean region, India's near neighbourhood, were pushing unviable investments, creating neocolonial dependencies and potential political turmoil in a part of the world that had an impact on India. They were also regarded as a political check on India's own and legitimate aspirations.

All this background is well known. What is the state of play now? Three points are worth considering:

First, the Chinese were genuinely surprised by the total and absolute absence of the Indian government at the BRI Forum. They said as much in informal conversations with Indian officials at later events, including at the Shanghai Cooperation Organization (SCO) summit in Astana. In a sense, they were misled – or allowed themselves to be – by commentary, analysis and feedback from sections of the strategic community in New Delhi.

Some in this community are old interlocutors of the Chinese; some, notably, are part of the current establishment. Not everybody believed that, in the end, Modi would stand his ground and simply refuse to send anyone to the BRI Forum. Indeed, the degree to which the Indian prime minister sees the BRI as a strategic challenge to India and to his own legacy has been underestimated.

What Modi can do about this and whether he can promote Indian connectivity and infrastructure projects and maritime capabilities to sufficient levels to provide workable alternatives – even if not absolute equivalents, for that is both difficult and unnecessary – to BRI is another matter. The fact is the Chinese misread his and his government's mood. That alone would require a Chinese reset, at least in tactical terms, and Beijing would need diplomatic antennae in the Indian capital to be upgraded in some form.

Second, India has clearly interpreted BRI as unacceptable Chinese expansionism. More than as a 'Marshall Plan for Asia' – as at least one wide-eyed Indian commentator described it – BRI is being looked upon as a series of bilateral projects between China and individual countries that are being packaged to resemble a multilateral framework.

'This is not multilateralism,' explained one Indian official. 'The New Development Bank is multilateral. Even the Asian Infrastructure Investment Bank is a multilateral institution, as there are internationally recognized norms governing it as well as multi-country ownership. BRI is not multilateral. It is Chinese owned and Chinese governed. Participation and co-financing by others and by genuine multilateral institutions is being thwarted by Beijing.'

Third, the rise of BRI is a direct consequence of American strategic confusion in Asia and the unstable nature of the early Donald Trump administration. In such a scenario, which allies can India turn to for support? In Europe, there is discomfort with Chinese attempts to divide and rule the European Union (EU). In conversations with the Indian leadership, both the Germans and the French have indicated wariness with a potentially Chinese shaped and led world order.

Yet, they are – at least the Germans are – alive to gains from short-term commercial contracts that may arise as part of the BRI. For now, they have left India to do the talking publicly. Despite Brexit, the benefit to India from a united EU, its integrity underwritten by Paris and Berlin, is greater today than in the past. Similarly, in the east, India's belief that the unity of the Association of Southeast Asian Nations (ASEAN), such as it is, must be sustained for as long as feasible despite Chinese attempts to carve up the Southeast Asian grouping, is more pronounced today.

Whatever their long-term prospects, both ASEAN and the EU are considered bulwarks to China in their current form. Indian investment – political and otherwise – and engagement with both specific countries in these associations as well as the entities will likely intensify. In that sense, unlike the early years of the first decade of the new millennium, India is now rediscovering 'Old Europe' and its original 'Look East' friends. These regions were, together, once the route to America. Today, they are simply the alternative route.

2

Friends with (Risky) Benefits

KRITI M. SHAH

There has been plenty written in recent times about the 'all-weather' friendship between China and Pakistan. While historically, Sino–Pakistan relations have been of a military nature, the China–Pakistan Economic Corridor (CPEC) has put their economic relations at the forefront. The USD 62 billion network of roads, oil and gas pipelines, dams, ports, industrial and agricultural projects connect the Western Xinjiang province of China to Gwadar in Balochistan, giving China direct access – across the subcontinent – to the Arabian Sea and new markets. The project has the potential to deepen the relationship between both countries, while simultaneously changing the geopolitics of the Asian region. Even though China has developed a close military, economic and political relationship with Pakistan, there are some inherent road bumps in their relationship that will test their 'shared interests' and 'adversity-tested' friendship.[1]

It would be an unfair assessment to believe that China's close relationship with Pakistan, and more specifically the billions of dollars in investments, emanates from Beijing's altruistic nature. The fact is that China's approach to Pakistan is derived majorly from its strategic interests in South Asia. While CPEC will flush billions into the struggling Pakistan economy and rapidly speed up its development infrastructure, it is also one part of China's vision to rewrite the rules for the next era of globalization, through its One Belt One Road (OBOR) project. China's interests in Pakistan, therefore, can be categorized as threefold: secure its economic development and connectivity projects in the region, contain the rise of Islamic extremism, and control Indian power in the region.

Pakistan offers Beijing opportunities for newer markets, trade, investment, energy supply routes and an easier access to the Indian Ocean via the Gwadar port. This is a faster, more cost-efficient route, rather than Chinese ships leaving its eastern coast and sailing south, around the Southeast Asian subcontinent, to enter the Indian Ocean. In addition to securing its economic and trade interests, China is determined to suppress militants and radicals in Pakistan that threaten to radicalize and that have destabilized China's own Muslim population. While China does not want groups such as the Afghan Taliban to destabilize Afghanistan, it continues to 'strike deals' and appease them through the Pakistani military.[2] Instead of using its influence with the Pakistani military and civilian establishment to crack down on militants and terrorists, it uses Pakistan's loyalty to ensure that groups do not target Chinese interests, and instead focus their activities against India and Afghanistan. The launch of Operation Zarb-e-Azb in Pakistan in 2014 saw the army carry out large-scale military operations against militants in the northwest tribal regions of the country. While these operations were interpreted as being due to American pressure to crack down on Taliban safe havens, it is more likely that Islamabad was coaxed by Beijing into being a 'supporter' of the US war on terror in Afghanistan. The army's operation focused on targeting members of both the Pakistani Taliban that regularly threatened the domestic stability of the country, and foreign militants – such as the Uyghur militants who were members of the East Turkestan Islamic Movement (ETIM), targeting China.[3]

Simultaneously, groups such as the Haqqani network and the Afghan Taliban were given free rein to carry out subversive activities in India and Afghanistan. Beijing has, on numerous occasions, come to Islamabad's defence at the United Nations and other global bodies, lobbying for it against India. This is because it sees such militant groups as the required hedge against growing Indian power and has therefore considered them vital to its own national security interests.

Such a policy promises to have long-term security implications for the region. Present Chinese logic dictates that by investing in infrastructure, agriculture, industry and transport, there will be a significant growth in Pakistan's sluggish economy, thereby alleviating challenges posed by poverty, lack of education, militancy and radicalization, thus transforming Pakistan forever. While that may have an impact to a certain extent, an argument can also be made that, just as economic development can bring about an improvement in domestic security, the reverse is also true – domestic insecurity can hamper economic development. Pakistan continues to remain a safe haven for militants to train, recruit and orchestrate terror plots across the world. Pakistan's crackdown on the Tehrik-i-Taliban (TTP) has resulted in backlash from factions and splinter groups of the militant organization. The Islamic State, which operates from the eastern province of Nangarhar in Afghanistan, has also successfully demonstrated its ability to launch attacks in Pakistan. Even if Beijing has struck the right chord with the military establishment in Rawalpindi, ensuring that militants will not attack China, its billion-dollar investments in the country remain in jeopardy.

Up until now, 'managing tensions' in South Asia has been in Chinese interests. It has, however, risked improving relations with India by consistently shielding Pakistani terrorists. While CPEC may bring the short-term gains that Beijing seeks, developing a multi-billion-dollar project in a terror-infested country is a disaster waiting to happen. The security of CPEC and Chinese nationals in Pakistan have been Beijing's foremost concerns. Lt Gen. Qamar Bajwa, in one of his first acts as Inter-Services Intelligence (ISI) chief, travelled to Beijing to reassure the Chinese on the same.[4] While China may make demands of Pakistan, the onus is on Islamabad to keep its promises.

By not forcing Pakistan's hand to cut ties with all militant groups, China is playing a risky game, one where it stands to lose more than a few billion dollars. As Hillary Clinton once reprimanded Pakistan, 'You cannot keep snakes in your backyard and expect them to only bite your neighbours.' The statement could have very well been directed at China. If Beijing truly wants its connectivity projects to be a roaring success, it must first ensure that Pakistan no longer maintains ties with extremists. This will allow its border regions to develop in a stable and secure environment.

3

China's Surreptitious Advance in Afghanistan: A Multidimensional Move

SHUBHANGI PANDEY

Given the dysfunctional state of affairs in war-torn Afghanistan for as long as one can remember, and the country's strategic location on the world map, it is unsurprising to witness a fast-growing Chinese interest in the region. The progressively deteriorating security situation in Afghanistan – and the potential risks that it could pose to Beijing's long-term economic and strategic endeavours – is an unsettling prospect for China. The geographical proximity between Afghanistan and the Muslim Uyghur province of Xinjiang in China is, however, the most crucial motivation for greater Chinese involvement in the region, one may argue.

International media outlets and intelligence agencies worldwide have been circulating reports for a while now, pointing towards the creation of a Chinese military base in the Wakhan Corridor of the Badakhshan Province of Afghanistan. Although historically China has not been one to embark on militarization programmes on foreign soil and has stoutly denied the rumours about building an Afghan 'mountain brigade', the example of Djibouti aptly brings to the fore China's newly adopted strategy of leveraging economic influence to further its strategic objectives.[1]

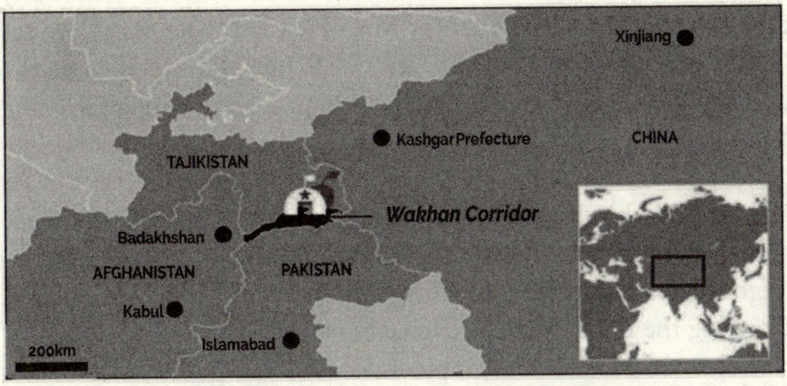

Image Courtesy: South China Morning Post

On 6 September 2018, the Afghan Ambassador to Beijing stated in an interview with *Reuters*, that China was all set to train Afghan soldiers on Chinese soil, in an effort to counter Islamic State (ISIS) and Al-Qaeda militants attempting to infiltrate Xinjiang through the northeastern border of Afghanistan, the mountainous Wakhan Corridor.[2] As per recent reports published by the *South China Morning Post*, despite straight-faced denials, China is very much in the process of building the military training camp in Wakhan and intends to station at least one battalion of troops at the base, along with requisite weapons and military equipment, upon completion of the project.[3]

In March 2018, the International Crisis Group too released a report affirming the discreet presence of Chinese soldiers in the Gorno–Badakhshan Autonomous Region (GBAO) of Tajikistan that borders both the Wakhan Tract in Afghanistan, and the Xinjiang Province in China.[4] Chinese military activity in Afghanistan therefore, needs to be understood by juxtaposing their projected strategic intent of countering Islamist radical forces targeting the Uyghur Muslims of Xinjiang, with their larger objective of expanding the scope of their strategic and economic influence towards Central Asia.

At the recently held meeting between the foreign ministry delegations of China and Pakistan in Islamabad, it was collectively decided to extend the ambitious China–Pakistan Economic Corridor (CPEC) project towards the 'west'.[5] While the specifics of the expansion were not made public, China's foreign minister, Wang Yi, had announced earlier in 2018 that Afghanistan would certainly come under the purview of CPEC, which is part of President Xi Jinping's flagship Belt and Road Initiative (BRI). Over the last three years, China has provided USD 70 million worth of military aid to Afghanistan, and USD 90 million worth of development assistance, targeting the Badakhshan province in particular.[6] [7]

Given the current strategic predispositions and policy predilections, financial and material assistance to Afghanistan is likely to reflect an upward trend in the foreseeable future as well. By establishing a physical presence in the region, China will become far better equipped to broker a peace deal between the militant factions operating in the various regions of Afghanistan and the government apparatus of the country, overtaking India as the frontrunner in the peace-building process, and taking a step towards acquiring international recognition as a legitimately benign global power. In keeping with their aspirations to single-handedly exploit the strategic leverage of Afghanistan, China has successfully convinced India to jointly partake in a limited capacity building programme in Afghanistan, which has left Kabul considerably disappointed with New Delhi, hitherto their foremost development investor in South Asia.[8]

China, however, seems to be striving to achieve a diplomatic equilibrium of sorts. Unlike most other states, it is viewing the chronic instability in Afghanistan as an opportunity to make considerable strategic headway, while at the same time playing the diplomatic card by projecting the intent of synthesizing a truce between the various warring entities in the region. Moreover, China has thus far fared well in retaining Pakistan as an 'all-weather' ally, by consistently allaying Pakistani fears and insecurities regarding growing Sino–Afghan closeness, while simultaneously integrating Kabul in its strategic calculus.

Having said that, the most important factor leading to fast-paced militarization of Badakhshan is the threat that the exiled Uyghur fighters of the East Turkestan Islamic Movement (ETIM) – now known as the Turkistan Islamic Party – operating out of Afghanistan, pose to strategic stability in China. The Uyghur Muslim province of Xinjiang, as it stands today, has been explicitly termed by Chinese authorities as the festering ground for three menacing evils that their society is confronting – separatism, terrorism and religious extremism.[9] Adding to this, there exists the dangerous possibility of radical elements hailing from foreign lands, such as the ones mentioned earlier, using Afghanistan as a launch pad to establish insurgent links with the already vulnerable Uyghur inhabited areas of China. Military operations in Afghanistan will therefore be imperative for China to counter militant activities of groups such as the ETIM, to instal a system of checks along their western border, and secure a watertight security mechanism with Tajikistan, Afghanistan and Pakistan.

The above notwithstanding, China's forward policy in the Wakhan Corridor needs to be assessed with a critical eye. Although on one level it seems to be motivated primarily by the threat of radicalization, China's interest in the region is also contingent on the strategic role that Afghanistan is capable of playing, in the larger scheme of things. Despite vehement Chinese denial, there seems to be sufficient evidence to indicate a definite military build-up in the region that China sees as an opportunity to arrogate to itself the role of a balancing force in the region's dynamics. In other words, China is viewing the chronic instability in Afghanistan as an opportunity to make considerable strategic headway, while pursuing both domestic and foreign policy objectives.

4

Decoding the China–Bangladesh Relationship

JOYEETA BHATTACHARJEE

There are various facets to Sino–Bangladesh ties. The two countries share defence, economic, political and people-to-people ties. China and Bangladesh have reconciled with the past and their relationship has grown in every sector.

China–Bangladesh connections have undergone a dramatic transformation from a formerly adversarial relationship to an enduring strategic partnership. During the liberation of Bangladesh in 1971, China supported Pakistan. Post-liberation, China even vetoed its entry into the United Nations.[1] Since then, the bilateral relationship has undergone significant transformation. Today, Bangladesh considers China an all-weather friend and trusted ally. During Chinese President Xi Jinping's visit to Dhaka in 2016, the two countries established a strategic partnership.[2]

Diplomatic relations between China and Bangladesh were established in January 1976, just a few months after the assassination of Sheikh Mujibur Rahman, the leader of Bangladesh's freedom movement and the country's first prime minister, in a military coup in August 1975. The military dictatorship that succeeded Mujibur Rahman is credited with enhancing Bangladesh's ties with China. In 1977, military dictator General Ziaur Rahman visited China, the first visit by any Bangladeshi head of state to China.[3] The visit gave major impetus to the relationship and it has grown steadily. There has been a consistency in Bangladesh regarding its policy towards China. In 1991, democracy was restored in Bangladesh and democratic governments since then have backed the two countries. The democratically elected leaders have been visiting China regularly.

Defence ties between the two countries is considered a major strength of the relationship. China is the only country with which Bangladesh signed a defence agreement. China is the biggest arms supplier to Bangladesh. Bangladesh defence forces are equipped with Chinese arms including tanks, missile launchers, fighter aircraft and several weapons systems. In July 2017, Bangladesh purchased two Ming-class submarines from China. Besides, China provides training to officers of the Bangladesh army. Bangladesh's dependence on Chinese arms has made the army a major supporter of the defence relationship.[4]

It is worth noting that, after liberation, the Bangladesh army had inducted repatriated officers from the Pakistan army who were familiar with Chinese arms. Because of this familiarity with Chinese arms, the Bangladesh army preferred sourcing weapons from China. Also, the friendly prices offered by China made the sourcing of arms from them lucrative.[5]

Economic ties are an important aspect of bilateral relations. China is Bangladesh's biggest trading partner with bilateral trade above USD 10 billion. However, the trade balance favours China with the trade gap between China and Bangladesh worth USD 9 billion approximately.[6] Bangladesh pressed for concessions to reduce the deficit and China obliged, giving duty-free access to Bangladeshi products. However, despite these concessions, there is no visible change in the deficit. China is also investing in Bangladesh, mainly in manufacturing.

Development cooperation forms an important part of any bilateral relationship. China is a major development partner of Bangladesh in infrastructure. China is building bridges, roads, railway tracks, airports and power plants. Chinese developmental assistance mostly comes as lines of credit. During President Xi Jinping's visit in 2016, China promised to give USD 24 billion dollars in economic assistance to Bangladesh, primarily as lines of credit, for approximately twenty-four projects.[7]

These development partnership initiatives have helped China popularize its image in Bangladesh and it is now able to portray itself as a friend seeking the well-being of the Bangladeshi people and the progress of the country. China has wisely capitalized on this popularity to gain political advantage by convincing Bangladesh to back its entry into the South Asian Association of Regional Cooperation (SAARC) as an observer and has convinced Dhaka to join the Belt and Road Initiative (BRI).[8]

In addition to these initiatives, Beijing is providing scholarships to students to study in China and encouraging Bangladeshis to learn Chinese. Furthermore, there is flight connectivity between Beijing and Dhaka via Kunming in Yunnan.

A crucial reason for the growth of Sino–Bangladesh relations is due to a national consensus in Bangladesh. China has skilfully created a perception in Bangladesh that it is politically neutral and non-interfering, and it has done so by refraining from commenting about Bangladesh's internal issues in public.

Bangladesh claims that economic considerations are the crux of this relationship. For Bangladesh, Chinese investments are a godsend, as it needs them for developing its infrastructure. Bangladesh aims to become a developed nation by 2040 and to achieve that target the country needs to develop its infrastructure and boost economic productivity.

China's main interest is Bangladesh's 160-million-strong market. Besides, Bangladesh is a good outsourcing destination for its manufacturing industries because of the cheap labour the country offers. Again, ports in Bangladesh are an important motivation for China because it offers an alternative route for China to reduce its dependence on the Straits of Malacca for the supply of its energy. Given Bangladesh's geographical proximity to China's Yunnan province, its ports can be easily accessed for the supply of energy resources.

Nevertheless, there is an India factor responsible for the bonhomie between China and Bangladesh. A large section in Bangladesh supports stronger ties with China to counterbalance India. For China, developing ties with Bangladesh gives it a presence in a major country in South Asia, which is India's backyard. Bangladesh could work as a bridge to access Indian markets for its products. Again, Bangladesh's strategic location, especially its proximity to the Siliguri Corridor – a narrow strip of land connecting India's northeast region to the rest of the country – is also a motivating factor. Indian security analysts suggest that China might leverage its relationship with Bangladesh to watch India closely in the event that major hostilities break out between China and India over their disputed border. Many in Bangladesh, however, have observed that such assumptions are far-fetched, as the country wants to maintain good relations with both India and China. Bangladesh Prime Minister Sheikh Hasina herself has said that India should not be worried about the country's relationship with China.[9]

Although China–Bangladesh ties remain strong, there is evidence to suggest that Bangladesh might not be wholly subservient to all the Chinese diktats. For example, Bangladesh had refused to accept the Chinese conditions on the construction of the Sonadia deep-sea port in 2014.[10] But as China's clout continues to grow in the wider South Asia and Indian Ocean region, Bangladesh cannot be expected to remain immune to it and the ties can only be expected to grow in the future.

5

India Faces the China Wall in Its NSG Drive

ARKA BISWAS

India has continued its diplomatic efforts to join the Nuclear Suppliers Group (NSG) since submitting its formal application for membership in 2016. While New Delhi has been hopeful that all remaining forty-eight members of the group would support its membership application, there has been no optimism over China joining the consensus. Beijing has explained its opposition to India's entry to the group citing potential issues because India has not signed the Treaty on the Non-Proliferation of Nuclear Weapons (NPT). But arguments from New Delhi highlight that Beijing's opposition should be largely viewed as political – its commitment to support Pakistan diplomatically and its objective of curtailing India's rise as a regional power.[1] Despite hints from Beijing that it might be open to discussing India's prospective inclusion in the NSG, developments in the bilateral relations make that prospect bleak. A geopolitical tussle between India and China has ensued and the two neighbours have been at loggerheads on several issues. As long as the two foreign policy objectives of the incumbent Indian government – confronting

China politically and securing India's NSG membership – remain in conflict with each other, it is unlikely that New Delhi will receive Beijing's nod for the NSG.

Since India submitted its NSG membership application, Beijing has publicly expressed its objection to it. In fact, at the beginning of the Seoul plenary of the group in June 2016, Chinese diplomats were quoted saying that India's membership application was not even on the agenda of the plenary.[2] Beijing explained that its opposition to India's entry was due to the detrimental effects on the NPT.[3] Inclusion in the NSG, Beijing believes, would affirm India's status as a nuclear weapon state; since the NPT – the framework that holds the nuclear non-proliferation architecture – allows only the five designated nuclear weapon states, India's admission to the group would undermine the treaty.

Beijing has further added that if India's membership application is to be considered, it should not be treated as an exception and a principled approach should be adopted that applies to all membership applicants that are not party to the NPT. China's 'principled' opposition to India's entry has been viewed as political, especially as Pakistan – the only other country not party to the NPT and interested in joining the NSG – applied for membership to the group a week after India, with support from China. The attempt of linking India's membership application to that of Pakistan's resulted in a flurry of writings from India accusing China of infusing politics into the NSG and compromising the objective of universalizing the norms of nuclear non-proliferation.

While Beijing's official mouthpiece dismissed such accusations and called the Indian reportage 'self-centred' and 'self-righteous', it also noted that it is open to having a mature conversation with an Indian government that 'behaves decently and is willing to communicate'.[4] Some Indian experts also noted that, as Beijing had committed itself so strongly to its opposition to India's NSG membership, it was difficult for it to change its stance at short notice at the Seoul plenary of 2016 and that Beijing could be more flexible in the future.

This argument was reinforced when Indian and Chinese officials met in September 2016 and thereafter in October 2016 with India's NSG membership on the agenda.[5]

However, developments in India–China bilateral relations since have only hardened Beijing's opposition to New Delhi's NSG membership bid. While securing India's entry to the NSG has been a priority for New Delhi, the Indian government has focused on another of its foreign policy objectives – to confront China politically on all fronts available. New Delhi has allowed the Dalai Lama to visit the state of Arunachal Pradesh, territory that is claimed by China; and opposed the China–Pakistan Economic Corridor (CPEC), which passes through the disputed territory in the state of Jammu and Kashmir, and a part of China's Belt Road Initiative (BRI), among others. All these developments have strained relations between India and China.

India has made significant efforts in getting China on board for its inclusion in the NSG, be it Prime Minister Narendra Modi raising the matter with President Xi Jinping or New Delhi assuring Beijing that it will not block Pakistan's entry to the group should other members concur. To top it all, there have been speculations that New Delhi has asked Moscow to convince Beijing or else it will put on hold the memorandum of understanding (MoU) with Moscow on the construction of nuclear reactors at Kudankulam 5 and 6 (although the Indian government officially denied putting such pressure on Russia). These efforts, however, are unlikely to bear any fruit for New Delhi so long as its foreign policy priorities – of joining the NSG and confronting China geopolitically – continue to be in direct conflict with each other. Until India has sufficient leverage to moderate China's behaviour on either of these fronts, it will continue to face the China wall in its NSG drive.

6

Doklam Impasse: Why Confrontation with the PRC Matters

KARTIK BOMMAKANTI

The 2017 crisis over the Doklam plateau provides important confirmation that confrontation with the People's Republic of China (PRC) and potential for force remains a possibility in Sino–Indian relations. Much has been written about why and how this crisis emerged in the Bhutan–India–China tri-junction without probing the larger implications it portends for conflict and cooperation between India and the PRC. What remains unaddressed is why and how their protracted boundary dispute renders Sino–Indian relations fragile, despite a burgeoning trade relationship. The Doklam impasse invites examination of two very relevant conceptual issues connected to relative and absolute gains on the one hand, and on the other, how reputational factors were important in determining the outcome of the crisis.

Relative vs. Absolute Gains

There is a veritable division between two schools of thought. The first, which the liberals subscribe to, highlights the pacifying role that economic interdependence plays in reducing conflict between India and the PRC. The second, the realist camp, contends that if the potential for force exists, their capacity to maximize cooperation will remain stunted. The standoff in Doklam only indicated that regardless of the argument advanced by liberal institutionalists, the prospects of absolute gains from open trade and greater economic intercourse mitigating the possibility of conflict and generating cooperation are limited. If anything, the Sino–Indian standoff gives empirical support to realist claims that relative gains are more important than absolute gains in international politics.[1]

Indian liberal institutionalists who express optimism about Beijing's claim that the Belt and Road Initiative (BRI) represents 'win-win' economic cooperation[2] between the two Asian giants should be sobered by current tensions. Notwithstanding the fact that some suggest that India stands to lose little in military terms if the PRC controls the Doklam plateau – the relative gains argument is apt in this case. India sees China's control of the Doklam plains as disadvantaging it as it reduces the distance between the plateau and the Siliguri Corridor. Critically, the PRC effort to alter the status quo in Doklam enervates the Indian army's capacity to concentrate strength. In any case, Beijing and New Delhi agreed that any territory under dispute at tri-junctions, as is the case with Bhutan and Myanmar, would be resolved following confabulation with Thimphu and Naypyidaw. Therefore, regardless of the merits of those who argue that there are no intrinsic Indian interests at stake, the *perception* of the other side gaining an advantage also matters in highlighting the significance of relative gains. This has important implications because relative gains over their disputed boundary are likely to override any aggregate or absolute gains that they make through trade and economic intercourse.

Reputation over Doklam

Some in India have suggested that the PRC's current strength actually gives it reason not to escalate the Doklam crisis.[3] If that is the case, why did Beijing precipitate the crisis in the first place? Was it triggered to test India's resolve and the extent of its support for Thimphu? For China, sovereignty claims evoke a visceral nationalist yawp. India, for its part, sees its security jeopardized by the PRC's road construction on the Doklam plains. Sovereignty and security are difficult issues in international politics, because they denude opportunities for cooperation, but equally constrain Beijing and New Delhi to defuse tensions. More importantly, while analysts recognized that Beijing's aim is to 'drive a wedge' between India and Bhutan,[4] few have considered how reputational factors influence the persistence of the crisis. Reputation in international politics works through two mechanisms: the first is dispositional and the second is situational. Dispositional factors relate to an actor's behavioural characteristics, such as intentions and motivations.[5] Situational factors are context specific to the extent an actor's conduct is driven by the constraints and opportunities inherent in the situation.[6] In some cases, both dispositional and situational attributes may be evident as is in the Doklam impasse. Chinese motives have drawn a response, because India holds some military advantage in the area, which Beijing wants to limit, and situational factors have played a role in New Delhi's response arising from competing territorial claims between Beijing and Thimphu and not between India and the PRC. By precipitating the crisis in Doklam, Beijing was only testing how credible India's support is for Bhutan even if New Delhi had no direct territorial claims over Doklam.

This situation should be familiar to many, particularly Westerners, in that it highlights the extent to which a strategic patron can come to the defence of its ally when the latter is threatened. What exertions will the patron endure on behalf of its ally, as is the case between the US and its allies? Indeed, the Doklam impasse had put India in a veritable hornet's nest, because New Delhi could neither forsake defending the territorial claims Bhutan has over Doklam nor could it ignore Chinese moves to shrink its operational-military space. Beijing, for its part, was attempting to kill two birds with one stone. First, since India was not an actual or legitimate claimant to the territory in dispute, China could assert internationally and through shrill rhetoric that New Delhi should back off. Second, it exerted pressures on India from a military standpoint, both in having to come to the defence of its ally as well as restricting India's options in defending the Siliguri Corridor. The Siliguri Corridor is a twenty-five-kilometre-wide stretch of territory, which connects the rest of India to Northeast India. The corridor is vulnerable to Chinese military interdiction. Moreover, if India backed down in the face of Chinese duress, the danger was it would be potentially setting itself up for further Chinese tests of Indian resolve along the rest of the Line of Actual Control (LAC).

7

The Sobering Arithmetic of a Two-Front War

ABHIJNAN REJ

As relations with both China and Pakistan continue to deteriorate, Indian policymakers now find themselves contemplating the unpleasant possibility of a 'two-front' war with both countries.[1] Whether such a war would be overtly collusive or not between China and Pakistan – that is, whether they would pre-plan a joint attack on India or take advantage of strategic opportunism – it is clear to many in positions of authority that the Indian military remains fundamentally unprepared for such a challenge.[2] But it can also be argued that a two-front force ratio (of Pakistani and a fraction of Chinese inventories to India's) has evolved and varied considerably over time, as China continues to rapidly modernize as well as numerically increase its military (through significant increases in defence spending)[3] and Indian military preparedness flounders.

In this article, such an evolution and variation of a two-front force ratio is quantitatively examined using time-series data constructed from ten International Institute for Strategic Studies (IISS) *Military*

Balance[4] volumes, from 2008–17. (A convention: given that the volumes publish data from the year before, the data reported below will correspond to the volume from the following year. For example, data quoted here for, say, 2010 would be from the 2011 volume, and so on.) The key finding of the article is that this force ratio, never in India's favour to begin with, is currently rapidly shifting in favour of the adversaries, even after considering smaller fractions of the Chinese military involved in a two-front conflict.

Before presenting the results, a caveat is in order. The article works with only seven equipment variables and a simple bean count. Therefore, a much more granular study is necessary for a firm establishment of the results. Having said that, the results that do appear are disturbing and portend ill for India were there to be a future collusive threat from Pakistan and China. It also points to an urgent need to make qualitative and quantitative improvements in the Indian military.

Background

A two-front war could start against India in three different ways. One, Pakistan takes advantage of an India–China conflict. Two, China engages in strategic opportunism in an India–Pakistan conventional military engagement. Three, China and Pakistan together collude to launch a surprise coordinated attack from both India's east and west. Out of this, the first is the most probable given that China would be hesitant to be seen as being either opportunistic or overtly aggressive at a time when Beijing engages in a hard sell of its global aspirations throughout Asia. This also seems the case because of the simple fact that if China were to want to take on India directly, it could very well do so without Pakistani assistance. The likely possibility, therefore, is a border war between India and China which Pakistan exploits to open a front across Kashmir to compensate for its inferior force ratio vis-à-vis India.

To see this, consider Figures 1 and 2, which plot the ratios of Pakistani and Chinese main battle tanks (MBT) and the ratios of the two countries' combat capable aircraft to India's, respectively.

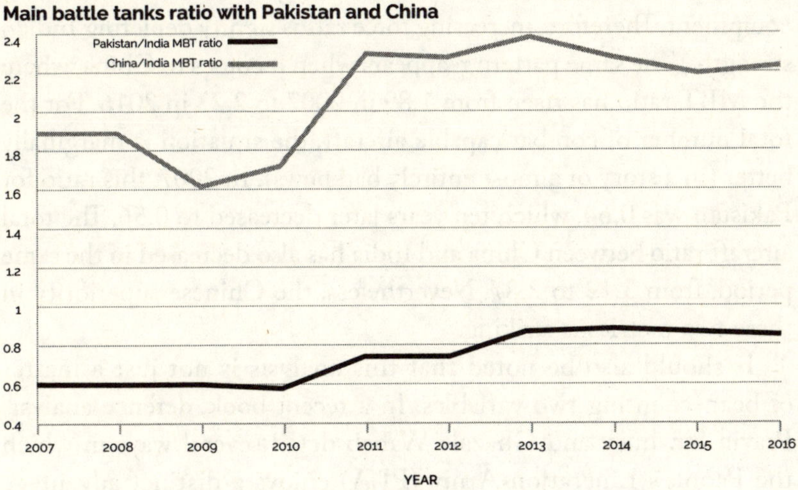

Figure 1

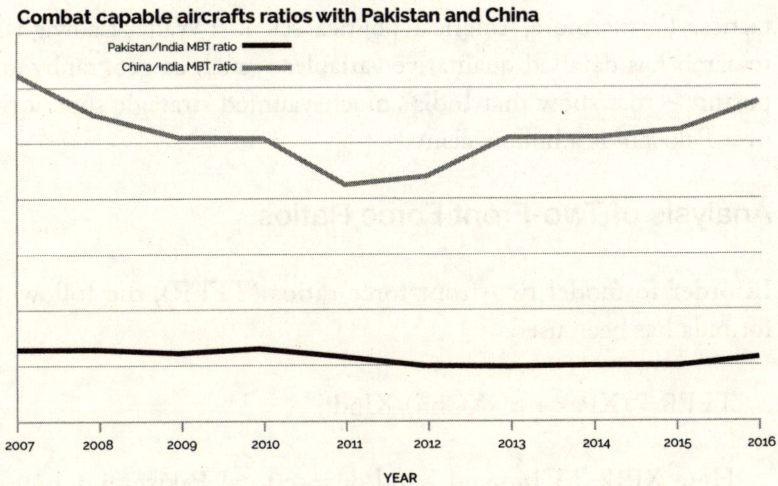

Figure 2

In terms of the ratio of Pakistani MBT to India's, India has steadily lost its advantage. In 2007, this ratio stood at 0.61, which by 2016 had risen to 0.85. (The simplest way to read force ratio numbers is to see them as the adversary's strength given one unit of Indian equipment. Therefore, increasing force ratios signify depleting Indian strength.) The same pattern reappears when it comes to China, where the MBT ratio has risen from 1.89 in 2007 to 2.23 in 2016. For the total number of combat capable aircraft, the situation is marginally better (in a story of almost entirely bad news). In 2007, this ratio for Pakistan was 0.64, which ten years later decreased to 0.56. The total aircraft ratio between China and India has also decreased in the same period, from 3.12 to 2.87. Nevertheless, the Chinese superiority in these two metrics is striking.

It should also be noted that this analysis is not just a matter of bean-counting two variables. In a recent book, defence analysts Pravin Sawhney and Ghazala Wahab detail several ways in which the People's Liberation Army (PLA) enjoys a distinct advantage over India, such as leveraging integrated theatre commands as well as a unified rocket force that replaces antiquated artillery-based tactics.[5] Furthermore, American political scientist Walter Ladwig III's research has detailed qualitative variables – such as geography and posture – that show that India's much-vaunted strategic superiority over Pakistan is a hollow claim.[6]

Analysis of Two-Front Force Ratios

In order to model two-front force ratios (TFFR), the following formula has been used:

$$TFFR = (XPak + \alpha \times XChn)/XInd$$

Here XPak, XChn, and XInd denote total Pakistani, Chinese, and Indian equipment of a certain type X respectively, which could vary. In other words, X could be MBT or fighter aircraft or some other equipment. The coefficient α is a number between 0 and 1 and specifies the fraction of Chinese equipment to be used by that country against India in a two-front war. In this article, α = 0.2, 0.3 or 0.4, meaning that it considers cases where China uses 20, 30 or 40 per cent of its equipment of a certain type against India. Please note that such choice of values is illustrative; the actual value of α will depend on other factors such as terrain and availability of supply lines. (Following conventions on how force ratios are calculated, it is assumed that India and Pakistan will deploy all its equipment of a certain type in a conflict between them.)

The time series for the main battle tank TFFR is given in Figure 3.

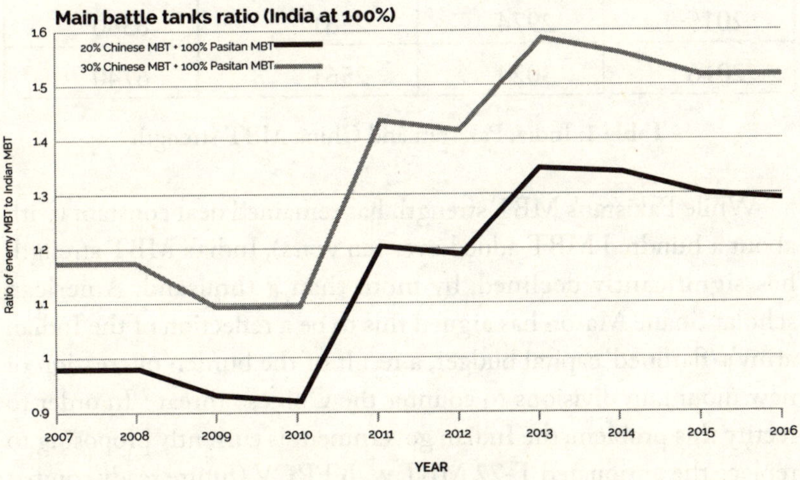

Figure 3

Two things stand out about this graph: one, how the TFFR has dramatically changed since 2010, and two, how Pakistan stands to gain vis-à-vis its MBT force ratio in the event of an India–China conflict (compare Figure 1 with 3). In order to understand the first point about Figure 3 better, it is instructive to look at the raw numbers behind it, in Table 1.

YEAR	INDIA	PAKISTAN	CHINA
2007	4059	2461	7660
2008	4065	2461	7660
2009	4047	2461	6550
2010	4117	2386	7050
2011	3233	2411	7400
2012	3274	2411	7430
2013	2874	2501	6840
2014	2874	2531	6540
2015	2974	2561	6540
2016	3024	2561	6740

Table 1: India, Pakistan and China MBT strength

While Pakistan's MBT strength has remained near constant (with about a hundred MBT added over ten years), India's MBT strength has significantly declined, by more than a thousand. American scholar Shane Mason has argued this to be a reflection of the Indian army's 'flatlined' capital budget, a result of the burden of creation of new mountain divisions to counter the Chinese threat.[7] In order to rectify this problem, the Indian government is currently proposing to replace the antiquated T-72 MBT with FRCV (future ready combat vehicles), although this is far from fruition at the present (2017).[8] The decrease in the number of Chinese MBT can be explained by a general reorientation of the PLA under President Xi Jinping away from being a ground-centric force and towards greater naval and air capabilities for the People's Liberation Army Navy (PLAN), People's Liberation Army Air Force (PLAAF) and the People's Liberation Army Rocket Forces (PLARF).[9]

It is the second point about Figure 3 that is more striking. Assume, as one of the plots in that figure does, that China deploys 30 per cent of its MBT ($\alpha = 0.3$, in the formula above) in a conflict with India. India's overall MBT TFFR has depleted from 1.09 in 2010 to 1.52 in 2016 – a 39.4 per cent decrease of the force ratio in this scenario. Therefore, Pakistan may indeed find it convenient to launch a limited attack in Kashmir in the event of an India–China war and forestall a counteroffensive by India along its western borders by leveraging the changed MBT ratio. This is in sharp distinction to the somewhat favourable Pakistan–India MBT ratio depicted in Figure 1, which would have prevented Pakistani adventurism to begin with, had China not been a factor.

The second TFFR is that of artillery strength, and the corresponding time series is depicted in Figure 4.

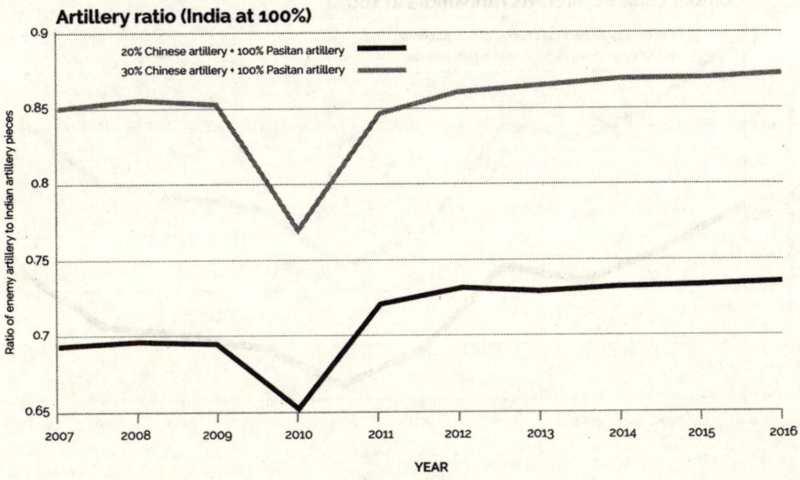

Figure 4

Again, the same story as with the MBT is true here. Even at 20 per cent Chinese deployment, the artillery TFFR increased from 0.69 in 2007 to 0.73 nearly ten years later. What could be perceived as a silver lining – that this is the only TFFR that is less than one for India – is not really so. During this period, the Indian artillery declined to 1,618, but it is the dramatic reduction in Chinese artillery making the TFFR what it is. (Pakistan's artillery strength has shown very modest growth in this period: 4,291 in 2007 to 4,472 in 2016.) Between 2007 and 2016, PLA reduced its artillery pieces by 4,482. This reduction is reflected in recommissioning of the PLA Second Artillery Corps as the PLARF in December 2015.[10] It suggests a move away from artillery pieces and into short- and medium-range precision-strike missiles in order to have the same tactical effect. In India, no such move is anticipated at the present.

The TFFR for total number of combat capable aircraft are given in Figure 5.

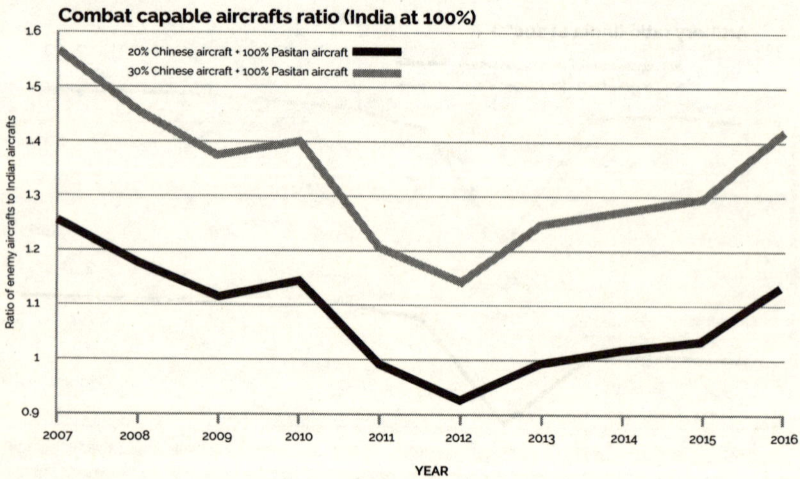

Figure 5

In order to unpack the TFFR, it is important to look at the raw numbers (Table 2).

YEAR	INDIA	PAKISTAN	CHINA
2007	565	360	1762
2008	603	383	1653
2009	632	383	1617
2010	665	426	1687
2011	798	453	1693
2012	870	423	1903
2013	866	422	2193
2014	881	450	2239
2015	881	450	2306
2016	803	451	2307

Table 2: A comparison of the three countries' combat capable aircraft

However, it is the serious depletion of the Indian Air Force's strength – from 870 to 803 combat capable aircraft, between 2012 and 2016 – along with a more than a 21 per cent increase in the number of such PLAAF aircraft in that period – that explains the plot. Just as in the case of the MBT TFFR, it is instructive to compare Figure 5 with Figure 2 in order to note the tremendous force multiplier the PLA is for the Pakistan military. In 2016, the Pakistan–India ratio went up from 0.56 to a TFFR of 1.14 in the event of a two-front conflict, assuming a 20 per cent Chinese involvement.

The variables considered so far may be – to some eyes – too crude to tell a fuller story. In order to examine this claim, consider two finer variables: the total number of armoured combat vehicles which can transport an infantry squad (sum of armoured personnel carriers and infantry fighting vehicles), and the total number of fighter planes (including those with a ground attack role). To start with, consider the TFFR of armoured combat transport vehicles in Figure 6.

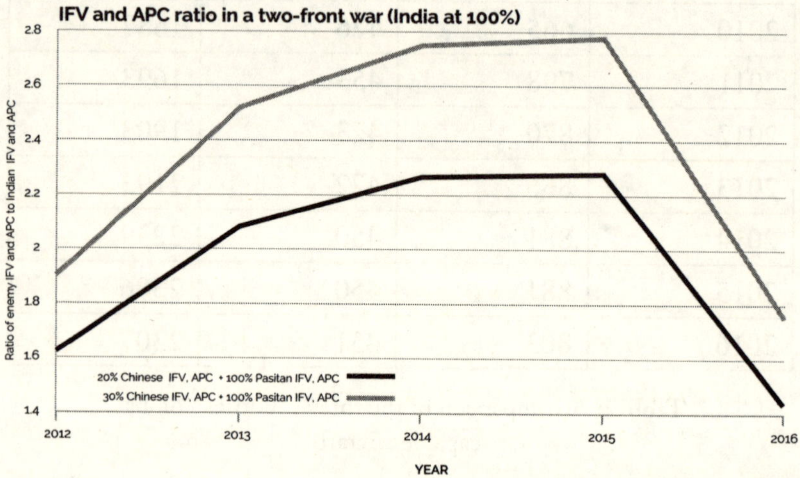

Figure 6

In 2012, at 30 per cent Chinese involvement, the TFFR for infantry fighting vehicle (IFV) and armoured personnel carrier (APC) stood at 1.62. This decreased to 1.43 in 2016. Part of the reason behind this welcome development was the rapid ongoing mechanization of the Indian infantry[11] that has led to a massive induction of IFV between 2015 and 2016, from 1,455 to 2,500. (The Indian Army no longer uses the APC at its disposal; Pakistan, on the other hand, has only APCs.) The Chinese and Pakistani numbers of armoured combat transport vehicles remained relatively stable in this period.

The second finer-grained metric – of the number of fighter aircraft, possibly with ground attack roles – is examined in the time series of Figure 7.

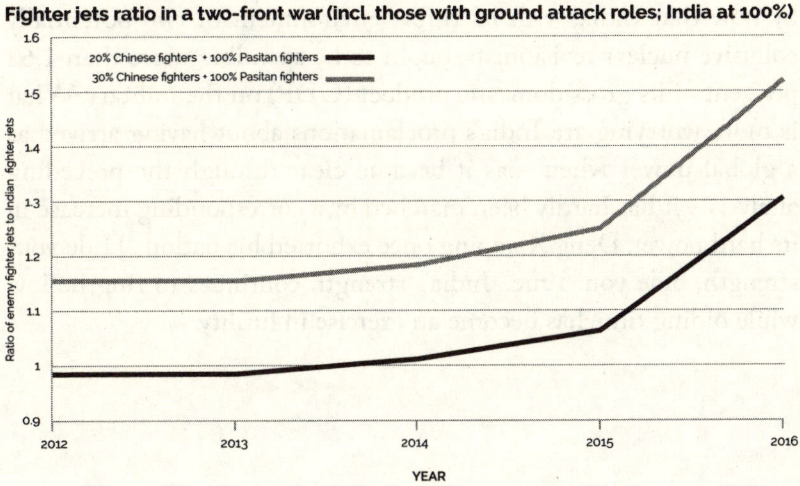

Figure 7

This is perhaps the most depressing plot of the lot. In 2012, India's fighter aircraft with ground attack roles (FGA) and fighter jets for aerial combat (FTR) strength together stood at 799. By 2016, this had depleted to 613 while the Chinese numbers in the same category remained stable. There is extensive commentary about the poor shape of the Indian air force caught as it is, in various bureaucratic turf wars and public controversies around acquisitions. Whatever be the reason, if the IAF depletes at the rate at which it has been thus far, fighting a two-front war will soon become a theoretical impossibility. Air Marshal B.S. Dhanoa noted in 2018: 'Our numbers are not adequate to fully execute an air campaign in a two-front scenario. The probability of a two-front scenario is an appreciation which you need to do. But, are the numbers adequate? No.'[12] The current analysis confirms his claim.

Notwithstanding the drawbacks that come with a bean count, the analysis presented in this paper disabuses the claim that the Indian military is ready to fight a two-front war, chest-thumping from some politically-motivated actors aside. It has become a trite observation by now that India, with its threat environment of two potentially collusive nuclear revisionists, ought to be spending more than 1.62 per cent of its gross domestic product (GDP) on the military. What is more worrying are India's proclamations about having arrived as a global power when – as it became clear through the preceding analysis – it has hardly been matched by a corresponding increase in its hard power. Deng Xiaoping once exhorted his nation: 'Hide your strength, bide your time.' India's strength continues to ring hollow while biding time has become an exercise in futility.

8

The Future Trajectory of Sino–Indian Water Relations

SONALI MITTRA

China's effort to portray itself as a credible and peaceful neighbour has been unsuccessful in more than one way. Nowhere is it more evident than in the case of water sharing of the Brahmaputra river's upper stream, the Yalu Zangbu. The stoppage of data sharing on the Brahmaputra during and after the Doklam standoff[1] and lack of clarity on the intent behind the thousand-kilometre-long tunnel to transfer water from Yarlung Tsangpo – as the Yalu Zangbu is known in Tibet – to Xinjiang[2] betray China's self-declared 'responsible' behaviour involving transboundary waters. While hydrological data sharing has been resumed after the eleventh meeting of the India–China Expert Level Mechanism (ELM) on transboundary waters recently (26–27 March 2018),[3] critical questions arise on the future trajectory of Sino–Indian water relations. What are the emerging geopolitical implications of sharing water from the Brahmaputra between China and India?

Departure from the Past

Diplomatic interactions on water cooperation between China and India have not always followed the contours of their geopolitical relationship. Ideally, a cordial relationship between the riparian countries is directly proportional to the possibility of cooperation over transboundary waters. But this has not always been the case.

With the improvement in relations, politically, in the 1950s, joint water and flood management and disaster prevention were the driving factors for collaboration between India and China. All talks on water cooperation were stalled during and much after the 1962 Sino–Indian war. As the relationship recovered, China and India signed the first memorandum of understanding (MoU) on sharing hydrological information on the Brahmaputra/Yalu Zangbu River in 2002.[4]

The political water equation was aligned until the early 2000s, after which water and political exchanges began to be delinked, at least superficially. In the later period (2002–12), a conflictual water relationship had minimal influence on the broader political relationship. Indian apprehensions on the impact of the Chinese Zangmu dam on the upper reaches of the Brahmaputra[5] were on a high at the time when China and India were developing a border resolution mechanism,[6] economic and strategic partnerships, and resuming bilateral army exercises.[7]

At other times, there have been instances when, despite tense political relations, water cooperation has advanced quite smoothly. In 2013, immediately after the Chinese incursion into the Depsang valley in Ladakh,[8] China and India renewed and extended the 2002 MoU on data sharing on the Brahmaputra River.[9] The progress continued over the next few years with regular meetings under the ELM. In 2015, China and India signed another MoU on sharing water-flow data on the Langqên Zangbo/Sutlej River,[10] despite political upheavals.

Departing from the past, the delinking of political and water-related interactions is unlikely to continue. A negative spillover effect on water cooperation is more likely as the the Sino–Indian boundary conflict intensifies. As is already evident in the case of the Doklam standoff when China held up the flood season data on the Brahmaputra, cross-border rivers would be used as a strategic means to influence boundary negotiations.

The Emerging Geopolitical Overtones of Water Cooperation

Historical trends may seem to indicate that tensions over the Brahmaputra form a small subset of the broader political relationship between China and India. However, going forward, laxity and mismanagement of the water relationship will have more severe geopolitical implications for India.

Sino–Indian water dynamics are loosely tied to India's relationship with its other riparian countries: Bangladesh, Pakistan, Nepal and Bhutan. Indian demands over the rights and entitlements to the Brahmaputra river is labelled 'hypocritical' by Bangladesh, Pakistan and even Nepal, who have similar 'lower riparian' grievances. India already has a strained relationship with Bangladesh over the long overdue Teesta Waters Treaty[11] and clashes with Pakistan over hydropower dams and reduced flow of water in the Indus River.[12] Therefore, while India negotiates with China on the rights of shared rivers, it will have to be balanced, strategic and fair so as not to set unrealistic expectations from its lower riparian countries.

Another trend likely to influence India's geopolitical position is China's shift in preference from bilateral to multilateral water cooperation – leaving India in an uncomfortable position. In line with its periphery policy (neighbourhood policy),[13] in 2016, China established the Lancang–Mekong Cooperation (LMC) with the six Mekong countries as an alternative to the Asian Development Bank (ADB)–led Mekong River Commission (MRC), which China denounced all along.[14] Beijing is pushing for a similar China-controlled multilateral setup in the Brahmaputra basin. Since 2010,

China has been advancing its engagement with Bangladesh on water management, hydrological data sharing (on Brahmaputra), flood control and disaster reduction.[15] China is also set to finance a series of hydropower projects in Pakistan under its Belt and Road Initiative (BRI), including one in the contested territory between India and Pakistan.[16]

India, on the other hand, continues to prefer bilateral agreements with its riparian nations. It has maintained discretion in its engagement with its eastern (Bangladesh) and western (Pakistan) riparian neighbours. Despite efforts to improve diplomatic ties with Bangladesh and Pakistan, India fears Chinese encirclement and confinement to a weak negotiating position.

Finally, China's aggressive activities on the upstream of the Brahmaputra may feed into its 'salami slicing' strategy.[17] The southeast Tibetan region and Northeast India are two of the most underdeveloped regions in both the countries. As per the international law of prior appropriation,[18] China can claim a greater share of the Brahmaputra river if it can utilize the water first to transfer it to its arid regions, produce electricity, or use it for agriculture. As China develops this part of the southeastern Tibetan plateau, it will not only be able to strengthen its military reach but may as well reinforce its territorial claim on Arunachal Pradesh, which Beijing refers to as 'Southern Tibet'.[19]

The Way Forward

Sino–Indian water relations have undeniably improved over the years and survived deep political tension. However, in the coming future, the basin countries will face hard challenges owing to climate change, reduced flow of water, upsurge in demand for water and increase in the frequency of disasters, among others. Besides these, both China and India will continue to engage each other more intensively on border issues, economic ties and strive to sustain their geopolitical interests and influence in the region. Undoubtedly, the future trajectory of Sino–Indian water relations point towards increasingly difficult negotiations – one that is more complex and intertwined with fluctuating geopolitical realities. For the Brahmaputra river, India must develop a more proactive strategy, as opposed to the reactive approach being used now. India must be as assertive as it is over the BRI or during the Doklam standoff, and more innovative in setting the standard for best practices in water sharing by focusing more on building India's own competence and capacities in managing cross-border rivers. Consequently, India will be able to establish a more cohesive and resilient position in negotiations with China.

9

'Weather War': The Latest Addition to the Sino–India Conundrum?

APARNA ROY

Reports of China embarking on the world's most ambitious cloud-seeding programme should not surprise India. China has been carrying out successful weather modifications and control and exercises for a decade. During the 2008 Summer Olympics held in Beijing, China, for the first time, fired a barrage of 1,110 cutting-edge military rockets into its evening clouds to make the opening ceremony precipitation-free.[1] However, the recently announced project aimed at bringing artificial rain to an area three times that of Spain[2] has been planned over the Tibetan Plateau, giving India reasons to be wary.

Tibet is the source of Asia's most important rivers, including the Indus, Ganges, Brahmaputra, Irrawaddy, Salween and Mekong.[3] Flowing through China, Laos, Myanmar, Nepal, India, Pakistan and Bangladesh, the rivers constitute a lifeline for nearly 3.4 billion people (46 per cent of the world's 7.06 billion population).[4] Since the plateau could be considered a shared ecological frontier, an anthropogenic change over the fragile ecosystem would have severe ramifications not just for lower riparian India, but other neighbouring South and Southeast Asian countries.

According to the *South China Morning Post*, China's reliance on 'cloud seeding' – the use of aircraft to spray chemicals like silver iodide, potassium chloride and sodium chloride into the clouds to aid precipitation – is a part of its climate change mitigation strategy. China's climate models have projected that the Tibetan plateau is likely to suffer severe droughts due to an estimated rise in temperature and decrease in regional rainfall.[5] While the prediction could be held true, the need for the Tibet region to rely on such artificial rain-making techniques is questionable. As the largest store of accessible freshwater outside the North Pole and South Pole and often referred to as Asia's water tower, the Tibetan plateau is hydrologically quite self-sufficient.[6]

An increase in water content in the rivers originating in the Tibetan plateau would be devastating for the lower riparian. Every year, the average amount of rainfall during the monsoons cause rivers such as the Brahmaputra or the Yarlung Tsangpo in China to overflow, leading to subsequent destructive floods in India's Northeast.[7] According to state government data published in September 2015, the floods and erosion have cost Assam 2,753 human lives and an economic loss of Rs 4,659.472 crore.[8] The flooding in 2017 caused the death of 157 people and devastated twenty-nine districts in Assam. According to the state disaster management authorities, in the past five years, flooding has killed about 500 people.[9]

India should therefore seek to strengthen its monitoring capabilities in the Northeast and border areas through geospatial technology that includes Global Positioning System (GPS), Geographical Information System (GIS) and remote sensing technologies for accurate weather forecasts and data gathering.[10] This would enable India to keep a strict vigil of Chinese activities as well as prepare for an effective counter-response.

To secure the lives of its 3.5-billion population in the fragile ecosystem of Brahmaputra – in the wake of China's cloud seeding ambition in Tibet – India should develop its own hydrological models for flood prediction, even as we continue to receive flood warning data from China. Examining the flows of the rivers regularly, both flood season as well as non-monsoonal flow data, from its own hydro-meteorological stations can enhance India's capacity to detect any suspicious activity upstream that could possibly culminate in a natural disaster in India.[11]

China's new project involves placing thousands of chambers on the Tibetan plateau, burning solid fuels to produce silver iodide. The iodide would act as condensate for water molecules in the air, which would fall to the earth as rain or snow.[12] According to a chemical engineer studying atmospheric aerosols at Columbia University, silver iodide, even in its non-toxic form, has significant potential to disrupt the aquatic ecosystem as it enters the groundwater as rain.[13] A study in 2016 by the Wyoming Weather Modification Pilot Programme found that possible consequences of cloud seeding include rain suppression, floods, tornadoes and silver iodide toxicity. Moreover, the mechanism is unreliable over a long period or on a large scale. A growing body of literature substantiate that not only does cloud seeding fail to achieve the desirable effect, it also could generate harmful consequences.[14]

Geo-engineering experts caution that an artificial manipulation of the weather to produce rain in one area could have unintended consequences, such as low rainfall elsewhere.[15] It would therefore be in China's and India's interest to mutually engage in a joint, thorough scientific study to obtain reliable data from the area. Beijing and New Delhi will have to undertake seeding trials that could guide the use of technology and develop a framework to carry out Environmental Impact Assessments (EIA), before tens of thousands of additional chambers are built across the Tibetan plateau to implement the project over an area of about 1.6 million square kilometres.

However, India's concern should be not just the environmental threat, but the likelihood of significant strategic implications.

The Sino–Indian bilateral relationship has remained tense in recent years owing to their ongoing boundary dispute, trade imbalances and military standoffs between the two countries at the Himalayan plateau of Doklam. Speculations are rife that China may use its weather modification technology as a strategic weapon against India to distort weather and unleash floods and droughts during times of conflict.[16] Such a strategy is not new. Used during the Vietnam War by the name of Operation Popeye, the strategy was to increase rainfall during the monsoon season to make the terrain muddy and difficult to traverse for enemy fighters.[17] While in the Sino–Indian context, such speculation has remained theoretical so far, given India's experience, their practical application cannot be ruled out. China has already begun to employ unconventional tools of coercive water diplomacy by denying flood-warning data on the river Brahmaputra to India during the Doklam standoff, leaving the latter vulnerable.[18]

Insofar as the strategic implications of weather modification are concerned, India should ensure that China does not breach the UN's Environmental Modification Convention (ENMOD) prohibiting states from 'engaging in military or any other hostile use of environmental modification techniques having widespread, long-lasting or severe effects as the means of destruction, damage or injury to any other State Party'.

An important way forward for India is to build on its environmental intelligence (EI) capabilities, because any form of decision-making would require a holistic view, integration of research across the components of cloud seeding, as well as its interactions with the surrounding regions and the downstream ecosystem. The Ministry of Environment and Forests (MoEF) should lead the creation of a platform for observation, modelling and data management.

Given that China is increasingly employing such unconventional means of diplomacy across the region, India should accordingly prepare its respective cadres.

10

Indian Media and China: Changing Discourse

RAKHAHARI CHATTERJI,
ANASUA BASU RAY CHAUDHURY

P.N. Haksar, principal secretary to Prime Minister Indira Gandhi from 1967–73, once remarked, 'It is true that we Indians have looked at China through western eyes ... [W]e have inherited stereotyped images of China ... the same is true of the Chinese looking at India as well. The time has come when it is imperative for us to try and understand each other directly.'[1] Observer Research Foundation's project on understanding China delves into this matter – to find out how the two countries directly perceive each other. Two recent publications titled 'Indian Media's Perception of China: Analysis of Editorials' and 'Indian Regional Media's Perception of China: Analysis of Select Editorials' from the *Assam Tribune* and the *Arunachal Times* are part of the study, making an attempt to present how the national and regional print media has looked at China during the years 2012–14. The national newspapers chosen from India, based on circulation, are: *Times of India*, *Hindu*, *Indian Express*, *Economic Times* and *Financial Express* while for the regional media, the selection has been restricted to *Assam Tribune* and *Arunachal Times*, published from bordering states of Assam and Arunachal Pradesh respectively.

In each of the newspapers, the authors have looked at the editorial pieces relating to China – as these articles are indicative of a newspaper's authoritative perception. There is no doubt that the print media in India, despite the strong presence of electronic media, enjoys enormous reach and has great impact on the minds of its readers – enriching their information, shaping their perceptions and providing them with choices. Hence, the media has a role and a responsibility in communicating proper understanding between neighbouring countries. Pranab Mukherjee, while serving as India's external affairs minister, highlighted this point. Addressing the media, he said:

> In many ways, the media is the torchbearer of better people-to-people contacts … [O]ne sentence from any of you has the potential to reach millions. It can correct a wrong; it can create an image; it can plant a seed of understanding.[2]

The three-year period was selected in the report because it saw leadership changes in both countries, and these leaders – Xi Jinping and Narendra Modi – appear similarly assertive in strengthening the bilateral relationship. They are also making efforts to resolve border and trade disputes between the two countries. The same period also marked the beginning of China's One Belt One Road (OBOR) initiative on the one hand and on the other, the transformation of India's earlier Look East policy into the Act East policy.

Before going into the issue of the print media's perception of China as projected through their editorials, two other issues were explored. It was necessary as well as interesting to know how much attention the print media paid to China-related issues, and secondly, it was also important to know if Indian media's areas of concern vis-à-vis China could be identified and if it would be possible to classify those areas in terms of editorial themes or categories.

The study on national media argues against conventional wisdom about the Indian media's portrayal of China. The total number of editorials published by these five newspapers on China-related issues available on their web editions during these three years stands at 167 – of which thirty were published in 2012 and forty-one in 2013. In 2014, there was a sharp rise in the number of editorials, as the total number came to ninety-six. Compared to 167 editorials in the five national dailies, the editorial count was eighty-nine for the two regional dailies (thirty-one for the *Arunachal Times* and fifty-eight for the *Assam Tribune*), i.e., per newspaper frequency was about 30 per cent higher for the selected regional dailies during this period. Starting with only eleven editorials in 2012, the number of editorials shot up to thirty-eight in 2013 and remained in that neighbourhood with forty editorials in 2014.

To identify the editorial themes in the selected national and regional newspapers, it was necessary to decipher the substantive thrust of an editorial. While dealing with quantitative representation wherein the study had to convert the textual information into quantities, caution was taken to avoid or reduce subjectivity. A group of researchers coded the textual material separately as well as jointly with the objective of attaining as much intersubjectivity as possible. The editorials studied covered a wide spectrum of issues ranging from geopolitics, strategy, the India–China border, international institutions, trade, economy, environment and even Chinese domestic issues. The selected section of the Indian print media showed a consistent interest in China to the extent that for the entire period covered by this study, it devoted slightly more than 15 per cent of editorial pieces to China. Further, editorial attention showed an increasing trend.

It is worth mentioning in this context that most perception studies usually do not consider the factor of geographical proximity in understanding perception. The present study, however, finds that distance from/proximity to the border can have its impact on what issues are considered most urgent. Thus, examination of the regional newspapers finds that the *Arunachal Times*, published from Arunachal Pradesh, the northeastern state bordering China, shows greater interest in India–China border issues while it published fewer editorials on ecology, economy and even on China as a rising power. The *Assam Tribune*, on the other hand, appeared highly sensitive to China's rising power in the neighbourhood and the threat of muscle flexing near the border, followed by its concern for border issues – including the diversion of Brahmaputra water.

While analysing editorials, both in quantitative and qualitative ways, the authors found there was neither consistent antipathy nor over-concern with a single issue, though the print media's perception of China (both national and regional) seemed dominantly negative. A deeper reading of the texts of the editorials under each theme for the national press revealed that 42.5 per cent of the total number of editorials could be labelled as positively disposed towards China while 57.4 per cent looked at China negatively. The highest concentration of positive editorials was found in the *Hindu* (61.2 per cent) while the highest number of negative editorials was in the *Indian Express* (69.8 per cent). This, of course, is a binary view of perception and this way of looking at it may conceivably conceal varieties of nuances within what have been called positive and negative perceptions. One way to get around this problem was to classify each type of perception in terms of its intensity of expression.

The study on national media found that out of the seventy-one positive editorials in national dailies, 28 per cent (twenty) could be qualified as 'strongly positive' while out of the ninety-six negative editorials only 25 per cent (twenty-four) could be labelled as 'strongly negative'. So, the newspapers wrote, proportionally, nearly the same number of editorials which could be labelled as 'strong/positive' or 'strong/negative'. At the same time, while a greater number of editorials in national media portray China in a negative light in general, in three-fourths of such editorials the point is moderately or weakly made.

Contrary to national media's perception of China, where the gap between positive and negative perception was narrow, the regional media demonstrated a huge gap between its positive (24 out of 89) and negative perceptions (65 out of 89) of China. The *Arunachal Times* wrote only 29.03 per cent with a positive projection of China as against 70.96 per cent editorials that were negative. The *Assam Tribune* was even less charitable: its positive editorials constituted only 25.86 per cent as against 74.13 per cent of editorials with a negative tone. All the positive editorials in the *Arunachal Times* were written with weak or moderate intensity (more weak than moderate) while 19 out of 22 negative editorials were strong or moderate (more strong than moderate). So, when the *Arunachal Times* was writing negative editorials it was doing so with a lot more assertion than when it was making a positive point about China. The *Assam Tribune's* position was somewhat different: 86 per cent of its positive editorials were moderate or weak, nearly evenly balanced, in contrast to 73 per cent of its negative editorials which were strong or moderate. That is, its editorials, whether positive or negative, tended to be moderate and not extreme. This slight but noticeable difference between the two newspapers from these two Northeast Indian states could well be because of the existential threat posed by China to Arunachal Pradesh through official de-recognition of its belongingness to India.

While analysing the national and regional dailies' perception it needs to be admitted that although the selection of national print media is more or less robust, the same cannot be said about the regional media where only two newspapers could be selected. Furthermore, although the period covered was not long, it was considered good enough to make a beginning. Despite these limitations, the study could come to some interesting observations. First, it became quite clear from the above presentation that the print media, both national and regional, dominantly perceived China in a negative light. It was also true that the regional media, represented by the two newspapers from two states in the bordering region of India's Northeast, as contrasted with their national counterparts, were distinctly more negative and were becoming increasingly so over these years. At the same time, there was an increasing tendency to be more discerning about issues and more forthright in pointing out areas where cooperation was possible and achievable. For such cooperation, the national press had identified connectivity and collaboration on economic and environmental issues as possible arenas. The regional press, apparently, was less enthusiastic about such cooperation.

Second, it is noteworthy that not only did the national and regional perceptions differ; even that the regional perception was internally fragmented: the print media representing the two northeastern states differed in terms of importance given to different themes as well as in terms of the intensity with which they projected China negatively or positively.

Third, the editorials in the regional newspapers certainly conveyed the idea that even though they represented two states from the bordering areas with historical and contemporary problems with China, they were not overwhelmed by its presence. The regional press did not think they needed to be overly concerned with China even though the publishers were, in the border regions.

Finally, it is also necessary to point out that broadly, the regional media's views overlapped with those of the national media. Thus, both the national and the regional media thought it appropriate to pay more attention to themes like China as a rising power and the border issue, among other themes or issues.

PART 3
China and the World

1

The State of Play in Sino–Japanese Relations

K.V. KESAVAN

Japan and China have just recently commemorated the forty-fifth anniversary of the normalization of ties between them. Their partnership, one of the biggest in the Indo-Pacific, has a great bearing on the peace and stability of the region. Their bilateral trade, with a volume of about USD 300 billion, is one of the largest in the whole region. In a closely integrated and interdependent Indo-Pacific territory, it is not appropriate to look at Sino–Japanese ties only through their narrow bilateral framework. Their strategic and economic interests go far beyond to impinge on a variety of regional and global issues, including maritime security, regional economic development and global climate change, to mention only a few. As many analysts acknowledge, it is hard to think of peace and stability in the Indo-Pacific region without cordial relations between China and Japan. Yet, tensions between the two in recent years have raised serious concerns about the future and the consequent implications for the region as a whole.

The expression 'economically warm and politically cold' is perhaps very apt to characterize their equation in recent years. Bilateral relations have been marred by historical and territorial issues and they have been further exacerbated by the nationalistic approaches adopted by both countries. Yet, they have maintained a fair level of economic interaction. Their economies have a high degree of complementarity with differences in their industrial and technological capabilities. This provides considerable scope for cooperation in several spheres. China is Japan's biggest trading partner as well as the biggest destination for Japanese investment.

In contrast, in the political sphere, Sino–Japanese relations have been severely strained by historical and territorial issues, and quite often, political tensions tended to threaten the prospects of economic cooperation. During 2001–05, when Prime Minister Junichiro Koizumi was at the helm in Japan, his visits to the controversial Yasukuni Shrine brought bilateral ties to the lowest point, but their economic ties remained not only steady but showed substantial growth in trade and investment. Japan's official development assistance (ODA) continued to flow to China for its economic development.[1]

During his first tenure as prime minister in 2006, Shinzo Abe selected China as the first country for his official visit abroad and signed a joint statement with his Chinese counterpart that underlined the importance of fostering 'mutually beneficial relations based on common strategic interests'[2] which became a diplomatic template for subsequent Japanese governments. This was followed by several positive developments such as defence dialogue, reciprocal naval visits, and joint training for search and rescue missions.

But Abe's tenure ended abruptly in 2007 itself and was followed by a series of short-lived cabinets until 2012. The Democratic Party of Japan (DPJ), which was in power during 2009–12, could not carry on any meaningful dialogue with China. On the contrary, the Senkaku/Diaoyu Islands issue, for the first time, assumed serious dimensions following the collision of Chinese and Japanese ships in 2010 and later, upon the nationalization of the islands by then

Prime Minister Yoshihiko Noda. From then on, the Senkaku/ Diaoyu issue suddenly changed the whole tenor of relations between China and Japan. In a bid to assert its rights, China started sending its surveillance ships close to the territorial waters near the islands almost daily. On some occasions, Chinese aircraft also violated Japan's airspace In addition, China also started harping on pre-war military excesses committed by the Japanese military in China, e.g. the Nanking incident and the 'comfort women' case. The situation in the East China Sea became so tense that many in Japan and the US feared that a military clash could occur due to miscalculation or accident.

Abe, who came back to power in December 2012 with a comfortable majority in the Japanese Diet, took a strong position on the Senkaku Islands issue. In addition, his visit to the Yasukuni Shrine in December 2013 followed by a series of security measures he undertook, strained bilateral ties and led to China's termination of all important exchanges with Japan, including summit level meetings.[3]

In the meantime, China's assertive maritime activities in the South China Sea drew a lot of global attention and Japan, the US and their allies strongly criticized China's construction of artificial islands in the area. In various regional forums, Abe strongly advocated that all nations have the right to freedom of navigation in open seas and that no country can change the status quo by force.[4] Abe also extended security-oriented economic aid to countries like the Philippines and Vietnam. His strong stand on the South China Sea issue, including his support to the International Arbitral Tribunal's verdict was denounced by China as unwarranted, since Japan was not a party directly involved in the dispute.

Despite the prolonged tension and turmoil in their bilateral relations, one should also note there have been indications in recent months of a desire from both countries to slowly resume normal exchanges. Influential Japanese leaders such as Yasuo Fukuda, Masahiko Komura and Toshihiro Nikai have maintained close links with the ruling establishment in China and they have played a key role in arranging meetings between President Xi Jinping and Prime

Minister Abe on the sidelines of some regional forums. Although the first two meetings held on the sidelines of the Asia-Pacific Economic Cooperation (APEC) meeting at Beijing in 2014 and later at Jakarta in 2015 were not marked by any particular warmth, the third meeting held at the time of the G-20 gathering at Hangzhou in September 2016 proved to be quite significant, as both leaders underlined the need to develop normal relations and move forward.

In the last week of May 2017, the fourth round of dialogue was held in Tokyo and it was co-chaired by Chinese State Councillor Yang Jiechi and Japan's National Security Advisor Shotaro Yachi. Both sides exchanged views frankly on bilateral and regional issues and reaffirmed their resolve to enhance cooperative relations. They also showed eagerness to resume high-level economic dialogue, which had not been held since 2010.

The year 2018 indeed opened with better prospects for bilateral relations. In January itself, Prime Minister Abe in his policy speech at the Japanese Diet expressed his strong desire to usher in a new era of cooperation with China. He even showed his readiness to extend support to the Belt and Road Initiative (BRI).[5]

In a reciprocal gesture, in April, Chinese Premier Li Keqiang also called upon both countries to create a favourable environment for high-level exchanges and 'help bilateral relations return to the track of healthy development'.

Soon, more significant developments followed. The first one was the resumption of the bilateral, high-level economic dialogue in Tokyo in April, which had not occurred since 2008. Chinese State Councillor and Foreign Minister Wang Yi visited Tokyo on 16 April 2018 to chair the meeting of the dialogue along with his Japanese counterpart Taro Kono. Wang Yi stressed that the changing global economic situation provides numerous opportunities for closer Sino–Japanese cooperation. In response, Taro Kono agreed that economic cooperation was an important driving force for both countries to plan and expand their engagements from a new perspective.[6]

The second was the visit made by Chinese Premier Li Keqiang to Tokyo in May to attend the Japan–China and South Korea trilateral, which had not met for more than two years due to strained relations between the three East Asian countries. The trilateral forum met during unprecedented political and strategic developments caused by the thaw in ties between South and North Korea, and between the US and North Korea. The forum carried considerable significance for Prime Minister Abe, who was feeling sidelined in the whole flurry of diplomatic activities concerning the prospects of peace and denuclearization on the Korean Peninsula.[7]

Li Keqiang's visit certainly gave an impetus for exchanges of visits at the highest level. Shinzo Abe visited China in October 2018 to pave the way for President Xi Jinping's visit to Japan in 2019.

To conclude, in the pursuit of their bilateral engagements, both Japan and China have adopted a pragmatic policy of separating politics from economics. Currently, there is a strong realization that it is essential for both countries to maintain 'mutually beneficial relations based on common strategic interests'. There is considerable stability in their economic relations and leaders of both countries are strongly inclined to further boost these ties. But strategically, there are serious problems – the Senkaku/Diaoyu issue and the freedom of navigation in the East and South China seas pose challenges to both countries.

2

Europe and China: Dependent but Ungrateful?

BRITTA PETERSEN

With China's economic strength and the relative weaknesses of many smaller European countries, it is justified to see a 'divide and rule' strategy in China's public diplomacy – a serious threat to the European Union (EU) that is already suffering from internal frictions.

In August 2017, German Foreign Minister Sigmar Gabriel decided to turn the tables on China. In a speech in Paris, he warned Beijing to stop all efforts to divide the EU and adhere to a 'One-Europe' policy.[1] Alas, he did not suggest how to enforce this new confrontational policy, if he intends to.

He could learn from the Communist Party of China (CPC) how Beijing makes sure that nobody questions the One-China policy. In February 2018, German carmaker Daimler-Benz was forced to apologize for 'insulting the feelings of the Chinese people' by publishing the sentence: 'Look at situations from all angles, and you will become more open' in an advertisement.[2] A seemingly harmless quote – but made by China's favourite enemy, the Dalai Lama.

Daimler's kowtow led to fierce criticism in Germany but the critics probably don't drive Mercedes.

Demonizing His Holiness and forcing everyone who wants to do business with China into submitting to the One-China policy has been a well-known strategy for decades, but it is not the only one anymore. A new report[3] launched by two German think tanks, the Global Public Policy Institute (GPPi) in Berlin and the Mercator Institute for China Studies (MERICS), could well serve as a wake-up call. 'Authoritarian Advance: Responding to China's growing Political Influence in Europe' gives a detailed insight into China's political-economic toolbox and a stern warning.

Europe needs to 'act swiftly and decisively' if it wants to stop the 'momentum of Chinese influencing efforts', recommend the authors. 'After all, China's political model is based on an authoritarian regime intent on strengthening a deeply illiberal surveillance state at home while also exporting – or at least trying to popularize – its political and economic development model abroad.'

The report triggered the expected reaction by the CPC's international mouthpiece, the *Global Times*. 'Misguided academics promote China–EU confrontation,' reads the headline of an article[4] that would have made Mao Zedong proud. A maybe-not-so-expected reaction, reported the Swiss newspaper *Neue Zuercher Zeitung* (NZZ). According to the NZZ article,[5] the *Global Times* prides itself on having indirectly contributed to the removal of Sebastian Heilmann as head of MERICS by pointing out that his publications are 'too political' and 'not objective'. The Mercator Foundation that runs MERICS denies these allegations.

Uncontroversial in Europe is that China is slowly but steadily adding political instruments to its already powerful economic muscle. While Russian attempts to influence public opinion and decision-making in Europe have drawn much attention and criticism, China focused for a long time mainly on questions of domestic importance, such as Tibet. But Beijing's public diplomacy has, of late, become more assertive. This shows in the ever-growing number of Confucius

Institutes in Europe (currently 160), newspaper supplements, media cooperation, invitations for journalists and attempts to invest in crisis-ridden European media outlets. The Chinese Students and Scholars Association (CSSA) has become infamous for trying to bring Western universities to court for events that allegedly insult the feelings of CSSA members.

While many of these measures are legitimate and within the framework of a democratic state, the problem is that China does not reciprocate them and strongly curtails the work of foreign organizations on its own turf. Adding China's economic strength to the relative weakness of many smaller European countries, it is justified to see a 'divide and rule' strategy in China's public diplomacy. It is therefore a serious threat to the EU that is already suffering from internal frictions.

One of the new Chinese instruments of public diplomacy is the '16+1' framework that was created by China in 2012 to encourage Central and Eastern European (CEE) member states and accession candidates to participate in infrastructure projects with China, not least the Belt and Road Initiative (BRI). The 16+1 format makes use of both the desire of smaller European countries to fill financial gaps in times of shrinking aid from Brussels, and the wish for easier access to do business with China – something that larger countries such as Germany and France already have, in the form of bilateral dialogues.

Some of the smaller European countries see China as an alternative partner to the EU, a highly problematic development for which the EU must blame itself partly. The case of Greece can serve as an example and a warning. The country became the main victim and, indeed, scapegoat of the European financial crisis[6] between 2008–15.

As a result, the cash-strapped country turned to China and became one of its first partners in the BRI. China's largest shipping company COSCO acquired 67 per cent of the Piraeus Port Authority in Athens, Greece's main port, and invested in many other infrastructure-projects, mainly in the energy sector. There is also institutional cooperation between the *Athens News Agency-Macedonian Press Agency* (AMNA) and the Chinese *Xinhua*.

When Greece blocked an EU statement on human rights in China at the United Nations (UN) in June 2017, European critics accused Athens of 'being in the pocket of China'. But the EU has much reason to introspect, because relations with Greece were heavily strained by the harsh treatment it received from the Eurogroup during the financial crisis. China stepped in when Athens was bankrupt. This threw the doors wide open to China's political influence in the otherwise EU-friendly country.

But Europe is now slowly waking up to the challenge. The president of the European Commission, Jean-Claude Juncker, recently offered the Western Balkan states a perspective to join the EU by 2025.[7] Countries like Serbia might indeed have feared that their accession to the EU could be postponed *ad calendas graecas* – and thus turned towards China as well.

More complicated is the situation in Eastern Europe, where right-wing populist governments in Poland, Hungary and the Czech Republic are not only less sensitive to human rights issues but even promote 'illiberal democracy'[8] themselves, such as the government of Viktor Orbán in Hungary. For Warsaw, Prague and Budapest, China has become a useful tool to show Brussels that there are alternatives to unwelcome meddling. According to a new report by the European Council on Foreign Relations (ECFR), the bilateral relationship between Hungary and China 'has become intensely political since the 2011 financial crisis'.[9]

While business between the two countries is still weak, Budapest apparently tries to please Beijing through pre-emptive obedience. In February 2017, Hungary refused to have its name added to an EU letter written to condemn the torture of Chinese human rights lawyers and did not sign the joint statement of the UN Human Rights Council in March 2016. In April 2017, the first Chinese think tank in Europe, the China CEE Institute, opened its doors in Budapest.

However, the annual 16+1 summits have not yet triggered the desired influx of cash into the CEE region. According to a study by Ernstand 10, China contributes to less than 5 per cent of foreign direct investment (FDI) in Europe and that mainly goes to larger countries like Germany, France and Italy.

These countries therefore struggle to find the right approach vis-à-vis China. The French China-expert, François Godement, criticized French President Emmanuel Macron during a state visit of China's President Xi Jinping to Paris in 2018. According to Xi, Macron overstepped 'the line between pragmatism and cynicism' by signing a common communique with Xi that stressed the commitment of both countries 'to the protection of human rights and essential liberties'.

The former German ambassador to China, Volker Stanzel,[12] who is also a board member of the Academic Confucius Institute in Göttingen, points out that the challenge for Europe lies in the fact that a rule-based international order and respect for human rights are core substances of European enlightenment. Yielding towards China therefore 'needs to have limits'.

But even oil-rich Norway, a former champion of human rights, has recently started soft-pedalling China. Beijing froze all political ties with Oslo following the decision of the Nobel Prize Committee to award the Nobel Peace Prize to Chinese dissident Liu Xiaobo in 2010. Norway, which is not a member of the EU, came out of the cold after a number of goodwill gestures in 2016 and started to negotiate a separate free trade agreement with China.[13] Since then, the government in Oslo has been extremely cautious to comment on Liu, even after his death in 2017.

If rich countries such as Norway succumb to pressure from Beijing, it is not a surprise that poorer ones fall in line or actively seek support from China. Even Australia was deemed as 'dependent on China' but 'ungrateful' by the ubiquitous *Global Times* after the government had published a critical paper on China's role in the Pacific region.

The EU, therefore, urgently must bring its own house in order. Decreasing competition among EU member states, taking smaller members and Eastern European countries more seriously and reviving a spirit of solidarity among Europeans is the best insurance against the Chinese 'divide and rule' strategy. An EU initiative to track Chinese investments and public diplomacy has already started and is a step in the right direction. There is nothing wrong in doing business with China but avoiding economic dependency must be a strategic goal for the EU.

3

China's Rapid Growth in Africa: Lessons For India

MALANCHA CHAKRAVARTY

China's rising economic interest in Africa has caught the attention of scholars, journalists and policymakers all over the world. Although the literature on China's role in Africa has proliferated, most studies present a dichotomous understanding of China's role in Africa, either as a 'threat' or as an 'opportunity'. In fact, some scholars have even labelled Chinese economic engagement with Africa as the 'new scramble' for African resources. Having said that, there are scholars who regard China as the new economic frontier that is making a great contribution towards African development. Within India, many experts routinely emphasize the need for India to counter China's growing influence on the African continent by building closer links with Africa. Others have expressed concerns over 'China's deep pockets' and India's inability to match China's soft loans for infrastructure. Sadly, there is very little Indian scholarship devoted to the issue of China–Africa relations. Given the importance of both China and Africa for India, this is indeed quite disappointing.

This essay tries to highlight some features of Chinese economic engagement with Africa which are often ignored by Indian scholars. Firstly, Chinese economic engagement with Africa is not limited to resources. Although trade in resources such as crude oil and copper account for the bulk of the trade between China and Africa, and China has sanctioned infrastructure-for-resource loans worth billions of dollars to resource-rich countries such as Angola and the Democratic Republic of Congo, it would be wrong to dismiss China's growing economic engagement with Africa purely as a means of acquiring resources. There are many African countries which lack resources, yet their economic ties with China are growing like never before. Ethiopia, an agricultural country in East Africa, is a case in point. Bilateral trade between Ethiopia and China grew at a rate of 63 per cent per annum between 2002–12 and currently China is the country's largest export destination. It is interesting to note that sesame seeds, a product which has been introduced in Ethiopia recently, accounts for about 85 per cent of the exports to China, followed by leather and leather goods.[1] Moreover, contrary to the belief that only oil producers like Nigeria, Angola, Sudan and Equatorial Guinea have been major recipients of Chinese soft loans, Ethiopia has also received huge volumes of Chinese loans for infrastructure. As per figures from China AidData, the total value of Chinese official financial flows to Ethiopia was about USD 3.6 billion in 2012.[2] Ethiopia has also been a major recipient of Chinese foreign direct investments (FDI). Chinese investment in Ethiopia is dominated by the private sector and is primarily directed towards the manufacturing sector, particularly the leather sector.

Secondly, China is making a huge economic impact on Africa through its trade, development finance and investment flows. Demand for African exports was one of the most direct channels through which China affected Africa. Chinese demand had a huge quantitative impact on most African countries and led to unparalleled growth in exports from countries such as Angola, Democratic Republic of Congo and Ethiopia. In fact, Chinese demand was significant enough to affect world prices and led to improvements in terms of trade for these countries. Therefore, the emergence of China as the main export destination played an important role in reviving their economies during the 2000s. Sub-Saharan Africa's exports to China grew remarkably from 2000 onwards, at a compound annual growth rate (CAGR) of over 22 per cent and by 2013, it exceeded sub-Saharan Africa's exports to the United States.

What is often ignored by Indian experts is the fact that there has been a phenomenal increase in China's exports to Africa, particularly manufactured exports. Indian experts rarely regard Africa as a market for Indian-manufactured products and prefer to focus on India's long-term commitment to African development, development cooperation initiatives like Indian Technical and Economic Cooperation (ITEC) and lines of credit (LOC) as well as the need for African votes for a permanent seat in the United Nations. On the other hand, China has effectively penetrated the African market. Imports from China overtook those from the US in 2004 and by 2013, China's share in sub-Saharan Africa's imports was about 14 per cent. There was a dramatic growth in imports of Chinese-manufactured goods from the early 2000s onwards and China is now sub-Saharan Africa's largest source of manufactured products. There was a dramatic growth in Chinese-manufactured exports to countries such as Angola and the Democratic Republic of Congo, countries which are usually known for the huge 'infrastructure-for-resource' loans from the Chinese Exim Bank.

In 2009, China accounted for just 2.9 per cent of Angola's manufactured imports but by 2013, China replaced Portugal as the largest source of manufactured goods for Angola with a share of 38.9 per cent. Similarly, the Democratic Republic of Congo's imports of manufactured goods from China have grown tremendously and China now accounts for over a quarter of the country's manufactured imports.[3] Ethiopia's case is particularly unfortunate because India has lost market share to China. In 2000, India was the largest exporter of manufactured goods to Ethiopia with a share of 19.1 per cent, followed by China at 13.1 per cent. However, China overtook India in 2003 and by 2012, it accounted for over 31 per cent of Ethiopia's manufactured imports, whereas India's share declined to 14.9 per cent. China currently accounts for over 50 per cent of Ethiopia's imports of leather products, textile yarn and fabrics, and cork and wood products, and nearly 90 per cent of Ethiopia's footwear imports.

Similarly, Chinese investment flows to Africa have also rapidly increased in recent years. According to the World Investment Report 2016 published by the United Nations Conference on Trade and Development (UNCTAD), China was the fourth-largest investor in Africa in 2014.[4] China's FDI stock increased more than three-fold from USD 9 billion in 2009 to USD 32 billion in 2014 and China overtook South Africa as the largest investor from a developing country in the region. While most of the Chinese investments in Africa are indeed led by large state-owned enterprises which typically invest in infrastructure and resource sectors, increasingly many private Chinese enterprises have also set up operations in many African countries. Scholars like Jian-Ye Wang and Jing Gu assert that, increasingly, it is the Chinese private sector – rather than government ministries – that is leading China's economic exchange with Africa. These enterprises typically invest in the manufacturing and service sectors. The main reason behind the growth of Chinese FDI in Africa's manufacturing sector is the increased pressure of industrial restructuring in coastal China, which is driving labour-intensive firms to Africa. Proximity to Europe and access to cheap labour are important pull factors in the case of African countries like Ethiopia. The presence of India's private sector has also grown very rapidly but the actual volume of Indian investments in Africa is much less than that reported by the Indian media. This is largely because the bulk of the Indian investments in Africa are directed towards Mauritius, a tax haven, and is round-tripped back to India.[5]

However, the most striking feature of China–Africa relations is the unprecedented growth of official finance from China to Africa. Although conceptual differences make comparisons between

Chinese development finance and official development assistance (ODA) from OECD (Organization for Economic Cooperation and Development) countries difficult, many estimates suggest that Chinese financial flows to sub-Saharan Africa are now comparable in scale to traditional ODA from OECD countries. Chinese finance is predominantly channelled through the China Exim Bank in the form of concessional loans for infrastructure development. Chinese companies are also building vital infrastructure including dams, ports, roads, railways and bridges in Africa. According to a study by the World Bank, over thirty-five African countries have engaged with China on infrastructure finance deals. Given sub-Saharan Africa's critical shortage of infrastructure, this is China's biggest contribution towards African development. Indian LOC are also largely directed towards infrastructure development in Africa, but it is quite clear that India can't match China in terms of scale. Therefore, India's development cooperation must be directed towards a few niche areas. India also needs to ensure better implementation of its LOC – they often suffer from project delays.

In a nutshell, potential gains from closer economic ties between India and Africa have not been realized fully. To revive its manufacturing sector and create jobs for the youth, India needs a more active strategy to expand its manufacturing sector. India's ailing manufacturing sector really can't afford to ignore Africa's growing middle class. Secondly, given that India can't match China's deep pockets, its development cooperation must be more strategic. India needs to focus on a few niche areas and ensure better implementation.

4

Taiwan Faces PRC's Increased Pressure Tactics, More Countries Cut Ties with the Island

H.H.S. VISWANATHAN

Ever since Tsai Ing-wen took over as president of Taiwan in 2016, the People's Republic of China (PRC) has been putting relentless pressure on the island. The establishment of diplomatic relations by Panama with the PRC on 12 June 2017 was a big setback for Taiwan in its efforts to maintain its international standing. What was worse, Panama did not officially inform Taipei before the announcement was made; reports suggest that the Taiwanese government learnt about it first from the media. The Panamanian president said, in a televised interview, that Panama was upgrading its commercial ties with China to full diplomatic relations and added that, 'I am convinced that this is the correct path for our country.'[1] Predictably, the reaction from Taipei was swift and strong. Its foreign minister said, 'Our government expresses serious objections and strong condemnation in response to China enticing Panama to cut ties with us confining our international space and offending the people of Taiwan.' The official spokesman said that Taiwan would not compete with China in what it described as a 'diplomatic money game'.[2]

PRC and Panama have substantial commercial relations. China is the second most important customer of the Panama Canal. But the decision to cut ties with Taiwan goes far beyond mere commercial interests. The root cause is China's growing suspicion of Tsai Ing-wen's intentions. Ever since she came to power in 2016, China has been increasing its pressure on the island. She and her party, the Democratic Progressive Party (DPP) have always been a thorn in China's flesh because of their preference for an independent Taiwan.

Earlier, in December 2016, the Democratic Republic of São Tomé and Principe switched diplomatic ties from Taiwan to the PRC. In May 2018, both the Dominican Republic and Burkina Faso switched their recognition to PRC. Now there are only eighteen countries which recognize Taiwan, most of them being in the South Pacific Islands and the Vatican. In Africa, only one country – Eswatini (formerly known as Swaziland) has relations with Taiwan.

China's attitude towards Tsai's government hardened after the then US president-elect Donald Trump's phone conversation with her. The situation was further aggravated by Trump's subsequent comments questioning the rationale of US's One-China policy, which is sacrosanct for the PRC. That was like a red rag to a bull and China reacted angrily implying tough retaliatory actions. Trump, after taking over as president, did retract his statements and even compensated by the Mar-a-Lago Summit but, as far as China's increasing suspicion of Taiwan is concerned, the damage was done.

The 1992 Consensus

Compare this to the situation a few years ago when Ma Ying-jeou of the Kuomintang (KMT) party was in power in Taipei. He and his party had always believed in One-China, even though the interpretations of what that meant differed between the PRC and Taiwan. During that period, the two sides had also had an informal agreement that they would not poach into each other's diplomatic ties. But Tsai Ing-wen and the DPP are a different kettle of fish. They have not endorsed the so-called '1992 Consensus' which, according to the PRC, is the fundamental pillar of China–Taiwan relations. The crux of the consensus is, 'Both sides agree that Taiwan belonged to China, while continuing to disagree on which China.'[3] It was a KMT government that signed the consensus.

However, DPP's position is very clear. It maintains that Taiwan does not belong to any part of China, and should be independent. The position is also a logical corollary of the fact that DPP supporters are mostly native Taiwanese with hardly any connections to the mainland. The PRC, on its part, has not given up the option of using force to unify China. They have, from time to time, reiterated the three conditions for use of force – declaration of independence by Taiwan, indefinite postponement of unification talks and stationing of bases by foreign countries in Taiwan.

Other Pressure Tactics

Forcing countries to cut diplomatic ties is not the only instrument that China is using. In the recent past, China has used its clout to keep Taiwan out of several international fora where it has participated in the past. Here are a few examples:

- In September 2016, the International Civil Aviation Organization (ICAO), a UN agency, declined to issue an invitation to Taiwan to participate as an observer, even though they had done so the previous year.
- In November 2016, International Criminal Police Organization (Interpol) rejected Taiwanese participation in its general assembly.
- In May 2017, in Perth (Australia), the Chinese delegation to a Kimberley Process Conference on diamond trade blocked Taiwanese participation as an observer, although they had

received a formal invitation from the organizers. The Chinese delegation went on to disturb the proceedings of the inaugural session until the Taiwan delegation was asked to leave.

- Again, in May 2017, at the World Health Assembly's annual meeting, China tried to block Taiwan's participation, where it had been an observer since 2009.
- China also put pressure on Nigeria to shift the Taiwan trade office from the capital, Abuja, to the commercial city of Lagos.

There has also been cartographic pressure on Taiwan. Until recently, the PRC's official maps used to show Taiwan as 'Zhonghua Taiwan', but now they have changed it to 'Zhongguo Taiwan'. This is not mere semantics. Although both terms mean 'China' in a generic sense, 'Zhongguo' is normally associated with the PRC. The nomenclature is very dear to China. For example, the PRC objects to the term 'Mainland China' because it could imply the existence of another China. The politically correct term for the PRC is 'Chinese Mainland'.

It is unlikely that China will ease the pressure if Tsai continues to remain in power. Their hope is that in the next election in Taiwan the KMT party will come to power and defuse the tensions. It is also felt that the US is not doing enough to prevent the isolation of Taiwan. Could they have used their influence to encourage the above-mentioned countries to continue their relations with Taiwan, is a question raised by many. China's growing global clout is manifest in the manner in which it has been successful in isolating Taiwan, and if the past is any guide, the future is going to be even more difficult for Taiwan's political aspirations.

5

Great Power Politics and the Tragedy of OBOR

GAYATHRI IYER

China's One Belt One Road (OBOR) initiative – the mammoth sea and road infrastructure linking Asia, Europe and Africa – is being pursued as an inclusive 'international capacity cooperation' initiative.[1] It is pitched as an economic agenda where some of the manufacturing capacity of China is shifted to partner countries, resulting in a 'win-win' for all.[2] Its immediate manifestation in South Asia is in the form of the China–Pakistan Economic Corridor (CPEC), a project Beijing claims could trigger South Asia's rapid modernization. The façade of business connectivity, however, shrouds a hegemonic ambition to dominate Eurasia and shape a new world order.[3] China's gambit is fraught with risk, as it involves contradictions that cannot be easily reconciled.[4] The purported innocuousness of China's endeavour does not conform to the nature of great power politics and the contradictions do not bode well for its future.[5]

The first of these fault lines expresses itself through the nature of great power politics.[6] Given that great powers have both varied interests and enormous resources, it is not clear why Beijing will confine its ambition to infrastructure and connectivity.[7] Indeed, to ensure hegemony in Asia, China will need to exert both economic and military power.[8] Regardless of the fact that military prowess has ceded space to economics post the Second World War, hard power projection remains as relevant as earlier.

The United States' Marshall Plan[9] for the reconstruction of Europe was a typical example of an economics-heavy approach underpinned by military strength. Two factors underlay the primacy of hard power:

- First, states found themselves entering an investment trap where securing economic investments necessitated the introduction of military force.[10]
- Second, the propensity of great powers to exert economic influence and extract military commitments from partner states.[11]

Whether in Asia or Latin America, expansive US military presence has always followed the dollar.[12] Not without reason, therefore, within a few years of reconstruction efforts launched in Europe, the US was as involved in the continent militarily as it was economically.[13]

The same was the case with the erstwhile Soviet Union, where its clientele – whether in Africa or Latin America – was required to accept heavy military involvement. If OBOR is to be seen as China's twenty-first-century Marshall Plan, the expanding economic influence would require deeper military commitments from China. In fact, a recent Pentagon report signals these possibilities when it highlights the possibility of Chinese military bases in Pakistan.[14] OBOR's 'win-win' formulation runs contrary to historical evidence of the behaviour of great powers.[15]

China's own record in the last couple of decades is proof that it cannot escape this tragedy of great power politics.[16] In fact, its rising economic stakes in the past couple of decades have been concomitant with a shift in its military priorities. The shifting of its industrial manufacturing corridors from Hong Kong to Mainland China was rapidly followed by a near-simultaneous increase in its military bases in the South China Sea and the Arabian Sea to guard its own mercantile fleets.[17]

Post the 2008 recession, when the rest of the world was reducing its international investments, China's counter-cyclical strategic investment across several countries surged as it quietly started embedding its military capabilities in its infrastructure assets across countries. Although China claims its drivers for the investment in infrastructure assets hinge around economic and energy security, an eventual set-up of military outposts in various infrastructural investments is inevitable.[18] This is already under way with naval berthing and docking facilities in Seychelles, Sri Lanka and Gwadar in Pakistan.[19]

A purely economic enterprise like OBOR, therefore, cannot escape its own militarization; which raises the question of whether China can sustain OBOR militarily. The US's decline as the global hegemon, for one thing, is not as pronounced as Beijing would have liked. Despite growing fiscal problems and domestic upheavals, America still has the naval power that China does not.[20]

China's lack of maritime dominance in the wider Eurasian seas bears further emphasis to this fact. Historically, economic hegemony has been an inevitable result of naval hegemony: the most powerful maritime powers have always ruled global trade. The decline of the Dutch as an economic superpower prior to the Industrial Revolution is attributed to the security challenges its merchant vessel faced vis-à-vis Britain's success in exploiting the sea-lanes with its superior navy.[21] Later, the British acceded that position to the Americans. However, China's current naval power alone may not be able to match the American advantage as the US carriers are vastly more capable than China's.[22]

But such maritime powers also establish their hegemony through what Gramsci called the 'co-optation' of others: by building strong maritime coalitions.[23] Here again, China lags far behind. China is geographically at a disadvantage, compared to the US, due to its comparatively limited access to water – it is essentially a continental power. Most of China is surrounded by land and, taking Eurasia as a continental alternative, the geographical limitations of the region come in the way of a strong naval coalition.[24] The southern parts of Eurasia – the countries of Southeast Asia and the Middle East – have disparate geography, limited by mountains, deserts and not very navigable waterways.[25]

An India–Pakistan coalition is not visible in the near future nor is the Ganges basin navigable.[26] This leaves only the countries in the North European Plain, the Eurasian Steppe and the Yellow River basin as candidates for meaningful coalitions.[27] However, although the Northern European Plain and the Eurasian Steppe are adjacent, they have no warm-water navigable waterways connecting them among themselves or the Yellow River basin to make a strong naval coalition possible at this juncture.[28]

The alternative that China seems to be employing is to emulate the Soviet model used during the Cold War era. Since the time of Peter the Great, the former emperor of Russia, Moscow's quest for warm water ports has been a constant in its security policy.[29] Vladivostok, on the Russian east coast, was constructed with a vision to establish a major naval presence in the Pacific Ocean and to also help Russia solidify its presence and ties with China, North Korea, Japan and other countries in the Far East.[30]

The port has had a large military base and has been valued for being a diplomatic and economic outpost since the time the Trans-Siberian Railway connected it to the west, opening Russia's eastern coast to the valuable markets located in Europe, just like what OBOR aims to do for China now.[31] However, the continental nature of Russian power did not allow it to be a naval power of global consequence in any period in its history. The same tyranny of geography works to China's disadvantage.

Notwithstanding the continental nature of Chinese power and the constraints which follow, established great powers constantly endeavour to prevent the rise of any global competitors.[32] The same is the case with the rise of China as a great power with the OBOR initiative. In fact, China's grand plans have already initiated a counter-coalition against it. One can see this in the renewed interest in the US-Japan-Australia-India quad formation.[33] The US, increasingly apprehensive of the swift movement of the OBOR and Chinese influence, is striking alliances with India, Japan and Australia to join hands in military cooperation in the South China Sea in an attempt to balance the increasing Chinese military muscle in international waters.[34] The US has also freshly revived its major infrastructure projects in Asia – New Silk Road (NSR) linking South and Central Asia and the Indo-Pacific Economic Corridor linking South Asia and Southeast Asia.[35] Meanwhile, India and Japan have joined hands to embark upon multiple infrastructure projects across Africa, Iran, Sri Lanka and Southeast Asia.[36]

China may be bidding to create a new world order as all great powers aspire to do, but in the process, it also cannot escape the inadvertent consequences of great power politics: its rising economic profile would require a larger military footprint.[37] Militarization of OBOR, even though incidental, would lead to multiple troubles, exacerbated by China's relatively modest naval strength, its geographical limitations and necessities of the global balance of power. China may attempt to escape these pitfalls but its success is highly doubtful, because the process of great power politics creates its own realities and outcomes, which, many a time, are involuntary.

6

One Belt, One Road, and Now, One Circle

RITIKA PASSI

The last frontier for exploration is being breached.

In August 2017, a Russia-owned LNG (liquefied natural gas) tanker with a unique reinforced steel hull became the first vessel to travel from Norway to South Korea, through the Northern Sea Route (NSR) along the Russian Arctic coast, without the aid of an ice-breaking vessel, and that too in merely nineteen days. Earlier this year, the US government provided funding for a new icebreaker for the Coast Guard, the first new one in forty years. Finland and Norway jointly funded a study on the viability and profitability of an Arctic Railway project that would connect the Nordic region to the Arctic coast and offer pathways into Europe all the way to the Mediterranean Sea and along the Russian NSR to Asian markets.[1] The world's biggest shipping company, Denmark's Maersk, successfully sent the first-ever container ship, a 42,000-ton vessel, through the Arctic along the NSR in the second half of 2018.[2]

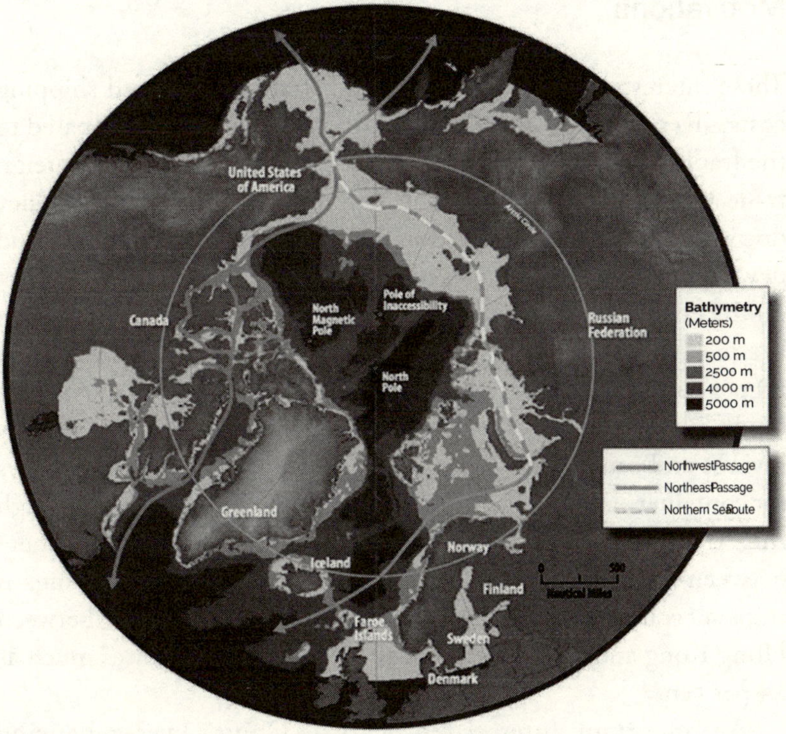

China, too, has staked a claim. A non-Arctic littoral – or, as it calls itself, a 'Near-Arctic state' – China released its official Arctic policy[3] at the end of January 2018, coming on the heels of increasing activity and visibility in the region in question, which is raising eyebrows and anxieties. The white paper declares China as 'an important stakeholder in Arctic affairs' and reveals an expanding playground in which China sees itself as a legitimate actor. Retreating ice in the Arctic and its repercussions – effect on local climate and environment, domestic agriculture and marine industries, waterway and resource development in the Arctic – are matters 'vital to the existence and development of all countries and humanity, and directly affect the interests of non-Arctic States including China'.

Motivations

These interests are both economic and strategic. Reduced shipping costs, given shorter routes between Asia and Europe as compared to the traditional Malacca Strait and Suez Canal route, benefit foreign trade and strengthen energy security for China. Indeed, as the policy document states: 'The utilization of sea routes and exploration and development of the resources in the Arctic may have a huge impact on the energy strategy and economic development of China, which is a major trading nation and energy consumer in the world.' Over 60 per cent of China's trade is seaborne[4] and it imports most of its crude oil via the sea, so even small differences in time taken imply savings and profits. For instance, it normally takes forty-eight days for container ships to reach Rotterdam from China. Passage through the Arctic would reduce Europe to Asia distances by anywhere between 20–40 per cent. There are even time and cost savings if ships set course from southern Chinese ports – the distance between Hong Kong and northwestern Europe is still shorter by as much as 14 per cent.[5]

An important, interrelated factor is China's ever-enhancing shipping power and increasing role in shipping finance.[6] China's state-owned shipping company, COSCO, is the largest shipping company outside of Europe, and China today lays claim to the third-largest merchant ship fleet in the world. This is reflective of not only the shipping industry's importance to China's economy, but also the key role China's growing merchant fleet and shipping finance industry are set to play in the rolling out of its maritime trade and infrastructure vision – including in the Arctic.

The Arctic also allows transportation through a more politically peaceable environment and is thus a more secure alternative to bottlenecked waters prone to piracy and dominated by a strategic competitor. Almost 70 per cent of China's energy needs are met by seaborne imports.[7] The lure of undiscovered oil and natural gas resources – anywhere between one-fifth and a quarter of untapped fossil fuel resources, potentially worth as much as USD 35 trillion – throw up alternative energy sources that China can tap and thus bolster its energy security. The US Geological Survey pegs 30 per cent of the world's undiscovered natural gas and 13 per cent of undiscovered oil reserves in the Arctic. Not to forget what are thought to be considerable deposits of mineable minerals – gold, silver, diamond, copper, nickel, titanium, graphite, uranium – and, crucial for the manufacturing of high-tech products like electric cars and smartphones, rare earth elements, such as lithium and cobalt. Clearly, at play is a longer-term vision to secure future trade routes to markets and resources.

The other strategic motivation implied is, of course, the desire to play a bigger role in trans-regional and global issues – and not just as a permanent member of the UN Security Council, a fact that is included in the policy document as a rationale for China jointly shouldering the cause of peace and security in the Arctic, or under a vision of a 'shared future for mankind', also liberally invoked throughout the document. The Arctic is a new sphere, previously inaccessible, where China wants to play a leading role, 'since the traditional areas are already taken by the old powers,' notes Jin Canrong at Renmin University of China.[8]

Critically, given the continued reality of climate change in the Arctic, the development of this region will see new technologies and 'economic biomes' come to the fore. This will not only catapult the Arctic as a major theatre of activity – economic and geopolitical – in the coming future but will also define science and sustainability in the twenty-first century.

Engagement

Given this context, it is hardly surprising that the Chinese white paper on the Arctic advances a 'Polar Silk Road' under the ambit of its broader Belt and Road Initiative (BRI), considering the starring role the BRI is already playing in advancing 'Xi-plomacy' (think the Two Centenaries and the 'Chinese Dream'). At first glance, the Chinese mandate primarily encourages its enterprises to develop shipping routes, including infrastructure construction, conducting commercial trial voyages and operating these shipping routes. Other areas, such as energy cooperation, blue economy and tourism, are not directly linked to the Polar Silk Road. But these are already existing fields of Chinese engagement under the BRI. Digital connectivity is also specifically mentioned. China is likely to use the BRI as a key vehicle to fulfil its stated policy goals ('to understand, protect, develop and participate in the governance of the Arctic'[9]).

While Beijing has been active in the Arctic since it bought its first icebreaker from Ukraine in 1994, recent years have seen an uptick in Chinese engagement. Not only has China's only icebreaker now navigated the three major shipping routes through the Arctic, in 2013, a Chinese ship carrying 19,000 tons of cargo became the first container vessel ever to transit the NSR to reach Rotterdam from Dalian in China – and that too, in a month, compared to the forty-five days it normally takes through the Suez Canal. China also became an observer in the Arctic Council, the highest-level body governing the Polar North, in 2013. In fact, Chinese President Xi Jinping even referred to China as an 'upcoming polar-region power' during a state visit to Australia in 2014.[10]

Research of navigational routes, as well as that of climate and environmental changes in the Arctic, and exploration of the region's potential resources are part of the ambit of this blue economic corridor. (An earlier paper by the State Oceanic Administration referred to the Northwest Passage as a 'northern link' in BRI.[11])

On ground, Russia's NSR is already a strategic area of cooperation between China and the largest Arctic state as part of the BRI – Xi and his Russian counterpart Vladimir Putin signed a joint declaration in July 2017 that invoked an 'Ice Silk Road' under which the NSR will be developed. (But note that the Chinese Arctic white paper does not highlight the NSR or any Arctic route as the preferred shipping route that Chinese companies will pursue.) The Yamal LNG project is the primary and largest Sino–Russian venture in this regard, which is expected to supply China with four million tons of LNG per year, transported through the NSR and reaching China in just fifteen days, less than half the time it would take using the traditional shipping route around Europe and through the Suez Canal.[12] The Silk Road Fund holds a 9.9 per cent stake, and the China National Petroleum Corporation, 20 per cent; Chinese banks have partly funded the project; and 60 per cent of the equipment has been contributed by Chinese companies. COSCO is the biggest non-Russian operator in these waters and has completed twenty-two commercial trips along the NSR between 2013 and 2018.[13] Engagement in Russia's Far East, including in oil and gas fields; construction of ice-class cargo vessels; and a deep-water port on the northwestern Russian coast are key Sino–Russian projects on the cards.

At the same time, China has also approached other Arctic littorals. While none of the other Arctic states are officially part of the BRI, they are members of the Asia Infrastructure Investment Bank (thus firmly within the scope of the BRI) and are actively engaged in Arctic projects that are likely to be subsumed under the BRI umbrella. For instance, Chinese mining companies are active in the Canadian Arctic and in Greenland. 2017 saw China particularly amplify its interaction with Finland, which is currently chair of the Arctic Council (it hands over chairmanship to Iceland in 2019). Xi Jinping became the first Chinese president to visit the Nordic state in twenty-two years. The first China–Finland Iron Silk Road began operating in November 2017, the first railway to link China with the Nordic region.[14] Both have jointly built a second Chinese icebreaker, set to enter into service this year.[15] And recently, China began discussing a 10,500 km fiber optic route across the Arctic to create the fastest digital highway between Europe and China as early as 2020.[16] The proposal involves Finland, Norway, Russia and Japan. Xi has even reached out to Alaska, making an unexpected stop on his way back home, post the China–US bilateral summit in April 2017.[17] There, he was apparently offered 'a generation's worth' of LNG supply by the governor.

BRI and International Law: Convergence or Clash?

China's Arctic policy – insofar as the ambition and the policy goals are concerned – is not a surprise. The inclusion of the BRI as a means of fulfilling China's stated aims in the Arctic necessarily means the appearance of similar parameters and principles – and indeed, 'respect', 'cooperation' and 'win-win result' form the basis of Chinese activity in this geography as well. 'Sustainability' is, understandably, given greater weight in this policy document.

In practice, what does the pursuit of an Arctic policy through BRI as a primary vehicle mean? The Chinese trade and infrastructure initiative has already gained nomenclature as the 'hardware' of Chinese power projection and an attempt to build a Sino-centric Asian and world order. As such, the Arctic, too, is being hardwired into a hub-and-spokes architecture, with China at the centre, that can then be supplemented with policies, norms and practices. These would include investing in infrastructure, buying foreign companies, competing for leases in oil and mineral extraction.

Against this context, the repeated stress on abiding by international law is noteworthy in the policy document. Given that China is a non-Arctic state, it has clearly used the principles of international law to justify an uncontested and unbarred entrance into the Arctic region: 'States from outside the region do not have territorial sovereignty in the Arctic, but they do have rights in respect of scientific research, navigation, overflight, fishing, laying of submarine cables and pipelines in the high seas and other relevant sea areas in the Arctic Ocean, and rights to resource exploration and exploitation in the Area, pursuant to treaties such as UNCLOS [United Nations Convention on the Law of the Sea] and general international law.'[18] The reiteration that Arctic shipping must be conducted in accordance with international law, further seems logical when considering existing territorial disputes among the Arctic littorals – such as the Northwest Route, which Canada sees as its internal waters, but the US claims as an international waterway. Clearly, for China to pursue its interests in this region, an understanding of Arctic waters as international commons – and thus freely navigable – is critical. Such an interpretation is possible through the UNCLOS framework.

China's implementation of the BRI on the ground and the intended use of the BRI to carve a different world order ('all roads lead to Beijing') stands as a counterpoint to the understanding of the Arctic as an international commons where, as indicated by the policy document, China will abide by all international legal instruments, treaties and mechanisms of pertinent institutions, like the International Maritime Organization. Indeed, as Chinese and polar politics specialist Anne-Marie Brady states, 'China's focus on becoming a polar great power represents a fundamental reorientation – a completely new way of imagining the world'[19] – and the polar region is one new strategic playground where China will build and prove its burgeoning power. Will this alternative world vision give right of way to international law and treaties? The short shrift given to UNCLOS closer home in the South China Sea could very well bely any true commitment on the part of China to accepted norms beyond, perhaps, an opportunity to allay concerns of revisionist designs.

Responses to China's official Arctic policy run to both extremes. Some are crying wolf and calling it a cover for a more subversive strategy; others believe China is only stepping up as a responsible nation, that any irresponsible activity will undermine its credibility – and that the policy itself is a clear statement against which to measure its behaviour. While China's capital is in high demand among the Arctic states as well – infrastructure investment needs are to the tune of USD one trillion over the next fifteen years[20] – commercial shipping through the Arctic is unlikely until at least 2040, given existing environmental, technological and financial challenges.[21] Matters of environment and sustainability, navigation security and dual-use infrastructure will become salient in the meantime. Chinese behaviour and actions will ultimately determine whether BRI implementation practices converge with the upholding of international law that China promises in its official Arctic policy.

7

What to Expect from China's New Development Cooperation Agency

SEBASTIAN PAULO

In March 2018, China's National People's Congress adopted a comprehensive reform package to reorganize and streamline government structures. Among the agreed changes, China announced the establishment of the International Development Cooperation Agency (IDCA). The agency is part of a broader effort to consolidate diverse parts of government involved in projecting China's influence abroad, especially in view of promoting the Belt and Road Initiative (BRI) more effectively. The IDCA's launch has sparked considerable interest around the world to know how this institutional innovation will affect the way China operates as a development partner. Definite answers will have to wait for the agency to be fully established. For the time being, the IDCA is probably a sign of government structures belatedly catching up with the reality of China's role as a leading provider of development finance.

Placed under the state council, China's cabinet, the IDCA will be responsible for the design, coordination, oversight and evaluation of development cooperation. Centralizing these functions under a single agency constitutes a significant change in a notoriously fragmented and opaque system. The agency integrates functions from the ministry of commerce and the ministry of foreign affairs that have until now led the complex interplay of countless ministries, agencies, policy banks and provincial governments involved in the implementation of China's development cooperation.[1]

The establishment of the IDCA underlines China's significance as a major provider of development finance, at par with the largest traditional aid donors. Most of its official finance is not aid as defined by the established donor club, the Development Assistance Committee (DAC) of the Organization for Economic Cooperation and Development (OECD). However, including less concessional types of finance, China committed more than USD 350 billion to 140 countries between 2000–14, coming close to the largest conventional donor country, the United States.[2] Adding the massive amounts of finance announced for the BRI, China's global ambitions have increasingly been stretching the limits of its unwieldy development cooperation architecture.

Development cooperation agencies have typically been associated with traditional donors, a label that China still rejects. Current reforms might nevertheless have partly been informed by dialogues that China has held with established donors over the past decade, especially in the China-DAC study group. With the publication of a white paper on foreign aid since 2011, and the new agency, China now shares some key characteristics with other donor countries. China has also started to engage in so-called triangular cooperation, implementing projects in developing countries together with OECD donors, such as New Zealand and the United Kingdom.[3] Last year, China and Germany opened a centre for sustainable development in Beijing to promote cooperation in Africa. This rapprochement with other partners has fuelled expectations of closer alignment with international practices.

Despite signalling some convergence with established donor practices, the IDCA does in no way herald the end of China's identity as a southern development partner. Development cooperation agencies are not exclusive to OECD donors. Other providers of South–South cooperation, such as Brazil and Thailand, have set up similar institutions.[4] In 2012, India created the Development Partnership Administration (DPA) under the ministry of external affairs. Although not an agency in the typical sense, this department fulfils comparable functions of coordinating and streamlining development cooperation. China is a latecomer in this regard, standing out above all, due to the unmatched size of its global engagement.

Although changes in China's development cooperation architecture follow international trends, domestic dynamics in China's state apparatus are also an important driver of current reforms. The IDCA is part of a broader effort to consolidate central control over the policies and instruments at the heart of China's global ambitions, notably the BRI. At the same time, concerns over social and environmental standards, risks to debt sustainability and other challenges faced by partner countries highlight that the success of China's global engagement ultimately hinges on its recognition as a reliable international partner.[5] Improving China's image as a major global actor will therefore be the main objective of the new agency.

International observers hope that a specialized agency will lead to improvements in China's development cooperation, such as better internal coordination, more transparency, and enhanced cooperation with other partners.[6] The shift away from the ministry of commerce also raises expectations that China's development cooperation will be less driven by short-term commercial interests and more by longer term, strategic considerations, including a stronger development orientation. To what extent these expectations will be fulfilled in a system that is largely about commercial lending remains to be seen. The appointment of Wang Xiaotao as the agency's first director might give some pointers to its future orientation. Xiaotao, the former deputy director of the National Development and Reform Commission (NDRC), China's macroeconomic management agency, which also hosts the office of the leading group overseeing implementation of the BRI, can be expected to maintain a strong focus on the BRI as a centrepiece of China's global engagement.[7]

Given India's doubts about China's flagship infrastructure and connectivity initiative, India's perspective on the new agency might differ from the so far mostly positive international reactions. The consolidation of development cooperation under a more strategic approach is likely to feed into Indian concerns. At the same time, a professional agency can open new opportunities for coordination and cooperation on matters of shared interests, for instance, as an interlocutor to discuss the need for collectively agreed standards, or to promote triangular forms of development cooperation. In April 2018, Indian Prime Minister Narendra Modi and Chinese President Xi Jinping, hinted, for example, at the possibility of Indo–Chinese cooperation with Afghanistan at their informal summit in Wuhan. The consolidation of China's development cooperation under the IDCA might facilitate such initiatives.

8

China Courts Latin America with Unrelenting Soft Power

KETAN MEHTA

The concept of soft power coined by American political scientist Joseph Nye in the 1990s has since become an intrinsic part of statecraft. While a society's culture and values were traditionally considered as soft power instruments, the dynamics of the term are now contested. It is even suggested that soft and hard power are two sides of the same coin.[1] Given the vagueness surrounding what constitutes soft power and its application, the Chinese interpretation of soft power has largely differed from that of the US.

China's soft power projection, referred to as 'the charm offensive,' encompasses all elements of soft power, except the security realm.[2] This is an expansive view of the term 'soft power', when compared to the limited understanding that the conventional notion entailed. As soft power largely works on perception rather than objective reality,[3] China's charm offensive attracts Latin America less because of its magnitude but more because of the hope that it generates investments. Being the second largest economy and holding more than USD 3 trillion of foreign exchange reserves, China's economic success has drawn the attention of the Latin American elites.

With the US preoccupied with events in the Middle East and elsewhere, China has moved into a realm formerly understood as the American backyard.[4] Resource-rich Latin American states entice China with opportunities to rev up economic growth and overcome the latter's dependence on the advanced markets of Europe and North America. China's interest in the region partly originates from the fact that out of the twenty-four states that recognize Taiwan, twelve are in Latin America.[5]

For a change, China, which historically competed with Taiwan for influence, has proceeded to conceive strategic partnerships with Brazil, Argentina, Chile, Mexico, Peru and Venezuela, much to the dismay of Washington. While Brazil and China are fellow member states in the BRICS group, seemingly sharing a coherent worldview over a range of issues, China and Argentina have even explored avenues to jointly develop advanced weapon systems. The China–Community of Latin American and Caribbean States (CELAC) forum, held in 2015, further highlighted that the prospects of the relationship are not just limited to economic fora.[6] This gives Beijing greater incentive to consolidate its position as a long-term partner to Latin American countries.

However, investments in Latin America's infrastructure – apart from the twenty Confucius institutions set up by the ministry of culture – have today become part of China's soft power arsenal. There is mutual interest evident in the China–Latin American relationship as reflected in recent developments: although Latin America has a limited role in the Belt and Road Initiative (BRI), which aims to improve connectivity between Asia and Europe, Chilean and Argentine presidents, nevertheless, attended the two-day BRI summit in Beijing in May 2017.[7]

On the occasion, then Chilean President Michelle Bachelet commented, 'We think there are a lot of projects that can link Asia with or through Latin America,' adding that both countries are exploring the opportunity to jointly invest in a Trans-Pacific optic-fiber cable system to improve digital connectivity between Asia and Latin America.

Bolivia, Chile, Ecuador, Peru and Venezuela are now prospective members of the Asian Infrastructure Investment Bank (AIIB), in which China holds 26.06 per cent of votes. Not surprisingly, as economic growth dries up in Latin America, China is the most sought-after source for investments. China has taken the lead in infrastructure development and plans to construct a Nicaraguan canal, a Trans-Amazonian highway and a two-ocean tunnel in Chile. As studies show, middle income countries (plentiful in Latin America) tend to gain from infrastructure investments[8] and the region is hopeful that Chinese investments would certainly narrow infrastructure gaps.

The investments in infrastructure are accompanied by significant investments in extractive industries in the Latin American economies. High-profile deals include a USD 5 billion steel plant in Brazil, a USD 4.4 billion commitment to Peruvian mines and USD 16.3 billion to develop the Junin block 4 in Venezuela's Orinoco oil belt.[9]

Putting aside the apprehensions that accompany China's growing investments in the region, Latin American public opinion about China has also undergone a change. Despite a limited understanding of China and a lack of interest in emulating the Chinese growth model, a significant number of Latin Americans see the rise of China not as a threat but rather as a contributing factor to the economic development of the region. In fact, as was evident in the 2013 Pew survey, titled 'global image of the United States and China', the latter was viewed most favourably in Latin America and Africa. Subsequent surveys have emboldened this observation.[10]

Gone are the days when Latin America used to be an insignificant region for China: due to fear of antagonizing the US which then had an imperative role in China's economic growth. Today, Latin America has outpaced Africa in terms of trade with China. In 2016, trade between Latin America and China amounted to over USD 216 billion[11] compared to USD 128 billion with Africa.[12] China, moreover, has become the largest trading partner of Latin American countries such as Brazil, Chile and Peru.

The current leadership, under President Xi Jinping, clearly attaches greater importance to relations with Latin America. As Xi aims to achieve complete modernization by 2035 and reclaim China's past glory, *fuqiang* (wealth and power),[13] Latin America is not merely an overseas market and investment destination. Winning the hearts and minds of the Latin American public in the future is indispensable for China if it seeks to narrow the gap with the United States. Merely cajoling political elites in states like Venezuela only translates into partial success. As Liu Yanhua, a councilor of the PRC's state council, acknowledged in a speech at a BRI seminar, China had faced backlash despite investing billions in infrastructure in some countries due to its lack of attention to the environment and local communities.[14]

9

Indonesia's 'Soft Balancing' Against China

PREMESHA SAHA

Despite Indonesia's huge archipelagic disposition, the maritime domain has, for long, been neglected in the policy calculus of the country. In the recent past, a change is being noticed, whereby Indonesia seems to finally realize and rediscover its 'long-neglected maritime destiny'. This was seen in 2014, with the public announcement by President Joko Widodo (also known as Jokowi) of his vision to turn Indonesia into a Global Maritime Fulcrum (GMF), given its strategic position, straddling the Indian and the Pacific oceans. This change can mainly be attributed to the 'great power contestation' in the Indian Ocean and the Western Pacific.

The fact that Indonesia is finally 'thinking maritime', can be seen from other moves being made by the country besides the ambition of turning Indonesia into a GMF. Indonesia, in July 2017, had renamed the waters northeast of the Natuna islands, at the far southern end of the South China Sea (SCS), the 'North Natuna Sea'. The Indonesian officials had also made it clear that only the part which falls under Indonesia's claimed exclusive economic none (EEZ) was being renamed. This EEZ, however, overlaps with China's infamous nine-dash line.[1] Although the Indonesians are not the first in the Southeast Asian region to rename their claimed zone in the SCS, what needs to be kept in mind is that this is being done by a country which has for long maintained that 'it is not part of the dispute in the South China Sea'.[2]

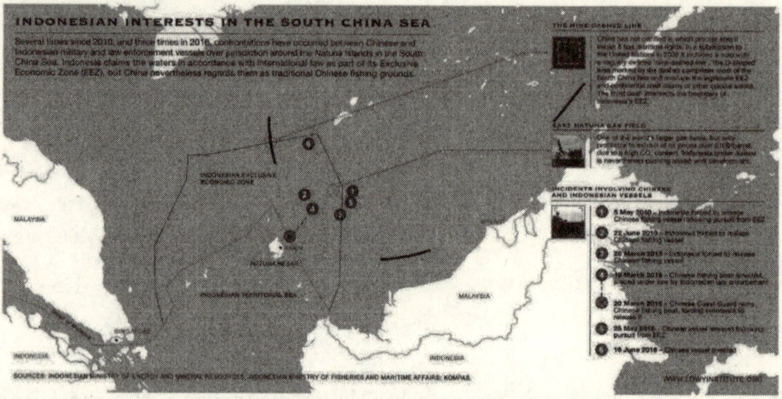

Source: Lowy Institute (https://www.lowyinstitute.org/the-interpreter/indonesia-s-new-north-natuna-sea-what-s-name)

There have been several incidents in the recent years in the Indonesian-claimed EEZ in the SCS. Indonesian fisheries enforcement or navy vessels have arrested Chinese trawlers in the overlapping claimant zone.[3] Although Indonesia still holds that 'it's a non-claimant state in the South China Sea dispute',[4] Indonesian President Jokowi has taken actions to beef up its military and law enforcement capacity in the area. He himself has made two high-profile trips to the military base at Ranai on Natuna Besar Island to demonstrate his interest in defending and protecting Indonesia's sovereignty over the islands and Indonesian rights to the resources in the adjacent EEZ.[5] Although these actions by Indonesia have not irked China too much, and the renaming carried no real legal force, it does reflect that the Indonesian diplomatic and political wing are learning to 'softly balance' against a rising China. His actions just indicated Indonesia's narrow territorial and economic interests around Natuna and not on the SCS issue. Therefore, the moves were fairly subtle in comparison to those of the Philippines, but just enough to ensure that Indonesia's interests were secured. Indonesia's actions, however, managed to make other countries like India, US, Japan, etc., realize that Indonesia is finally ready to take a stand on the SCS issue outside of the platform of the Association of Southeast Asian Nations (ASEAN).

In recent times, Indonesia has been bringing up the SCS issue in international fora as well. For instance, at the time of President Jokowi's visit to India in December 2016, it was reiterated in the joint statement that, 'Regarding the South China Sea, the two sides stressed the importance of resolving disputes by peaceful means, in accordance with universally recognized principles of international law including the UNCLOS.'[6] Even during the visit of the coordinating minister for maritime affairs, Luhut Pandjaitan, to India in May 2018, he asserted that 'there should not be any power projection in the South China Sea and that Indonesia has very carefully responded to the issue'.[7] Even while talking about Indonesia granting India access to develop the port of Sabang, located in the northern tip of Sumatra and near the Strait of Malacca, he said that, in his personal view, '[…] this will ensure a bit of a balance in the South China Sea. A balance of power can be maintained.'[8]

Indonesia is also one of the few countries in the Southeast Asian region that has embraced the Indo-Pacific concept. Indonesia is growing to take notice of strategic rivalries, and the growing strategic and economic importance of the Indo-Pacific region. In February 2018, a Chinese naval task force comprising four ships had entered the Indian Ocean from the Sunda strait for exercising in international waters close to Australia and had exited via the Lombok Strait. Earlier, in 2014, China held a three-ship naval exercise in the Indian Ocean, conducting a series of exercises including combat simulations. The task force had sailed through to the Western Pacific by way of the Lombok Strait near Indonesia's Bali island, approaching the Philippines.[9] Indonesia may not have issued official statements expressing its discomfort with these Chinese naval forces crossing its waters, but given Indonesia's sensitivity to maritime sovereignty, these exercises can also be one of the reasons for it to be willing to seek a balance of power (to counter a rising China) in the Indian Ocean and the Western Pacific.

Indonesia is maintaining the equilibrium well. It has been careful in not taking too strong an 'anti-China' stand on the SCS dispute and its naval advances in the Indian Ocean using its waterways, to be able to draw the benefits from the Chinese Belt and Road Initiative (BRI). Indonesia did participate in the Chinese flagship BRI summit and proposed projects worth USD 28 billion. Thus far, China has, through the BRI, made investments in the Jakarta–Bandung High Speed Railway project, and has signed contracts for investing in two hydropower projects, one power plant and a steel smelter (these contracts were signed during the visit of Chinese Premier Le Keqiang to Jakarta in May 2018). China's investments and aid to Indonesia have increased significantly, particularly in infrastructure projects, ranging from bridges and roads to power plants and high-speed rail. In 2017, China was the third-largest foreign investor in Indonesia, with investments amounting to USD 3.4 billion. According to Indonesia's Investment Coordinating Board (BKPM) chief, Thomas Lembong, China is investing heavily in Indonesia through the BRI. Both countries have agreed to jointly develop infrastructure projects in three Indonesian provinces specifically designated for the BRI: North Sumatra, North Kalimantan and North Sulawesi.[10]

China and Indonesia have continued to strengthen their cooperation since the signing of the Joint Declaration on Strategic Partnership between the government of the People's Republic of China and the government of the Republic of Indonesia on 21 January 2010. The joint declaration evolved into a joint communiqué between the two governments on further strengthening their strategic partnership when they met in Jakarta on 29 April 2011. The joint communiqué mentions boosting cooperation in political, economic (including trade and investment), defence and security, maritime cooperation, social and cultural, and regional and international domains. The joint communiqué clearly states:

> The parties undertake to continue to strengthen cooperation in the safety of navigation, maritime security, the Navy, marine scientific research and environmental protection, search and rescue at sea, ship building, marine fisheries, cooperation in areas such as capacity-building and to continue to strengthen coordination and cooperation in international forums such as the International Maritime Organization. Both sides agreed to work together to promote 'the blue economy', and continue to support the Indonesian Centre for Ocean and climate in mutually beneficial cooperation.[11]

After the 2011 declaration, the two countries conducted dialogue through the Bilateral Dialogue Forum on Politics, Law and Security. The forum met for the sixth time on 26 and 27 April 2017, and one of the discussions was about the alignment of the vision of the GMF and the BRI.[12] The two sides agreed to maintain high-level visits and close communication on key issues, integrate development strategies and promote cooperation under the BRI.[13] The dialogue could be the impetus for a plan of action for the implementation of the comprehensive strategic partnership between the governments, signed in Beijing on 14 May 2017.[14]

Starting 1 January 2016, Indonesian Port Corporation, PT Pelindo 4[15] expanded its export/import destinations from Makassar (originally only Xiamen and Hong Kong) and added Korea and Japan. Doso Agung, president director of PT Pelindo 4, announced the addition of the direct-call destinations since most of the export cargo from eastern Indonesia is to China, Korea and Japan. The addition of these direct-calls is expected to increase Indonesian exports to East China, Korea and Japan, i.e., countries with the largest economies in the Asia Pacific region. Direct-call has radically changed the map of national logistics because the export/import of cargo from East Indonesia, which was previously done through Jakarta/Surabaya via Singapore or Tanjung Pelepas, can now be done directly from Makassar to destination states, such as Hong Kong, Korea and Japan without double-handling or high costs.[16]

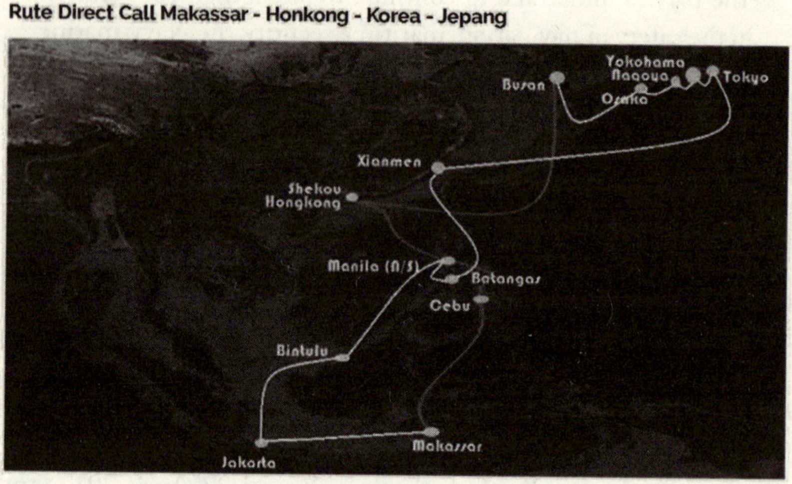

Figure 1: Direct-call route to East Asia [17]

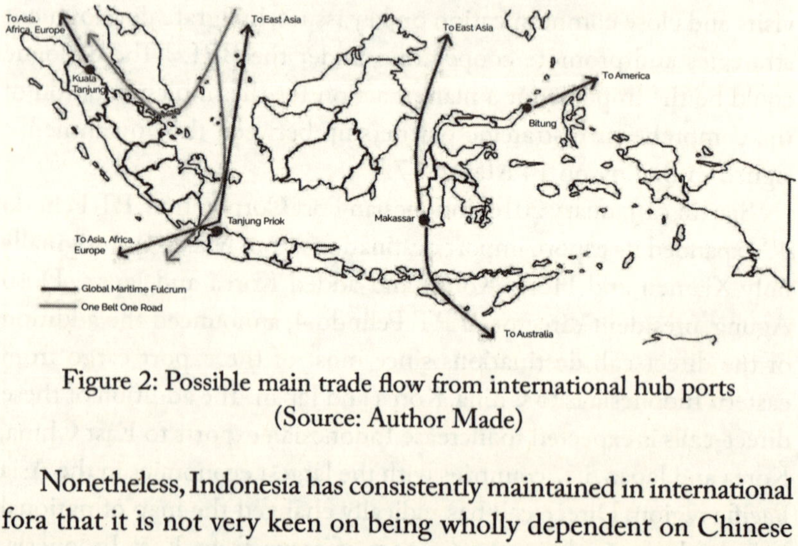

Figure 2: Possible main trade flow from international hub ports (Source: Author Made)

Nonetheless, Indonesia has consistently maintained in international fora that it is not very keen on being wholly dependent on Chinese investments. This was reiterated by Indonesia's coordinating minister for maritime affairs during his visit to India in 2018, 'We don't want to be controlled by the Belt and Road…'[18] This is also perhaps one of the reasons for Indonesia's proposal to grant India access to develop the port of Sabang.

Indonesia's 'soft balancing' is a clear shift from Indonesia's non-aligned foreign policy stand. Although Indonesia does not make a stern 'anti-China' rebuttal on volatile issues where its interests are at stake, it does not remain completely silent either. At the same time, it is able to draw Chinese investment using tact and diplomacy. It is clear to the world at large that Indonesia is awake upon every suit in strategic maritime realities and is able to skilfully and effectively liaise with super powers like China. Indonesia previously did not act in this manner – so now with consistent soft posturing, it is leading countries to believe that it is more interested in a balancing act than in a pro-China stance. In a way, this is actually helping Indonesia to reorient itself as an active player 'in determining the future of the Pacific and Indian Ocean region (PACINDO)'.

INDONESIAN INFRASTRUCTURE PROJECTS CONSIDERED STRATEGIC FOR BRI

No	Project	Sector	Investment (USD M)	Stage
1	Trans-Sumatra Toll Road	Transport	27,700	Pre-Construction
2	Sunda Strait Bridge	Transport	24,000	Planning
3	Bontang Oil Refinery	Energy	14,500	Planning
4	Jakarta-Bandung HSR	Transport	5,100	Awarded

No	Project	Sector	Invest-ment (USD M)	Stage
5	Central Kalimantan Coal Railway Network	Transport	2,300	Tendering
6	West Coast Expressway	Transport	2,000	Project Signed
7	Kertajati Airport	Transport	1,800	Tendering
8	Soekarno-Hatta Airport Train Express Line	Transport	1,800	Design
9	East-West MRT	Transport	1,700	Planning
10	Balikpapan–Samarinda Toll Road	Transport	875	Planning
11	Kulon Progo (New Yogyakarta) International Airport	Transport	700	Awarded
12	Surabaya Monorail	Transport	558	Planning
13	Kalibaru Port, First Container Terminal	Transport	393	Project Signed
14	Manado–Bitung Toll Road	Transport	330	Planning
15	Perbarakan–Tebing Tinggi Toll Road	Transport	303	Financing Close
16	Nusa Dua–NgurahRai–Benoa Toll Road	Transport	253	Financing Close

No	Project	Sector	Investment (USD M)	Stage
17	Southern Bali Water Supply	Water and Waste	219	Planning
18	Surabaya Tram Line	Transport	210	Planning
19	Umbulan Drinking Water Supply System	Water and Waste	151	Awarded
20	Batam Waste-to-Energy Plant	Energy	133	Tendering
21	Tangerang City Water Supply Project	Water and Waste	120	Project Signed
22	Bandar Lampung Water Supply	Water and Waste	100	Tendering
23	Bandung waste-to-energy Plant	Energy	68	Tendering
24	Bandung solid waste management improvement	Water and Waste	65	Tendering
25	West Semarang water supply	Water and Waste	56	Planning
26	Bogor and Depok solid waste management	Water and Waste	40	Planning

No	Project	Sector	Investment (USDM)	Stage
27	Way Rilau Water supply system	Water and Waste	38	Tendering
28	Palu water supply	Water and Waste	30	Planning
29	Medan water project	Water and Waste	25	Awarded
30	Tanah Ampo Cruise Terminal	Transport	25	Tendering
31	Lamongan water supply	Water and Waste	17	Planning
32	Maros water supply	Water and Waste	13	Planning
33	Jakarta MRT, Line 2	Transport	-	Planning
	Total		85,622	

Source: Pinsent Masons, August 2016, https://www.pinsentmasons.com/PDF/2016/obor/OBOR-Pinsent_Masons-2016.pdf

10

Rogue Nations: Assessing the China–Russia Relationship

KANAK GOKARN

The China–Russia partnership has so far defied categorization. Two formerly adversarial countries now enjoy a steady yet flexible relationship. Their growing engagement since the events in Ukraine in 2014 has revolved around the sale of military equipment,[1] Russian oil sales to China,[2] and increased Chinese financing for Russia amidst Western sanctions.[3] Moscow and Beijing generally agree on the shortcomings of an international order dominated by the United States and its allies.[4] Their relationship has caused a lot of concern, especially for the United States as was evident in its latest *National Security Strategy* (NSS).[5] However, there are certain underlying tensions within the relationship that place constraints on their bilateral ties. These relate to each side's national interests as well as their engagement with the international order. It must be said that the two sides have been adept at managing these tensions over the years, but they may affect the trajectory of their relationship in the long run.

The driver of these anxieties is the imbalance in the relationship. While both countries are significant actors in the international arena,

Russia's anxieties, in particular, stem from demographics as well as economics. China's population and GDP are almost ten times that of Russia. Russia's exports to China are primarily raw materials and hydrocarbons. Many analyses point to the tensions inherent to this buyer-seller relationship. As Russia becomes increasingly dependent on China for investments and as a market, the latter's power to negotiate favourable deals will only increase.[6] Thus, Russia will remain wary of overdependence on one country, particularly one with whom many of its interests overlap. Russia's tendency to balance various interests and preserve its strategic autonomy, while expanding its influence, must come into play. This would increase the likelihood of some degree of rapprochement with Europe,[7] especially given President Donald Trump's recent actions that have pushed Europe and Russia closer together. Since China's priority is its economic development, Western countries are more attractive partners,[8] even if Beijing does benefit from Russian oil. China's pragmatic approach to these imbalances has allowed the relationship to continue without seriously threatening the basis of their ties. Much depends on how it continues to deal with these pressures.

In Ukraine, an area Russia considers integral to its security, China refrained from directly criticizing or supporting Russia's actions. It abstained from the UN Security Council vote that would have declared the Crimean referendum illegal,[9] while issuing instructions to its domestic media outlets to refrain from connecting the issue to its own separatist problems.[10] While many Western countries responded to the violation of Ukrainian sovereignty by imposing sanctions, China criticized their usage but ultimately complied with them.[11]

Similarly, in the South China Sea, an area which lies within China's 'sphere of interest' but does not concern Russia directly, the latter has pursued its own interests. China's calibrated actions in the region are unlikely to invite the level of backlash that Russia's actions in Crimea did and the two have conducted joint exercises in the region.[12] But as Russia seeks to expand its footprint in the Pacific, evident in its modernization of its Pacific fleet, it may be drawn into the region.[13] It has engaged in its natural tendency to balance various interests, without giving the appearance of capitulating to any one power, by engaging with Vietnam.[14] Vietnam is wary of Chinese activities in the region owing to its boundaries being threatened, but Russia has cooperated with Hanoi militarily[15] as well as in the hydrocarbon sector.[16]

The pair's actions in Central Asia, where both desire significant stakes, will be important in the coming years. Russia sees it as an area that is key to its expanding influence. Although most Central Asian countries recognize their historic ties with Russia and the latter's economic power and security interests in the region, some have been less than enthusiastic about participating in Russia-led projects such as the Eurasian Economic Union (EAEU) and the Collective Security Treaty Organization (CSTO).[17] Russia's introduction of stricter immigration controls for the region has also proven to be a sore spot.[18] China instead prefers to offer economic growth as an incentive. The region is key for China's 'Go West' policy as well as their flagship project, the Belt and Road Initiative (BRI), to showcase its influence in Asia, but its benefits for the region are limited as Chinese firms prefer to employ Chinese workers.[19] Russia's role as a potential security guarantor in Central and West Asia is not challenged by this form of engagement. However, China's foray into the security sphere may be inescapable, and combined with its expansion into a historically important geographical area for Russia, this may affect the relationship in the long run.[20]

These tendencies – China's pragmatism and its recognition of the importance of the West, and Russia's balancing act and its aversion to outside encroachment in its 'sphere of influence' – will only exacerbate the imbalance. Russia's geopolitical weight has certain benefits for China, and China is emerging as a key economic partner for Russia. But their relentless pursuit of their national interests and their respective relations with the West might ultimately be more important than their relationship with each other, especially Russia's ties with Europe and China's ties with both Europe and America. Links between the governments and leaders may be close, but Russia's general affinity for Europe is greater. Further antagonizing the West is in neither Moscow nor Beijing's interest. Chinese policymakers have expressed apprehension about Russia's unpredictability, following its actions in Crimea and later Syria.[21] The convergence between China and Russia is over their opposition to the US-led system, but they do not yet define what their roles are to be in their ideal international order. American policies under President Trump may be pushing them closer together now, but this may be more out of expedience than a desire to build any sort of formal alliance. In any case, their relationship is a product of the current international context, so it is reasonable to assume a change in context could lead the two to re-evaluate their relations.

11

Contesting the Dragon: India and ASEAN Converge

MAYA MIRCHANDANI

The invitation to ten Association of Southeast Asian Nations (ASEAN) leaders and heads of government as chief guests on Republic Day in January 2018 focused conversations on new and emerging alliances, and ongoing tensions between India and China on the Doklam plateau, provide ample evidence that India's 2018's foreign policy focus was directed Eastward.[1]

Even though a Look East policy has officially – and some would argue, ineffectively – been in place for over two decades now, Ram Madhav – director of the India Foundation, and the BJP-led government's key foreign policy voice – announced at the Raisina Dialogue 2018 that 'India has to completely reorient its strategic mindset. A shift is needed from westward to eastward thinking. From land-based thinking to ocean-centric thinking.'[2] In this new world view, India, and its large peninsula jutting into the waters in the heart of the Indian Ocean, must expand its influence and reach from the eastern coast of the African continent to the western edge of the Pacific waters – not just to counter China, but to positively and clearly emerge as the leader of Asia. China's inexorable march across land and sea into North, Central and South Asia via the Belt and Road Initiative (BRI) and the Maritime Silk Route is seen by most as an attempt to encircle India and contain Delhi's reach and influence, making China India's single biggest security challenge; adding layers of complexity to the already complex and tenuous ties between Delhi and Beijing.

For India, with its history of troubled relations with China that range from a serious border dispute to water wars, the challenge has consistently been to remain engaged and avoid standoffs while asserting its own reach and power, both domestically and in the wider Asian region. When Prime Minister Modi went to Xiamen to attend the ninth BRICS (Brazil, Russia, India, China, South Africa) summit, everyone believed that a military standoff between the two countries had been averted by some deft diplomacy after seventy-three days of eye-to-eye confrontation between Indian and Chinese troops on the Doklam plateau.[3] For the better part of late 2017 and early 2018, Delhi and Beijing were locked in cold conflict on the Doklam plateau, located at the crossroads of India, Bhutan and China, but firmly in Bhutanese territory. However, the truth is that this confrontation is far from over.

Chinese intentions to build a road southwards from the plateau, giving it potential access to Gyemochen, seven kilometres south of Batang La – the watershed point at which the current tri-junction between Bhutan, India and China is marked – is anathema to Delhi. China's design to move the watershed to Gyemochen is clear – it is to force India's hand and insist a new boundary line be drawn east of Gyemochen, thereby putting Arunachal firmly into Chinese territory.

This has always been unacceptable to India. Before hypernationalist media in both countries could ratchet up the rhetoric and make headlines pushing for greater confrontation, which Delhi was determined to avoid, the ministry of external affairs hastily pointed out that India and China have 'mechanisms' in place to ensure things don't spiral out of control.[4] These 'mechanisms' led to Prime Minister

Narendra Modi's informal summit with President Xi Jinping in Wuhan in China in May 2018 – a meeting that left many puzzled about possible intent and outcomes, given recent history, as well as China's concerns over the 'Quad' grouping of India, Japan, Australia and the USA in the face of growing tensions between Washington and Beijing. But Delhi said Doklam wasn't discussed because it had been resolved and there was nothing to talk about.[5]

However, India cannot afford to presume that the resolution is permanent or that these mechanisms will work, especially, given that the 'disengagement' of 28 August 2017 does not appear to be accepted by large sections of the Chinese establishment. If anything, the presence of Chinese troops in Doklam – whether they returned after the disengagement, or continued in spite of it – indicates two things: one, that Delhi may want to employ mechanisms but has no real force and no one person to talk to on the Chinese side to de-escalate, and two, that the mechanisms mean very little, when time and time again the Chinese have shown utter disregard for India's concerns.

Chinese incursions, right from Depsang in 2013 and Chumar in 2014 (even as Xi Jinping and Narendra Modi walked on the banks of the Sabarmati river in Ahmedabad) must be taken in conjunction with an assertive Xi signalling an aggression and activism that Delhi has found hard to counter on its own.[6] In fact, analysts believe that the de-escalation over Doklam in August 2018 was more a result of the fact that Xi wanted to focus his attention on the 19th Party Congress and push for greater power domestically, as well as sharpen his image as a globally responsible leader ready to fill a vacuum created by Donald Trump's unpredictability and brinkmanship. With that in the bank, it was only natural that things would flare up with Delhi again.

India may well have asserted itself and its military interests by blocking China's Doklam adventure, but it would be ill-advised to assume that even the deftest diplomacy with Beijing will dial down these tensions anytime soon. If one looks at China's aggressive stance towards India in the context of other developments, it is safe to expect that the presence of ten ASEAN leaders in Delhi, all putting their heads together to improve regional cooperation, connectivity and security with India, in the Indian Ocean and in Southeast Asia has made Beijing more anxious. This invites the question: was this the reason for Beijing's renewed sabre-rattling on Doklam? After all, the timing is perfect.

ASEAN leaders, while in India, also looked to India for help in ensuring that access to sea routes remain open and not threatened in the face of Chinese expansionism. As countries like Vietnam and Philippines fight to secure areas like the Spratly Islands and the Scarborough Shoal from China respectively, for India, the focus has been on connectivity and development of sea lanes rather than on security, and Delhi has been clearly hesitant to take a position on Chinese aggression in the resource-rich South China Sea.[7] The waterway is a key sea-lane for global trade – more than USD 5 trillion worth of goods pass through its waters annually. This, along with its offshore oil and gas blocks, has led to the Chinese navy sallying forth – undeterred by international courts, which have rejected its claims on any of these islands.[8]

ASEAN nations would like to see India take a stand but the maritime security imperative in the Indian Ocean, from Delhi's lens, is not necessarily in sync with the geography of ASEAN. It lies closer to India's own coastlines and waterways. Looking eastward, India's imperative is economic – freedom of navigation (FoN) has predominantly guided engagement with ASEAN countries in the maritime domain and India's hesitation to support them vociferously against China is a thorny issue. Complicating things further is the proximity of some ASEAN nations to Beijing, and the fact that ASEAN functions on consensus, with veto powers to all members.

Seen against these realities, it is apparent that Delhi's advantage lies in fighting its own diplomatic war against Beijing via other routes, and new and unusual strategic alliances with ready partners. The 'Quad' formed in 2017, comprising India, Japan, Australia and the United States of America is perhaps the most significant of them all. In fact, the use of the term 'Indo-Pacific' in reference to the Quad, as opposed to 'Asia Pacific'(preferred by the Chinese) is more than just an acknowledgement of the threat of Chinese expansionism, in all but name.[9] While it reorients strategic thinking in this new direction, Delhi has also been forced to assure ASEAN leaders that its partnership in the Quad does not mean it will divert attention away from the regional grouping. No single ASEAN nation has openly endorsed it; in fact, many are inherently sceptical and some feel left out of an important strategic move that affects them directly.[10]

Also at Raisina 2018, Dino Patti Djalal of Indonesia's Foreign Policy Community echoed ASEAN concerns of being caught in the crosshairs of a new fight between China and what Beijing is viewing as an 'Asian' NATO.[11] For Indonesia and, indeed, the other nine ASEAN members, China is a reality – one that needs to be handled cleverly, and one they need to be able to live with. For India, however, the Quad threw up a world of opportunities to explore alternatives to China's BRI and Maritime Silk Route plans. India's Republic Day invitation to ASEAN nations was an attempt to garner diplomatic support for this initiative.

Beijing may flex its muscles in Doklam to portray India as weak to the very countries it is trying to engage with, but Delhi's gains will lie in balancing its diplomatic act with both East and West – engaging with the United States and Europe while asserting its own prominence and linkages with the wider Southeast Asian region. If it pulls this off, perhaps the mandarins of the ministry of external affairs do have China to thank for the coming together of strong democracies, big economic powers and regional heavyweights, all partnering for a common cause.

12

The BRI and Myanmar's China Debate

K. YHOME

Myanmar's diplomatic balancing is under stress in the face of the West distancing from Naypyidaw over the country's handling of the Rohingya crisis. As in the past, Naypyidaw is tilting towards its northern neighbour for both political and economic support and Beijing is fully leveraging the situation to its advantage.

After years of close strategic relations during Myanmar's military rule, China–Myanmar relations plunged into a phase of uncertainty when the Myanmar military regime decided to take the path of democratization in 2010. In the following years, Myanmar's suspension of two China-funded projects – the Myitsone hydropower project in 2011 and the Letpadaung copper mine in 2013 – marked the beginning of a troubled relationship.

Beijing recalibrated its policy towards Myanmar to suit the changing times – with the aim to arrest growing anti-Chinese sentiments in the Southeast Asian nation and to safeguard its core strategic interests, including limiting strategic ties between Naypyidaw and Washington.

When the Aung San Suu Kyi-led National League for Democracy (NLD) government took office in 2016, contrary to popular perceptions, it adopted a balanced policy towards China and the West. Beijing's Myanmar policy revision may have paid off.

The China–Myanmar Economic Corridor

Myanmar joined the Chinese Belt and Road Initiative (BRI) when State Counsellor Suu Kyi attended the Belt and Road Forum for International Cooperation in Beijing in May 2017. A memorandum of understanding (MoU) on 'Cooperation within the Framework of the Silk Road Economic Belt and 21st century Maritime Silk Road Initiative'[1] was signed during the visit.

Under the BRI scheme, two economic corridors – the Bangladesh–China–India–Myanmar–Economic Corridor (BCIM–EC) and the China–Indochina–Peninsula Economic Corridor (CIPEC) involve Myanmar, owing to its geographic location. Both Beijing and Naypyidaw recognize Myanmar's critical role in pushing forward these BRI projects.

Beijing proposed the China–Myanmar–Economic Corridor (CMEC) as part of the BRI at a time when Myanmar was increasingly under international pressure owing to its conduct in the Rohingya crisis.[2] Beijing is aware that Myanmar needs its political and diplomatic support to fend off mounting international scrutiny.

As Beijing's relations with Naypyidaw entered a difficult phase in the reform period, China began to push alternative corridors including the China–Pakistan Economic Corridor (CPEC), the China–Laos–Thailand road and railway corridors and, in recent years, the China–India–Nepal corridor under the BRI scheme. With Naypyidaw now more receptive to Chinese initiatives, Beijing is prioritizing the CMEC as it remains the shortest route for China to reach the Indian Ocean and beyond.

In early June 2018, a report citing a Myanmar official said China and Myanmar reached a '15-point MoU' on the CMEC.[3] The corridor will run from the Chinese Yunnan province to Mandalay in Central Myanmar and then south to Yangon and west to Kyaukpyu special economic none (SEZ) forming a 'Y-shaped' corridor involving basic infrastructure, construction, manufacturing, agriculture, transport, finance, human resources development, telecommunications, and research and technology to develop the CMEC, the report added.

As part of the CMEC, major roads and railways are being proposed to link China's Yunnan province with Myanmar's major cities. In March 2018, the two countries signed an MoU to conduct a feasibility study for the construction of two major corridors – the Mandalay-Tigyaing-Muse expressway project and the Kyaukpyu-Naypyidaw highway project.[4]

The Kyaukpyu Deep-Sea Port

A Chinese mega-project in Myanmar is the strategic Kyaukpyu SEZ in the Rakhine state of Myanmar. The USD 10 billion project involving the development of a new deep-sea port (USD 7.5 billion) and an industrial park (USD 2.5 billion) was awarded to a consortium led by a Chinese state investment company, China International Trust and Investment Corporation (CITIC) in 2015.

On 4 July 2018, Myanmar's planning and finance minister, Soe Win said Myanmar would ask China to reduce the scale of the project. The minister gave an economic argument for the need to downsize the China-led Kyaukpyu SEZ project saying that 'the bigger the projects, the bigger the responsibility to pay back'.[5]

Earlier in May 2018, Sean Turnell, a senior economic consultant to Suu Kyi expressed similar concerns about the project saying that the USD 7.5 billion price-tag for the deep-sea port was 'way, way, way beyond what [Myanmar] needs'.[6] According to Turnell, the Myanmar government has 'really taken notice' of Sri Lanka's experience when Colombo had to surrender Hambantota port, southeast of the island nation, to Chinese companies on a ninety-nine-year lease for the USD

1 billion debt from China that it was unable to repay after borrowing it from China for the construction of the port.

Some in Myanmar's policy circles play down the debt fear. On 30 June 2018, while attending the Third BRI Summit in Hong Kong, Myanmar's union minister for the ministry of the office of the union government and the chairman of Myanmar's investment commission, Thaung Tun, dismissed the fear of a 'debt trap'. Nonetheless, Tun said Myanmar was aware of 'what happened' in Sri Lanka and Naypyidaw would 'make sure' the Kyaukpyu port is 'a workable project', suggesting that Myanmar is not ruling out downsizing the project.[7]

Initial reports over the prolonged negotiations on the Kyaukpyu SEZ project suggested that Naypyidaw was unconvinced about the commercial viability of the project. This may be valid as Kyaukpyu, being some distance away from the country's biggest city Yangon, may not be able to generate rapid logistics demand.

Myanmar renegotiated a previous shareholders' agreement that gave Chinese CITIC an 85 per cent stake in the project, and only 15 per cent to Myanmar. The deal was widely viewed as unfair and raised concerns about the project landing Myanmar into a debt trap.[8] According to Set Aung, chairman of the Kyaukpyu SEZ's management committee, who is also the deputy planning and finance minister, CITIC would now take a 70 per cent stake with the remaining 30 per cent going to Myanmar.[9] Even so, concern shifted to the scale of the project. The key issue that seems to worry Naypyidaw most is the experiences of neighbouring countries.

As Myanmar's chief negotiator on the project with Chinese CITIC, Set Aung said he was 'very cautious in the negotiation process, mindful of what happened in other countries and to follow international standards'.[10] Under the new deal, the project would now 'start on a smaller scale' and expansion would be 'based entirely on demand'. On the financing side too, Set Aung has been cited as saying that loans taken for the project would be 'private loans, not government loans' with no sovereign guarantees. Set Aung believes that the new terms of the deal would protect Myanmar from falling into a debt trap.

Even so, Set Aung pointed out the need for careful examination of 'the details of each project' under the BRI and to evaluate if a project is 'necessary' for Myanmar. Moreover, Myanmar needs to continue its engagements with other players in the development of infrastructure projects such as the Asian Development Bank, the World Bank, Japan and other agencies, he added. This indicates that as Myanmar leverages the BRI for its own interests, it is also seeking other options to avoid overdependence on China. However, Myanmar's growing dependence on Beijing in dealing with the ethnic conflicts in the borderlands gives China an upper hand.

The Kyaukpyu–Kunming Railway

In 2014, the strategic rail project deal to link China's inland province of Yunnan, Kunming, to the Indian Ocean from Kyaukpyu expired. The agreement signed between the China Railway Engineering Corporation (CRECG) and Myanmar's railway ministry had failed to commence construction within the three-year stipulated time frame agreed under the deal. Reports suggest that Myanmar's concerns over 'social opposition, financial feasibility, distribution of gains and national security' were the key reasons for halting the railway project.[11] In October 2018, China and Myanmar signed an MoU to conduct a feasibility study to a railway linking Muse with Mandalay.[12]

Concerns are likely to continue to loom large about the implications of the troubled China–Myanmar borderlands on the mega-infrastructure projects under the BRI scheme. Myanmar's efforts to find peace in the border regions remain elusive. Beijing has been playing an active role in Myanmar's internal conflicts, though that has not brought about any progress in the peace progress so far.

With new projects proposed under the BRI scheme, Myanmar's strategic concerns will only grow, owing to its own experience and the lessons it is learning from neighbouring countries. These issues are increasingly shaping public opinion in Myanmar. Naypyidaw may seek alternative options to reduce dependence on Chinese investment. However, for now, with the unceasing internal conflicts in the borderlands and the need to ward off international pressures, Naypyidaw may go along with Beijing's initiatives.

China's long-term strategic interests of seeing Myanmar as a 'land bridge' to reach the Indian Ocean will continue to drive Beijing's strategy. This interdependency defining the relationship is unlikely to change in the near future.

However, China will face a dilemma sooner than later. In the short-term, Myanmar's internal conflicts may suit Beijing's interests as they create conditions for Naypyidaw to seek Beijing's support and generate tension between the West and Myanmar. However, continued internal conflicts in Myanmar will affect border stability with huge implications for the development of BRI projects and, on the other hand, may even invite other major powers to involve themselves in these conflicts.

13

Engaging Africa through Summits: The Chinese Experience

ABHISHEK MISHRA

The role played by summit meetings in the international politics and engagements of postcolonial Africa can be located within a context dominated by several interlinked factors, including the very process of decolonization. Formal powers and institutions were transferred from European to African states as they started attaining independence. In this context, newly independent African states began their international politics wherein summit meetings, or a series of ad-hoc meetings between heads of government became established means of voicing Africa's opinions, coordinating policies, and establishing diplomatic channels of communication.

Africa's Experience with Summitry

Big powers have engaged with African countries through multilateral forum summits for a long time. France was the first to engage with the continent way back in the 1970s. The US–Africa Leaders Summit took place in August 2014. Not only Western powers, but also Asian powers such as China, India and Japan have held summit meetings with African countries. Japan through the Tokyo International Conference on African Development (TICAD) launched in 1993, India through India–Africa Forum Summit (IAFS 2008, 2012, 2015) and China through the Forum on China–Africa Cooperation (FOCAC).

The experiences of these countries in engaging with African countries through summit meetings have been a success. Increasing numbers of African heads of state and governments have attended these meetings, thereby generating mutual trust and international awareness regarding Africa's developmental needs. These summits have led to more open, accountable, diverse and multifaceted engagement between Africa and the rest of the world.

China and Africa's engagement through FOCAC was launched on October 2000 at the first ministerial conference held in Beijing. FOCAC is part of a growing trend of South-South Cooperation that provides an alternative to traditional decvelopment assistance mechanisms. The second ministerial conference took place in Addis Ababa in December 2003, third in 2006 in Beijing, fourth in Sharm El-Sheik in 2009, fifth in Beijing in 2012, and the second FOCAC and sixth ministerial conference in December 2015 at Johannesburg. The 2018 FOCAC Summit was held in September in Beijing.

These summits have paved the way for China – although a late entrant like India – to make inroads into the African continent. China has set up industries and infrastructures in diverse fields in different parts of the continent. China is increasing its forays into Africa and has emerged as Africa's largest trading and investment partner.

China–Africa Partnership

China's trade and investment partnership is vital for both trading partners. China views Africa as a growing source of raw materials –

most importantly crude oil, iron ore and copper – which have helped fuel China's rapid infrastructure development. For Africa, China represents a major trading partner and investor that provides it with cheap consumer products, buys its natural resources, and helps build its infrastructure.

Over the past decade, China–Africa bilateral trade has been steadily increasing, punctuated by a slight slump and quick recovery from the 2009 financial crisis. However, weak commodity prices since 2014 have adversely impacted the value of African exports to China, even while Chinese exports to Africa remained steady.

China-Africa Trade

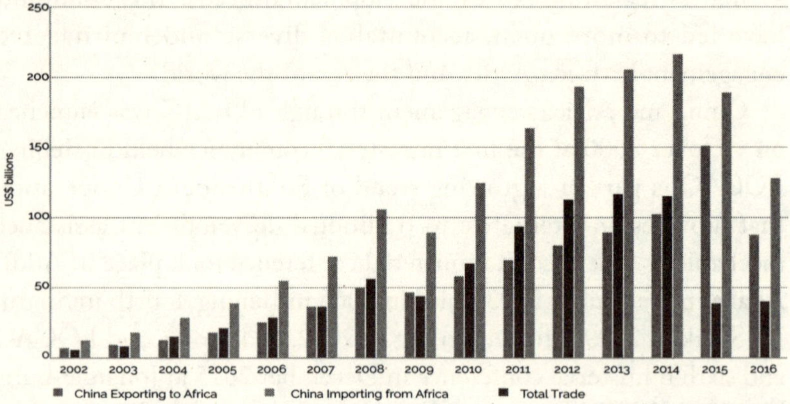

Source : UN COMTRADE 2017

China–Africa trade reached USD 220 billion in 2014 along with investments worth USD 32.4 billion, and was estimated to be about USD 300 billion by 2015.[1] According to the statistics by China Customs, in January–December 2017, the import and export value of China–Africa trade amounted to USD 170 billion, up 14.1 per cent year on year, 2.7 per cent higher than the general increase of foreign trade in the same period.[2] Among these, China's exports to Africa reached USD 94.74 billion, up 2.7 per cent. China's imports from Africa reached USD 75.26 billion, up 32.8 per cent. The trade surplus was USD 19.48 billion, down 45.2 per cent year on year.[3]

Forum on China–Africa Cooperation

Since its inauguration, the FOCAC has become a crucial component for institutionalizing China's relations with the African continent. The FOCAC is a multilateral platform for collective, pragmatic consultation and dialogue established jointly by Chinese and African leaders 'in order to further strengthen the friendly cooperation between China and Africa under the new circumstances, to jointly meet the challenge of economic globalization and to promote common development'.[4] The rhetorical focus is on equality, South-South cooperation, and mutual benefit.

The forum meets every three years and is held in Beijing or in an African country on an alternating basis. It charts out a three-year action plan which is carried out on a bilateral basis between countries and is monitored by a follow-up committee. The FOCAC has five guiding values which embody the spirit of South-South cooperation, namely – equality and mutual benefit, diversity in form and content, emphasis on practical results, pursuit of common progress, and amicable settlement of disputes.

China also seeks to engage with African multilateral fora. In the 2000 Beijing declaration of FOCAC and the 2003 Addis-Ababa Action Plan, China pledged its support to African Union (AU) and New Partnership for African Development (NEPAD). In 2006, an MoU was signed between the FOCAC and NEPAD secretariats.[5]

Both China and Africa are emphasizing on issues related to environmental protection, especially since the fifth ministerial conference in 2012. As trade and investments in Africa are increasing, there is a greater need to monitor damage to environment and loss of biodiversity. With a large growing population, water scarcity and poor soil quality, Africa's population is very susceptible to climate change. Therefore, Africa needs to balance sustainable development efforts with economic growth and poverty alleviation.

In this respect, under the framework of FOCAC, efforts are being made to hold a conference on China–Africa Cooperation in

Environmental Protection, set up the China–Africa Environment Cooperation Center, launch the China–Africa Green Innovation project, and establish a China–Africa Joint Research Center project which aims to support African efforts in implementing clean energy and wildlife protection projects, and enhance their capacity to access the Green Climate Fund.

2015 Johannesburg Summit

During the 2015 Johannesburg summit, China pledged to invest USD 60 billion in African states, which tripled the previous USD 20 billion commitment during the 2012 FOCAC summit in Beijing.[6] However, most of the funds are in the form of loans and export credits. The USD 60 billion includes USD 5 billion for grants, USD 35 billion for concessional loans and export credits, and USD 5 billion each for the China–Africa Development Fund and the Special Loan for the Development of African Small-and-Mid Sized Enterprises, and USD 10 billion for the China–Africa Industrial Capacity Cooperation Fund.[7] These funds are expected to help address the bottlenecks in Africa's economic and social development. The 2015 summit focused on key areas such as agricultural modernization, industrialization, trade and investment, and public health, among others.

Whether China will be able to implement its commitments at a fast pace and accord priority to important areas of cooperation will ultimately depend on China's bilateral relations with individual African countries. Although the FOCAC action plans outline cooperation projects multilaterally – that is, among China and several African states – China delivers on the projects bilaterally. This will make African state leaders and other stakeholders compete for these large sums of money. The African countries that have the most experience with risk assessment or project management are most likely going to be the biggest beneficiaries of Chinese development goals announced during the FOCAC. Given its current progress, China is on track to meet most of its financing commitments in areas such as industrialization, agriculture development and infrastructure.

2018 Beijing Summit

The FOCAC 2018 in Beijing attempted to increase strategic consensus between China and African countries in order to maintain friendship and consolidate the political foundations for their unity and cooperation. Building on the success of the 2015 Johannesburg summit, the FOCAC 2018 focused on synergizing the Belt and Road Initiative (BRI), United Nations 2030 Agenda for Sustainable Development and development strategies of individual African countries. The main focus of the summit revolved around dollar signs with China pledging another USD 60 billion in new financing to Africa.

Xi in his opening speech highlighted eight major initiatives for future China–Africa cooperation – infrastructure connectivity, trade facilitation, green development, industrial promotion, capacity building, people-to-people exchanges, healthcare, and peace and security.[8] While none of these initiatives are new, they represent an implicit response to charges that China is mainly interested in profiting off Africa. President Xi emphasized on a 'five-no' approach to China's African policy which includes 'no interference in African countries' internal affairs' and 'no attachment of political strings to assistance'. While the principle of 'non-interference' has long guided Chinese foreign policy, in practice, the principle has always been more flexible, both for reasons of economics and perception. While China has always maintained that its model of engagement with Africa is 'win-win' cooperation between two equals, there is still a long way to go for the diversification of African exports, especially of non-mineral products, to China.

14

Charting China's Approach to International Law

AARSHI TIRKEY

In the 1970s, China's foreign policy made a marked departure from the isolationist stand it adopted in 1949. Since then, it has steadily integrated into the international legal order by becoming a part of various international organizations, treaties and agreements. China's emergence as a key player in global politics implies that its actions, statements and opinions carry weight in framing and modifying both, future and existing, international legal norms. As countries aim to navigate a geopolitical future with decreasing US engagement and increasing Chinese influence, it becomes pertinent to know and understand China's evolving approach to international law.

Placing State Sovereignty at the Forefront

Simply defined, 'international law' refers to a body of rules derived from customs or treaties, which nations recognize as binding in their relations with one another.[1] Treaty and custom-based rules – such as those related to peace, conflict, boundary disputes, trade and navigation – help create a stable, peaceful and mutually beneficial rules-based international order. However, under realpolitik, countries instrumentalize international legal rules in pursuance of their own national and political interests. Back in 1945, the international community based on norms related to government recognition and state succession ostracized China. Under the leadership of Western countries, Chiang Kai-Shek's government-in-exile based in Taiwan was recognized as the official representative of China's seat in the UN, and not Mao Zedong's Communist Party of China (CPC) which was in de facto control of Chinese territory. For these reasons, China has treated international law with caution and considered it as a tool for economic exploitation and political oppression.

Consequently, China's general approach to international law has been drawn from principles enshrined in a 1954 bilateral treaty signed between India and China, known as the 'Panchsheel Treaty'. The treaty, which aims to govern bilateral relations between the two states, consists of traditional Westphalian principles like respect for territorial integrity and sovereignty, non-interference in internal affairs and mutual non-aggression. The core tenets of the treaty heavily emphasize the concept of 'state sovereignty', i.e., a state's full right and power to govern itself and control its affairs without any outside interference from any other state.[2] These principles have been frequently invoked by China to oppose outside interference in issues such as the Tibetan independence movement, which impinge on her sovereignty and territorial integrity.

Under international law, treaties are the primary legal instruments for governing and regulating relations between states. Once a treaty is in force, its provisions are binding between parties and its objectives must be performed in good faith. However, China considers certain treaties, known as 'unequal treaties', as non-binding. 'Unequal treaties', a term coined by China, refer to a group of treaties through which it was coerced to concede certain territorial rights to Western powers.[3] Given that the treaties were signed during the heyday of imperialism, China feels that the treaties violate its sovereignty and integrity since it negotiated them from an unequal position. This is a primary reason why China frequently contests the legitimacy of the McMahon Line that demarcates the territorial boundary between India's Arunachal Pradesh and South Tibet.

China does not follow international human rights obligations and avoids international scrutiny of its domestic human rights record. China's wariness arises from the use of these norms to interfere in the domestic affairs of states through public censure, economic sanctions and, in several cases, armed intervention and regime change. Beijing demonstrates an extreme reluctance to endorse UN action in response to human rights violations or humanitarian crises. A notable example includes the blocking of a UN Security Council resolution on the humanitarian crisis in Syria in May 2014.[4]

A Different Approach to Emerging Fields in International Law

The above position is in contrast with China's approach to newer and emerging fields of international law, such as space, trade, deep-sea mining, cyberspace and climate change. China's change in approach can be attributed to the fact that the process for framing newer rules is more inclusive and participatory, as it contains significant representation from developing and least developed countries. China has an equal say in framing these rules and, given the size of its economy, population, military and territory, its opinions and statements contain significant heft. Accordingly, China treats this as an ideal opportunity to promote its own vision for the global legal order. For example, China hosted the first World Internet Conference (also known as the 'Wuzhen Summit') in 2014 and advocated 'internet sovereignty' as a basis for cyber governance. Internet sovereignty, a mechanism that is already established in China, gives each country the right to govern and regulate its internet space as sovereign territory.[5]

As one of the largest economies in the world, China has continuously pushed for greater trade and economic integration through bilateral and multilateral free trade agreements, such as the Regional Comprehensive Economic Partnership (RCEP). Beijing has endeavoured to set up new multilateral financial institutions – the Asian Infrastructure Investment Bank (AIIB) and the New Development Bank (NDB) – as alternatives to the Western-dominated Bretton Woods system. However, even within the area of trade, economic and investment laws, states have flagged up concerns regarding transparency from China's end. China continues to adopt measures to promote its own sovereign rights in a covert manner, by utilizing gaps and lacunae in existing international trade and economic laws. Developments in the past, such as the yuan devaluation, or the lax intellectual property rights regime in Chinese markets, aim to further its economic interests at the cost of similar interests of others.

Beijing, thus, recognizes the utility of international law but assigns a 'functional' approach to it, and uses it to achieve benefits like economic and reputational gains.[6]

China's Vision for the Future of the International Legal Order

Previously, China's experience with colonialism and imperialism made it a hesitant participant in the international legal order. Its response to pre-established, traditional international legal rules was guided by concerns of state sovereignty and non-interference in domestic affairs. However, with newer and emerging fields of international law, China is eager to participate in its formulation to help realize its vision for the global legal order and to create space for the protection of its own national and political interests. With an increasing decline in US engagement with the rules-based international order, a vacuum has been created in global leadership. Given China's emerging role as a global heavyweight, it could effectively fill this vacuum and utilize this position to modify existing international laws and shape new ones, in consonance with its own vision for the international legal order.

The implications of such a trajectory for international law are many. For instance, on the one hand, it may help roll back 'liberal interventionism' by Western powers, under the guise of human rights protection. But on the other hand, it may end international scrutiny of domestic human rights abuse and help perpetuate crises like those of the Rohingya refugees. Although imperfect, international law has helped create a world governed by rules and norms and has made the global order more predictable and less chaotic. It remains to be seen whether the future trajectory of international law will indeed be shaped by China, given the dynamic nature of national and global politics, and the role played by emerging powers, like India.

15

The Politics of the Redback: Chinese Economic Statecraft and Global Finance

TUNEER MUKHERJEE

'Uneasy lies the head that wears a crown' best characterizes America's position as the hegemon in global finance.[1] The global financial system that we have today is the result of a combination of international monetary cooperation, diverse economic ideologies and collective financial innovation. The United States (US) for the last half a century has controlled the financial order via prudent macroeconomic management and shrewd statecraft. The relative political stability of the US and the way it designed the global economy in the post-war era makes American economic institutions best suited to handle global financial rubrics. Additionally, the International Monetary Fund (IMF), that monitors trade flows, and the World Bank, that helps provide financing for developing nations, are both headquartered in Washington, effectively making United States the de facto leader of the global economy. The currency instrument that realizes all of this is the US dollar (USD) – the *primus inter pares*, the first among equals, of the international monetary system.

The rise of the People's Republic of China (PRC) has initiated a change in this longstanding international monetary order. The absenteeism of the US in reorganizing the existing system of global economic governance has compelled policymakers in Beijing to pursue their own strategies to achieve economic leverage. The objective of traditional economic statecraft is to shore up a country's foreign policy objectives via the use of economic resources.[2] China's use of economic instruments to shore up its position as a global economic power is one that supplements the broader idea of the rejuvenation of the Chinese nation.[3] The incentive for the PRC is the ability to wield power beyond its immediate shores. There are three comprehensive strategies that the Chinese have employed to this effect: the first and most visible amongst them is the internationalization of the renminbi (RMB), the official currency of the PRC; the second is the establishment of Beijing-based financial lending institutions for developmental funding; and the third is the advocacy of free trade, and positioning itself as a leader of globalization in the aftermath of the election of a protectionist leader in the US. These strategies provide Beijing a wide range of tools with which it can pursue economic statecraft and exercise power abroad. While these measures might not change the fundamentals of global economics, there is enough potential to institute a parallel system of monetary cooperation.

The issue of the 'redback' (an informal term for RMB) is central to China's quest for global recognition. Zhou Xiaochuan's paper for the People's Bank of China (PBoC) titled 'Reform the International Monetary System', put forth a nuanced plan for the world to move away from the USD.[4] Xiaochuan demanded a more responsible US economic policy to protect the value of China's dollar-denominated assets and proposed measures to encourage the use of the Special Drawing Rights (SDR) issued by the International Monetary Fund (IMF) as a partial substitute to the 'greenback' (informal term for the USD). In 2016, the PRC finally followed up on this and published its foreign reserves total in SDRs.[5] David Marsh observed that this was a clear signal that the PRC was 'embarking, pragmatically but steadily, toward enshrining a multicurrency reserve system at the heart of the world's financial order'.[6] This move from the PRC was a natural follow-on from its plans to create a parallel financial lending system via the Asian Infrastructure Investment Bank (AIIB) and the New Development Bank (NDB). These two tools – an internationally accepted 'redback' and financial institutions under Beijing's control, give it the requisite arsenal to project economic influence and craft China's version of the crown – the Belt and Road Initiative (BRI).[7]

In October 2016, China achieved a breakthrough in its attempts to internationalize the RMB when the IMF included the 'redback' in its basket of reserve currencies.[8] The RMB joined the USD, the euro, the yen and the pound in the organization's SDR basket. The SDR essentially controls which currencies countries can receive as part of the loans granted by the IMF.[9] The PBoC immediately released a statement, hailing the inclusion of the RMB as 'affirmation of the success of China's economic development and results of the reform in its financial sector'.[10] This measure came on the back of an extremely vocal campaign from one of the candidates of the US presidential election, wherein he formally announced that he would label China a 'currency manipulator' if he came to power.[11] As things stood, China's currency regime was completely under state control, and therefore lacked the basic tenets required of an international reserve currency. Multiple restrictions on capital accounts in China limit investment options for foreign investors in the country and make it difficult for them to acquire financial assets inside China.[12] As earlier attempts to internationalize the currency were only limited to establishment of offshore financial markets, currency swap agreements with foreign central banks and the liberalization of the current account, policymakers reached a juncture where they had to make a crucial sacrifice if they wanted to internationalize the RMB.[13]

Basic international economics is based on the principles of the Mundell-Fleming model, and provides policymakers with the option to choose two out of three: free capital flows, a fixed exchange rate and monetary policy autonomy.[14] This 'impossible trinity' made it impossible for China to exert control over both domestic interest rates and the exchange rate of the RMB at a time when their capital account restrictions were getting porous.[15] The PBoC announced a move away from fixing the value of the RMB to let it be decided 'in conjunction with demand and supply condition in the foreign exchange market and exchange rate movement of the major currencies'.[16] This move was in direct contrast to earlier policies of controlling the value of the RMB to support the export-oriented trade regime. This did, however, give the RMB the requisites for inclusion in the SDR, but resulted in a downward pressure on the currency. This led the PBoC to further reform the currency regime with the introduction of 'counter-cyclical adjustment factor' and to tighten capital controls to address capital flight, as raising interest rates was considered too risky a move.[17]

As mentioned, another reason for China's proclivity to expedite the internationalization process was the concern among Chinese policymakers over their dependence on US monetary policy.[18] The centrality of the USD gives the US the ability to run skyrocketing trade deficits without any disciplinary constraints, as it can finance the difference through open market operations.[19] The USD and T-bills are readily lapped up by international investors, as they consider it to be the safest form of investment. As the 2007 financial crisis demonstrated, after multiple rounds of quantitative easing by the US Federal Reserve, capital flowed into the US as investors sought protection from market volatility.[20] The foreign exchange reserves of almost every country is denominated via the greenback. Consequently, these banks must also engage in open market operations to keep their currency values stable if the Federal Reserve changes its interest rates, effectuating a global dependence on US monetary policy.

Most significantly, a widely circulated RMB helps China achieve independence in its pursuit of economic statecraft. Policymakers in Beijing eventually want development banks backed by them to issue financial assets in its local currency to international partners. The establishment of new multilateral financial institutions, the AIIB and the NDB, serve to project Beijing's growing economic clout.[21] As the *Economist* posited back in 2014, 'China will use the new bank to expand its influence at the expense of America and Japan, Asia's established powers. China's decision to fund a new multilateral bank rather than give more to existing ones reflects its exasperation with the glacial pace of global economic governance reform'.[22] These institutions carry with them the support of many Western nations and can be used to issue financial assets that will then provide the biggest avenue of RMB circulation in international markets. Yet, data from Swift – the global interbank system that transfers trillions of dollars' worth of currency daily – shows that only 1.6 per cent of domestic and cross-border payments processed in December 2017 were denominated in RMB, whereas the USD accounted for nearly 40 per cent of cross-border payments during the same period.[23]

The final stroke in Beijing's grand plans for its currency is the BRI, through which it is sponsoring some 900 projects in sixty-five different countries.[24] The China Development Bank has already earmarked 890 billion USD for this purpose.[25] The economic strategy to spread the use of the RMB to the developing world through development assistance programmes and trade settlements will further enhance the role of the Chinese currency, subsequently raising China's profile in the rest of the world.[26] Then Beijing can efficiently deploy a range of economic instruments to further its foreign policy agenda. These instruments can be anything from limiting investments to imposing trade restrictions, freezing financial assets or shifting foreign currency holdings.[27] These further lead to enshrinement of Chinese influence in the domestic policies of these countries. The goal to global power seems less rocky when backed by the economic goodwill emanating from a strong, stable and widely used currency. The BRI also ensures the establishment of a Chinese-led infrastructure network that will serve neighbouring regions for a long time to come. Xi Jinping's speech at the World Economic Forum in 2017 made the world notice that the consequence of a protectionist

US was the ascendance of China as the advocate of global trade.[28] As the conversation in the US shifts to trade barriers, the trend in China is free-trade agreements.[29] This paradox of political ideologies in sync with economic considerations has created an air of uncertainty that the Chinese are savouring. They will do their best to take advantage of this vacuum in global economic leadership to further their interests.

However, there are multiple roadblocks to the RMB's acceptance as a global reserve currency, leaving Beijing with limited avenues. China has accrued USD 3.11 trillion of central bank reserves, from balancing its massive trade surpluses in the current account, making it the single largest holder of US Treasury Securities.[30] This phenomenon, also labelled the 'dollar trap', forces China to accumulate or lose reserves to adjust the money supply of the RMB to match supply and demand in the market in which the RMB and USD are exchanged. If China manages its currency, internationalization of the RMB will be insufficient in fulfilling Beijing's desire to decrease their dependence on the USD. Instead, if countries begin accumulating RMB reserves, Beijing must offset an equivalent additional amount of some other currency, which almost certainly means that China must hold more dollar reserves. China is yet to achieve the 'indispensable' status in global economics like the US and has weaker financial fundamentals when compared to the current hegemon. The restrictions and controls on China's economy means that it is unable to offer the liquidity required of a colossal financial system that transacts USD 5.1 trillion every day.[31]

The contentious nature with which it has operated controls on capital and fixed its exchange rate mechanism do not provide stability to the system.[32] In a system that is tied to the idea of a free and open global economy, Beijing's multiple territorial disputes, authoritarian regime and lack of government transparency pales in comparison to the American system of meritocracy and liberal democracy.[33] Moreover, economic ties with Beijing have not always resulted in the best outcome for some countries.[34] The terms and conditions associated with the BRI, and the lack of sustainable investment standards, cast doubt on a future global economy that revolves around China.[35] This, compounded by the fact that after the US government under Donald Trump imposed tough trade barriers on the US import of multiple Chinese products, there was a record eight-week drop in the exchange rate of the RMB to the USD, does not aid the international standing of the redback.[36]

In March 2018, China launched crude oil futures contracts priced in RMB on the Shanghai International Energy Exchange, and these contracts are the first RMB-denominated futures that foreigners can directly buy and sell.[37] This especially assumes significance at a time when China became the largest importer of crude oil in the world, and Beijing is attempting to settle bills for crude in RMB instead of the USD.[38] The day is not far off when an alternative currency will be used for global transactions of oil and gold. The idea of a super sovereign currency is novel, whether it be IMF's SDR or a new cryptocurrency of the Information Age, and as these currencies gain more traction, the world's dependency on the dollar will decrease.[39] Yet, as things stand, the USD is the world's negotiated currency, and if countries can acquire it in near-unlimited amounts, and the US can bear the brunt of an ever-widening fiscal deficit, the crown, as heavy as it may seem, will firmly be with the United States.[40]

PART 4

China's Economy, Society and Culture

1

The People's Republic: A Flawed Champion for Globalization?

MIHIR SWARUP SHARMA

It was the first visit to Davos by a paramount leader of the People's Republic of China (PRC) in 2017, and it surely could not have gone better. In any case, Xi Jinping would not have had to work too hard to distinguish himself from the two leaders who were simultaneously making news – Donald Trump, whose inauguration was fast approaching, and Theresa May, who was announcing Brexit-related details. But, even so, his speech was exceptional – one calculated to upend thinking about the global-trade-based liberal order.

Even rhetorically, it was unusual. PRC leaders' speeches are not overfull of references drawn from other global cultures, and Xi himself has a well-known penchant for Chinese history and mythology. And there was much of that in the Davos speech – but it drew also from Western writers such as Charles Dickens, underlining stylistically what he was trying to convey through its substance: that the People's Republic is ready to step up and play at least part of the role that the West is abdicating in terms of providing strategic support for globalization.

The World Economic Forum, home of the Davos Man and the mecca of globalization, lapped it up. As inward-looking, nativist movements sweep through the Western world, Xi appeared to be presenting himself and the PRC as champions of freer trade and more open borders, warning against 'locking oneself in a dark room'.

On one level, this should not be surprising. The decade and a half since Xi Jinping's country was admitted to the World Trade Organization has been a miracle for China as far as development goes. On the back of steadily expanding global trade in the early- to mid-2000s, China repeatedly doubled its per capita income and lifted millions out of poverty. The crisis of 2008 gave the Communist Party confidence that its own system of economic and political governance was more stable and better thought-out than traditional liberal capitalism. The PRC, thanks to the processes associated with globalization, became the world's second most influential economy and slowly began to accumulate military-strategic power to match. Naturally, it is reasonable that its leaders view an open, globalizing world as being in their own interests and would be seeking to support it.

For other countries, like India, who seek to benefit similarly from global trade and investment, this commitment is naturally welcome as long as it serves to counterbalance a movement in the West towards a more closed world.

Yet it is important, too, to not be carried away. As it stands now, the PRC cannot be the new liberal economic hegemon – nor would we want it to be. As a successor to the role the United States has traditionally played in this respect, the PRC is fatally flawed.

The reasons are quite clear and spring from the domestic political economy of China itself.

First, globalization has in recent decades been partly a financial phenomenon. The flows of capital across borders have helped stimulate economic growth in wide-ranging borders and resulted in global efficiency gains. Yet, while China has benefited greatly from such capital flows, it is important to note two things.

One, it continues to be a relatively hostile place to foreign capital it cannot completely control. The leadership in Beijing is aware of this; it was no coincidence that, almost at the same time as Xi Jinping spoke in Davos, news broke out that Beijing would lift some restrictions on foreign capital operating in the PRC.

Two, as a source as well as a destination of capital, it leaves much to be desired. Unlike the West, capital does not flow out of China looking for simply the best or safest return. Because of the statist nature of the domestic financial system, the accumulated savings of the PRC's inhabitants tend to be directed as much, perhaps more, towards investments of political and strategic worth. A country that is not properly financialized domestically, where savings cannot translate smoothly into liquid capital that follows its own reasoning, cannot step in easily to replace US capital if it, for example, returns home in response to Donald Trump's vast infrastructure spending plans.

Second, China itself is not able to support world trade in the manner the West has hitherto done. Again, the reason goes back to domestic political economy. Globalization's driving mechanism was internal domestic competition in the economies of the West. Private companies went out and discovered efficiencies in the rest of the world that would give them a leg up over their rivals. The Chinese economy does not yet work like that. Despite occasionally suggesting that promised market forces would be given greater play in the domestic economy, Beijing's leadership has been hamstrung by political obstacles to achieving that end. State-owned enterprises are difficult to displace politically, even though the private sector now provides 80 per cent of jobs in the PRC. Until a level playing field is achieved at home, it is perhaps too much to expect of private Chinese companies to go out and be standard-bearers of globalization elsewhere.

Finally, standard-bearers for globalization must admit it runs both ways. There are costs to being a hegemon, and the US was in the past willing to pay them – in terms of market access and preferential tariffs for poorer countries, for example. But the Chinese economy itself remains relatively closed. Work visas are not that easy to obtain; foreign companies report an ever more difficult operating environment; and services imports of the sort India would wish to export are, in effect, frowned upon.

There are solid reasons to welcome Xi Jinping's robust backing of the benefits of globalization. But it is, at the very least, premature to hail China as the new underwriter of the global liberal order. Liberal economics abroad depends crucially on open and free markets at home – and there is much that Beijing still must do to make those a reality.

2

China's Protectionist Tendencies Will Continue

PREETY BHOGAL

In this era of protectionism, China is trying to emerge as a supporter of free trade and open markets. During the World Economic Forum at Davos in 2017, Chinese President Xi Jinping advocated greater integration amongst world economies. If one were to believe his words, it is pertinent to ask: Is China indeed opening its markets to foreign competition or is its enthusiasm for multilateralism feigned just to position China favourably vis-à-vis the US?

In 1978, China launched the economic reform process of transforming its existing system of state-planning into a more liberal and market-based regime. This decision to liberalize the economy has played a significant role in China's economic development. Under its open-door policy (introduced as part of the reform package), Beijing encouraged foreign trade and investment. Nevertheless, the trade and investment promotion policy of China was largely driven by mercantilism – promoting exports more than imports by adopting protectionist policy measures to accumulate wealth (foreign exchange). The government consciously offered special concessions to export industries in the form of no duties charged on materials imported for export purposes, set up export-processing zones in provinces, and offered special loans for short-term or long-term financing, among others. In addition, these industries were given autonomy to retain a part of the foreign exchange earned from exports and employ it for reinvestment in the business. The government also provided a favourable exchange rate for converting foreign exchange to renminbi (RMB) to exporting industries during the 1980s (USD 1 for 2.8 RMB[1] as against the official exchange rate of USD 1 to 1.6 RMB). Regarding investment, foreign investors were encouraged to set up factories (either independently or jointly with Chinese firms) in export-processing zones for producing export goods using Chinese manpower. This resulted in dual returns for China – increased employment and better wages for domestic labour, along with productivity gains from using the technology, knowledge and capital of foreign investors.

China has selectively liberalized its economy – taking a piecemeal approach – opening only those sectors to foreign investors that were considered critical to the growth and development of its economy. These sectors included mainly labour-intensive manufacturing units, and other sectors in need of upgraded technology and infrastructure (energy and traditional industries). The bureaucratic red tape and complex procedures also acted as a barrier to inward foreign investments to China. This was, however, the story until the mid-1990s. As China advanced towards liberalization, there were some changes evident in its trade and investment regime.

Later, China opened the services sector to foreign investors and even slashed tariffs on some of the manufacturing and agricultural imports. The average trade weighted tariffs reduced from 40.6 per cent in 1992[2] to 9.1 per cent in 2001. The process of lowering tariffs, eliminating non-tariff barriers (quotas) and opening key services to foreign participation was strengthened upon China's accession to the World Trade Organization (WTO) in 2001 and is still ongoing.

In 2014, the trade weighted average tariff came down to 4.5 per cent[3]; however, it is higher than the tariffs of developed countries such as the United States and the European Union. China has reduced overall average tariffs since its WTO accession but for some sectors such as automobiles and agricultural commodities, high tariffs coupled with other trade-distorting measures[4] (export subsidies, state-trading) continue to be imposed. China has often been accused by many developing and developed countries of unfair trade practices viz., currency manipulation, intellectual property theft, dumping, foreign equity restrictions, etc., which act as barriers to free trade. For instance, the United States filed a complaint against China in the WTO for creating obstacles in terms of large capital requirements for the entry of US banks[5] in the market and excluding US telecommunication companies from doing business in China, among others. India has also levelled criticism against China for its dumping practices. Since 2005, the WTO has recorded about 43 per cent[6] of all export subsidy-related complaints against Chinese firms.

China's integration into the global economy has deepened over the past few decades; nonetheless, this engagement has invariably been a cautious one – protecting the interests of its domestic players over foreign competitors. China generally takes a different perspective on globalization and free trade – collaborating with and opening to countries which could benefit it. History says it all. Even the access of foreign investors to Chinese markets comes with many strings attached. In other words, China wants foreign companies to transfer technology in exchange of being granted permission to invest in the country. Although forced technology transfer of this sort is forbidden in China's WTO accession agreement, it is blatantly followed by China. Regardless of the restrictions placed on foreign investors, China can extract economic benefits by engaging with other world economies. This is attributed to the growing dependence of world economies on China for finance, infrastructure development, semi-finished goods, and finished products.

Chinese President Xi Jinping's championing of free trade and multilateralism at Davos in January 2017 seems mere rhetoric, given vast trade and investment restrictions imposed on foreign companies by China in the past. According to the Information Technology and Innovation Foundation's index, which ranks countries after assessing the impact of their economic and trade policies on global innovation systems, China ranks 44 out of 56 countries.[7] This indicates that China harms global innovation by adopting policies such as forced localization to trade and investment, export subsidies, or failure to protect intellectual property rights. These policies benefit only China and has a destructive impact on the global innovation system. Despite a restrictive policy environment in China, it cannot be denied that the selective liberalization model has worked for the country's growth. Over the period 1989–2017,[8] China registered compound annual growth rate above 13 per cent. As long as China receives sufficient benefits from its piecemeal liberalization approach, it will not be willing to make a transition to a more transparent, fair, liberal and rules-based trading system. It is unlikely that anything will change in China's trading regime.

Despite the rhetoric of President Xi Jinping, China was and will continue to be protectionist in the foreseeable future.

3

Pollution-Free Progress? Ambient Air Quality in India and China

SHALINI RUDRA, PRIYANKA SHAH

With GDP growth rates of over 7 per cent per annum, India and China are constantly in the news for being the fastest growing economies.[1] Such unprecedented acceleration is achieved at the cost of deteriorating ambient air quality across major urban centres in both countries. Several Indian and Chinese cities defy the World Health Organization (WHO) air quality standards and at times reach toxicity levels that are unfit for inhalation.[2] For instance, the WHO recommends that annual median concentrations of PM2.5 (fine particulate matter less than 2.5 μm in diameter) should be below 10 μg/m^3, but the levels in urban areas of India and China are six times higher at 66 μg/m^3 and 59 μg/m^3, respectively.[3] A WHO report[4] finds India and China[5] among the worst performers in air quality.[6] In fact, Beijing[7] and New Delhi[8] have been neck to neck in PM2.5 concentrations, but of late the Chinese capital has shown improvements.[9]

The dense concentration of PM2.5, in the presence of a deadly cocktail of other gases and unburned carbon particles, creates a photochemical smog that lingers on due to the meteorological conditions during winters. These fine particles pose a major threat to human health as they can not only settle deep in the lungs, but also enter the human bloodstream and can potentially lead to heart attacks, strokes and lung cancer. In 2015, PM2.5 contributed to over 4.2 million deaths worldwide with 52 per cent of these deaths occurring in India and China (1.1 million deaths in each country).[10] Globally, exposure to ozone-related pollution is responsible for over 2,54,000 chronic obstructive pulmonary disease (COPD) deaths. Approximately 71 per cent of such deaths occur in India and China. According to the 'Global Burden of Diseases' report, there has been a 17 per cent increase in premature deaths attributable to PM2.5 in China since 1990, and the figure for India is three times more.[11]

The challenge of addressing pollution is undeniable given the significant costs in terms of life years lost to premature deaths[12] and disability. While evidence on ambient air pollution leading to serious illnesses is plentiful, disruption in ecosystem services are also well recognized.[13] One attempt to quantify these found that the yield loss in wheat production, owing to high concentration of short-lived climate pollutants in India, was 50 per cent.[14] Another study found that poor natural light has slowed down agricultural output.[15] This could have detrimental consequences on the economies given that agriculture still contributes a large proportion of the GDPs of both countries. It is also threatening wildlife havens for migratory birds and other animals in Delhi.[16]

The special report by the Health Effects Institute notes that industrial emission, transportation, open biomass burning and coal-based power plants are some of the major sources of particulate pollution.[17] The rapid growth of automobiles and vehicular emissions have a cumulative impact on PM2.5 concentrations in both countries.[18] While coal-based power plants are important sources of ambient air pollution in China[19], biomass burning is a major cause of air pollution in India.[20,21] Excessive use of firecrackers in India also causes deteriorations in air quality in a short span of time.[22] Similarly, atmospheric suspension of dust particles from construction activities is another concern in cities. All these sources cause lingering health and environmental effects throughout the year. Thus, the key to reducing air pollution lies in controlling emissions from these sources.

The growth trajectory of both the nations has been different and has resulted in different kinds of emissions. While China's growth is mainly due to coal-based plants and industry-led, India has achieved its high growth rates due to specializing in services. Therefore, the kind of pollution abatement that is expected from both the sectors is also different. Studies have pointed out that recent restructuring and the slowdown of the economy has lessened the use of coal resulting in emission reductions. However, this comes at the cost of reduced industrial production and lagged growth in China's manufacturing sector.[23,24] India's problems, on the other hand, are related to both underdevelopment as well as income-led consumerism – agriculture-related crop burning at one end and high-growth induced conspicuous consumption at the other.

Policy Measures

Acknowledging the threat, both the countries have adopted a set of policies and regulation aimed at reducing emissions. The environment protection law (in effect since January 2015) of China is one such initiative to reform and regulate environmental quality with several short-term targets.[25] This has proven to be effective as resources can immediately be directed towards meeting short-term goals, it is easier to monitor progress and, unlike long-term targets, the interest of stakeholders is undistracted.

China has specifically emphasized stringent regulation of the industries (power plants) to improve emission standards.[26] Production activities in polluting industries such as steel and coal are now more sensitive to air quality standards. Often, production is curtailed to minimize emissions during specific seasons. Economic activities in the country are now increasingly diverting away from heavy industries and towards alternatives for clean energy. Similarly, effective policies on vehicular emissions, traffic management, promoting electric and hybrid vehicles, dust removal and green coverage have contributed towards the reduction of air pollution in the country.[27,28] In the latest attempt, Xin Guobin, vice-minister of industry and information technology, revealed that the government is mulling over imposing a ban on production and sale of cars using traditional fuels.[29] With huge subsidies flowing in for domestic automakers, the imposition of a ban on petrol and diesel cars will be seen as the government's move to tap into its large domestic market for electric and plug-in hybrid cars. China has also focused on the systematic monitoring of air quality standards and has improved data sharing for effective citizen participation.[30]

India has also been implementing effective regulations regarding pollution control. The ministry of environment, forest and climate change has specific focus on policies for promotion of clean technology, particularly vehicular emissions.[31] There are efforts for greater inter-sectoral coordination. For instance, the ministry of road transport and highways has identified several initiatives to modernize the government-owned as well as private vehicles and promote eco-friendly transport.[32] Similarly, the Pradhan Mantri Ujjwala Yojana (PMUY) aims at providing clean cooking fuel (LPG) to safeguard the health of women and children. There are also many state-level policy efforts. For example, Delhi implemented traffic regulations (e.g., odd–even rule) to reduce vehicular emissions during phases of high pollution.[33] Emphasis on CNG fuel is now an important feature of vehicular transport in Delhi. Punjab has provisions for subsidizing equipment purchases that increase the usage of crop residues.[34] Importantly, there is an increased emphasis on environmental statistics for quality monitoring – which is actively discussed by stakeholders and the media.[35,36]

In response to the deadly smog that covered Delhi in 2016, the Supreme Court enforced a graded response action plan.[37] The plan involves a series of interventions that are to be enforced through coordination among neighbouring states and pollution agencies, depending on the severity of pollution. Initially, this plan was lauded and compared to several others that were implemented by governments across the globe. Unfortunately, however, data from the Central Pollution Control Board (CPCB) reveals that since its implementation, air quality has not met WHO standards for even a single day.[38] This could be due to manpower, technical and/or institutional constraints faced by the pollution control agencies, which then prevent full-scale enforcement of plans.[39] Furthermore, the ban on sale of firecrackers in the capital that was passed in 2016 by the Supreme Court due to the lasting impact it has on air quality and health of citizens was lifted just before Diwali last year.[40] The top court said that banning the sale was an 'extreme step' and has restricted the sale of firecrackers to 500 shopkeepers along with certain other rules.[41] This is a disappointing move, given that extreme steps are indeed required to curb pollution levels in a city that has constantly been among the most polluted in the world. However, this is not to say that firecrackers alone cause poor air quality, but they certainly do contribute to the pre-existing pollution levels.

Thus, while there may be a plethora of policies and strategies to tackle the air pollution issue in the capital, there has been little to no improvement in the air quality standards. India may have taken steps towards the reduction of air pollution but has failed to display the kind of urgency that China has in recent years.

Potential for Sino–Indian Cooperation

Both India and China have drawn up effective measures to improve air quality. While reasons for air pollution vary considerably, there are a myriad of similarities in the nature of the challenges faced by the two countries. Therefore, several lessons can be learned from each other and there is great potential for bilateral cooperation between the countries in the area of pollution control. Furthermore, since environmental challenges like air pollution transcend national boundaries, it is even more crucial for the two neighbours to work together on this front.

At the September 2017 BRICS summit, in its declaration, China stressed on the importance of environmental cooperation to achieve sustainable development goals (SDGs), with 'concrete actions to advance result-oriented cooperation in such areas as prevention of air and water pollution, waste management and biodiversity conservation'.[42] Since China has made great strides in green technologies, an area for cooperation with India can be through the sharing of such advanced technologies, knowledge and experiences as well as 'green practices'. There should also be greater exchange of real-time data between the two countries.

Like China, India should also aim for short-term targets and tighter deadlines. A key component for any plan to successfully work is accountability. Pollution boards, state governments and officials involved in the implementation process should be held accountable – rewarded for good performance and penalized for poor performance.[43] India can also borrow China's innovative enforcement model, i.e., the anti-smog police that patrols streets to keep a check on environmental rule violations. Involving citizens in such a process would not only lead to an increased sense of ownership but could also generate employment.[44] Furthermore, it is important for the government to ensure that real-time air quality data is readily available to the public. There have been major infrastructural lapses including missing and delayed data, as well as non-functional air quality monitoring stations.[45] While such issues may seem trivial on the surface, they can have detrimental effects on the imposition of emergency measures (such as the graded response action plan) that are contingent on the availability of this data.

While China may have some lessons to offer, given the multifaceted nature of air pollution, it would be futile to implement a 'one size-fits all' policy. As Fu Jihong, deputy director general of the Shanghai municipal foreign affairs office, said, 'When it comes to environment protection, we must acknowledge that every city is different, with its own features and characteristics. The treatment of the environment must also take into consideration the specific needs of the city as well as the development requirements of the city.'[46]

4

China's Innovation Boom: Lessons for India

MEGHNA BAL

Until recently, the narrative surrounding China's technological growth was sustained more by responsive adaptation than original innovation. Most of China's top technology companies had Western counterparts. Alibaba, the Chinese e-commerce giant, was a hybrid of Amazon and eBay whereas Baidu, the search engine, was China's response to Google. Similarly, Facebook found its Chinese equivalent in Tencent.

Today we are witnessing a reversal of this movement of ideas. Currently, China's influence extends across a host of technology verticals around the globe. Imitations of its indigenously developed Meitu application, which beautifies selfies, are emerging all over the world, including in the United States (US).[1] Start-ups in the US are also replicating China's model for on-demand bicycle leasing.[2] The dating app Tinder has purportedly taken its inspiration from a Chinese app called Momo.[3] Even in India, Chinese smartphones are dominating the scene with a 50 per cent market share.[4]

Additionally, China's most fascinating online experiments are taking place beyond the borders of its traditional technology sector. Companies from 'real economy' industries like banking, real-estate, construction and agriculture are creating new commercial archetypes based on data science and the industrial internet.[5] Illustratively, the real-estate giant Vanke is spearheading the assimilation of online-enabled technology and services into digitized societies.[6] It is targeting the creation of cities which provide residents with amenities like parks, safe cuisine, mobility, health and learning services – all through the internet.[7]

Several factors have contributed to the growth of Chinese innovation.

First, the liberalization of the licensing framework surrounding the manufacture and sale of mobile handsets in 2007 catalysed the creation of a burgeoning domestic mobile industry.[8] New entrants flooded the market. Shanzhai handsets were now legitimized.[9] Their mobile phones were low-cost 2G phones that were imitations of the products of well-known brands.[10] Thus, the cost of smartphone handsets dropped dramatically. In 2009, handsets were available for as low as INR 9,761.[11] Over time, China's mobile phone industry expanded to include more players, further dropping the rates for smartphones. Today, Chinese smartphones cost less than half of what they did eight years ago. The meteoric rise of China's domestic mobile communications industry has put a smartphone in the hands of 75 per cent of its population.

Second, the country's one billion internet users provide the perfect test bed for new technologies and applications.[12] Only innovations that can prove their mettle can survive the highly competitive Chinese technology market.

Third, there is a top-down mandate for innovation in China. Its government invests heavily in the technology sector and is open to softening its stance on specific issues if it will allow for greater ingenuity. In 2012, for instance, China devoted almost 2 per cent of its gross domestic product (GDP) to research and development (R&D).[13]

Finally, China has a wealth of human capital in the technology space. A report by the Organization for Economic Cooperation and Development (OECD) states that 55 per cent of Chinese doctoral degrees are awarded in the areas of science, technology, engineering and mathematics.[14] According to the 2015 US News and World Report, which ranks universities around the world on different criteria, China's Tsinghua University has pipped the Massachusetts Institute of Technology (MIT) to become the top engineering university in the world.[15]

China's technological growth offers valuable lessons for India:

1. **Think Locally, Act Globally**: Both India and China have developed technological solutions to address domestic issues. However, Chinese tech companies have a much larger global footprint than Indian companies. Both the public and the private sector should look at ways through which India's tech sector can broaden its global reach. An encouraging development in this regard is that many countries are looking to emulate India's unique identity database, Aadhaar.

2. **Invest in Human Capital**: Government investment in research and development remains minimal in India. Studies suggest that India only invests about 0.9 per cent of its GDP on research.[16] Additionally, India's research landscape is hindered by excessive bureaucracy.[17] Most administrators at state educational facilities in India are politically appointed.[18] Many of these individuals have no real background in research.[19] Moreover, out of every 10,000 people in the country, only four are full-time researchers as opposed to eighteen in China.[20] With this context in mind, India must take concrete steps to reduce the red tape at its research facilities and chart out avenues for financing research activities in the country.

Although the challenges are significant, India boasts similar advantages to China as it has a large population, decent connectivity rates and distinctive scientific competencies. Additionally, India has also managed to execute digital initiatives that are serving as templates for the rest of the world. Like China, India must also find ways to export local innovation and reap its demographic dividend if it wishes to be a key player on the global technological stage soon.

5

Transition to a Low-Carbon Economy: China's Influence on Outcomes

LYDIA POWELL

As the world's largest energy consumer and carbon emitter, China's energy choices were expected to be at the centre of the global transition to a low-carbon economy.[1] China has exceeded expectations as the stylized facts below reveal.

In 2015 alone, China invested over USD 102 billion in low-carbon renewable energy, accounting for a third of global investments.[2] China is expected to invest about USD 360 billion in renewable energy by 2020 and terminate plans to build eighty-five coal-fired power plants.[3] China's investment of about USD 78 billion in renewable energy in 2016 was the largest in the world, accounting for 32 per cent of global investment in renewable energy.[4] The European Union (EU) as a whole, invested about USD 59 billion in renewable energy and the United States (US) about USD 46 billion.[5] China's investment in research and development of renewable energy, at about USD 2 billion in 2016, was close to the USD 2.2 billion invested by the EU, which leads the ideological narrative on the significance of a global low-carbon transition.[6]

China is expected to instal 36 per cent of global hydroelectric capacity, 40 per cent of all wind capacity and 36 per cent of all solar capacity between 2015 and 2021.[7] China will also account for 54 per cent of growth in nuclear capacity by 2040 and surpass the United States as the country with the largest nuclear power generating capacity by 2030.[8] China's state power grid corporation, which is the largest in the world, plans to develop a global grid that draws on wind and solar power from around the world.[9] Five of the world's six largest solar module manufacturers are in China and Chinese companies rank among the largest wind turbine manufacturers.[10] Chinese companies account for 50 per cent of the production of lithium which is critical for the manufacture of storage batteries.[11] Batteries are not only critical for managing the intermittency of electricity from renewable sources but also to power electric vehicles, which are seen as the future of transportation. Chinese firms also account for over 72 per cent of the production of rare earth minerals that are vital for the manufacture of renewable energy technologies.[12] China plans to reduce energy intensity by 15 per cent in its thirteenth five-year plan from 2016 to 2020.[13] China is the only developing country that has implemented efficiency standards for automobiles.[14] Out of the 8.1 million supposedly green energy jobs available globally, 3.1 million are in China.[15]

These figures could intimidate even the uninitiated, but when seen in the context of China's relative size and its level of industrialization, these investments and initiatives may be interpreted as rational responses to domestic compulsions rather than a calculated effort towards a global dominance of the future energy landscape. However, some of the consequences of the increased complexity in producing and using renewable energy may inadvertently leverage attributes such as the centralization of governance in China.

China's pace of industrialization was unprecedented but it was far less energy intensive than that of Western nations. While nineteenth-century United States and Britain needed fifty years to double their real income, China achieved the same feat in nine years – as it was able to use less capital per worker, leveraged by Western technology and know-how.[16] China's demand for thermal coal (and other vital natural resources) grew faster in nineteen years than the entire world's demand grew in the previous forty years.[17] Although China's economy increased eighteen-fold from 1980–2010, its energy consumption increased only five-fold. The energy intensity per unit of GDP declined by 70 per cent in this period.[18]

More recently, China's transition from an investment- and manufacturing-led economy to a service- and consumption-led economy has lowered demand for energy and reduced energy intensity of its economy substantially. China's working age population has been on the decline since 2012 and is forecast to fall by 23 per cent by 2050, which means that dependence on abundant labour is no longer possible.[19] Increasing productivity is the only option for China, which means improving energy efficiency and lowering energy consumption by moving away from low-end manufacturing. In 2016, China's service sector contributed 52 per cent of GDP and domestic consumption contributed 60 per cent of GDP growth.[20] China's changing growth model, along with global demographic and consumption trends, are accelerating the low-carbon energy transition.

The first major global energy transition that began with the Industrial Revolution was a quantitative and qualitative transition from almost no external energy to abundant external energy. In the United Kingdom, which was the first to make this transition from traditional biomass to fossil fuels, it involved the development of a wide range of technologies at the supply and demand end between the 1500s and the early 1900s.[21] The second significant transition that started in the early 1900s was when the share of coal in global energy supply had peaked.[22] The diffusion of steam engines, internal combustion engines and electric motors drove quantitative changes in the supply and relative shares of fossil fuels. The share of oil and gas increased at the expense of coal but it was not the scarcity of coal that led to the introduction of more expensive oil.[23] Technological shifts in demand, with consumers paying attention to convenience and cleanliness, drove the shift towards the delivery of refined petroleum and grid-based energy forms (natural gas and electricity) even though their cost to consumers was above those of alternatives.

The path towards a low-carbon economy may include improvement in the efficiency of energy conversion, the reduction of energy use and the substitution of fossil fuels with renewable energy. Although the low-carbon transition is described as a phenomenon at the level of primary energy use, its driver is energy consumption that prefers quality energy sources. This transition is path-dependent as initial conditions affect the pace of transition – e.g., resource availability and other geographic, climatic, economic, social and institutional factors leading to differences in spatial structures, infrastructure and consumption patterns. Initial conditions also influence the level and type of technologies used both at the consumer end and within the energy sector. China's initial conditions favour a quantitative as well as qualitative low-carbon energy transition.

China's industrialization, which began with the export of raw materials, continued on to the export of manufactured goods and is now progressing with the export of capital. The export of technology and knowledge of low-carbon energy technologies, capitalizing on the West's quest for decarbonizing the world, may be a rational final step to complete the process of industrialization in any country that is in the same growth phase as China's.

Unlike in the era that was dependent on fossil fuels, when a natural endowment of resources was important, the transition to low-carbon energy sources requires a knowledge-intensive industrial-production base (quality) and a large energy-consumption base (quantity), both of which are necessary to reduce the cost of transition. China scores in terms of both – quality, with an entrenched industrial production base, and quantity as it has the largest number of energy consumers. Relatively higher income levels of energy consumers, especially those in urban areas in China, also favour a quality transition for energy use. China's spatial power densities are particularly high, especially in urban areas due to the twin influences of high population density and high per person energy use. The correlation between declining carbon intensities and rising incomes is well known.[24] Low carbon intensities mean that more primary energy must be mobilized for conversion to high quality fuels such as electricity even if it means incurring the economic costs and the inevitable conversion losses. Increasing conversion of losses of the global energy system are not necessarily unique to the current low-carbon energy transition, but China is pursuing the transition at relatively low levels of per person incomes. This limits its ability to use markets as an instrument of change. China is thus greening capitalism using mandates rather than markets. Consequently, China is less dependent on instruments such as carbon prices and taxes, which are difficult to implement.

China's dominance in low-carbon technologies is not an exception to the trend of Chinese dominance in some other emerging sectors such as mobile communication, e-commerce and quantum cryptography, which complement the use of decentralized low carbon energy forms. In 2018, China had roughly 54 per cent of global capacity for refining polycrystalline silicon (solar grade), 87 per cent of capacity for production of silicon wafers, 69 per cent of manufacturing capacity for solar cells and 71 per cent of capacity for solar modules.[25] China's wind turbine manufacturers account for 60 per cent of global wind turbine manufacturing capacity.[26] In storage (batteries), China's dominance is stronger as it controls 80 per cent of manufacturing capacity globally.[27] Economies of scale arising from these exceptionally large manufacturing capacities in China reduced the cost of transitioning to low carbon technologies in Europe and other countries around the world, including India, by at least 60 per cent.[28]

But there are concerns over China's quantitative and qualitative power in influencing outcomes in the ongoing energy transition. The fate of renewable energy sources crucially depends on the power sector because electricity is still the main vector for renewable energy. The main features of a renewable energy system are lower intensity of energy sources, low efficiency of conversion, temporal and spatial discontinuity, dramatic change in the economic concept of energy scarcity, and a leading role for a network wherein energy, matter, information and monetary values circulate. This may lead to higher levels of complexity and control. The increasing significance of renewable energy and the related challenges of matching peaks in provision with those of consumption are likely to entail higher levels of state involvement in monitoring and controlling the consumption of energy at the individual level. While surveillance and control of energy supply and demand may be accepted in China, it may not be replicated by the rest of the world.

6

China as India's Main Bulk Drugs Supplier: Helplessness or Cautious Evolution?

OOMMEN C. KURIAN

Ever since China undermined India's Nuclear Suppliers Group (NSG) bid, regular calls to boycott Chinese goods are made in India. That many such appeals are made on social media using Chinese-made phones is a good example of the interlinked nature of the post-globalized world.[1] India may be the 'pharmacy of the world', but a substantial part of the bulk drugs[2] that are used to manufacture the medicines that India is famous for come from China. As Graph 1 shows, from about 23 per cent in the year 2000, Chinese imports peaked in 2007 at 59 per cent and are currently at 52 per cent. Among certain types of bulk drugs, the proportion of imports from China is even higher.[3] Given the strained relationship between the countries, this exceptional dependence has received policy attention in the past, and trimming bulk drug imports from China is a focus of policy discussions within the government and the media.

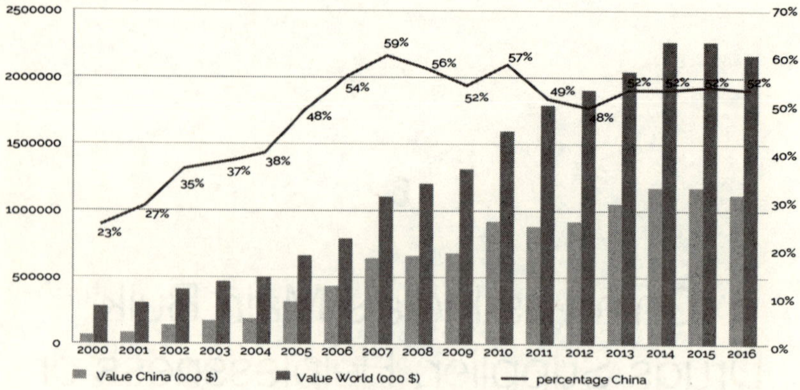

Graph 1: Bulk Drug Imports to India
Source: Comtrade Database

However, this familiar narrative often ignores the strengths of the Indian pharmaceutical sector. More importantly, it fails to mention that India is a major exporter of bulk drugs as well. Graph 2 shows that between 2000 and 2016, exports of bulk drugs have expanded many times over. Rather than being a hapless manufacturer of medicines wholly dependent on China for raw materials, India is itself a major exporter of bulk drugs. In fact, the latest data shows that in bulk drugs, India has a favourable balance of payments – in other words, India exported more bulk drugs than it imported, by a margin of USD 247,647,000 in 2016. In nine out of the seventeen years between 2000–16, India exported more bulk drugs than it imported, driven primarily by the outsourcing of bulk drug production by multinational companies.[4]

India's Pharmaceutical Industry

Over the last three decades, India has achieved remarkable improvements in health outcomes, but despite progress, the overall levels of health development remain low. Low prices of medicine

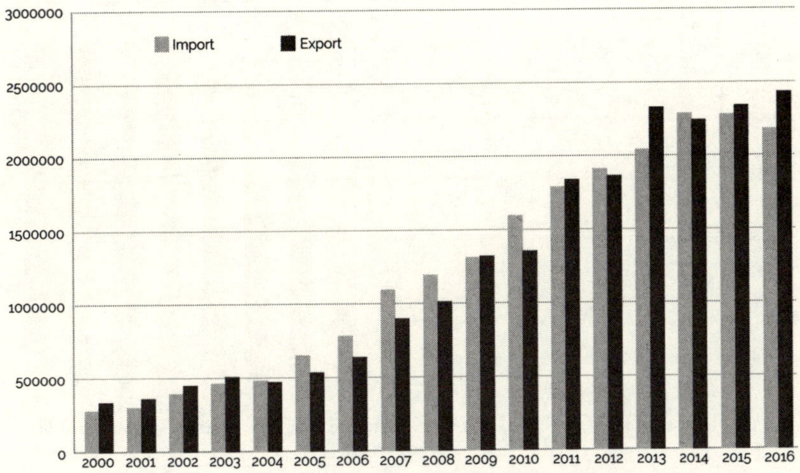

Graph 2: Bulk Drug Exports from India
Source: Comtrade Database

compared to many other countries are a major reason why India was able to improve the health status of its population, despite the incredibly low public spending on healthcare. Research shows that at the time of Independence, the Indian pharmaceutical industry had a low production base, heavy dependence on imports, domination by foreign firms and high prices of drugs.[5] Today, India is one of the largest pharmaceutical industries in the world – the third largest producer of medicines in terms of volume, and fourteenth in terms of value.[6] The growth of the Indian pharmaceutical industry, reflected in the growth of exports as shown in Graph 3, has been carefully driven by policy interventions at various levels. The current value of India's exports of pharmaceutical products alone is about six times that of bulk drug imports.[7] In all, at present, formulations make up much of pharma exports and bulk drugs comprise a majority in pharma imports.

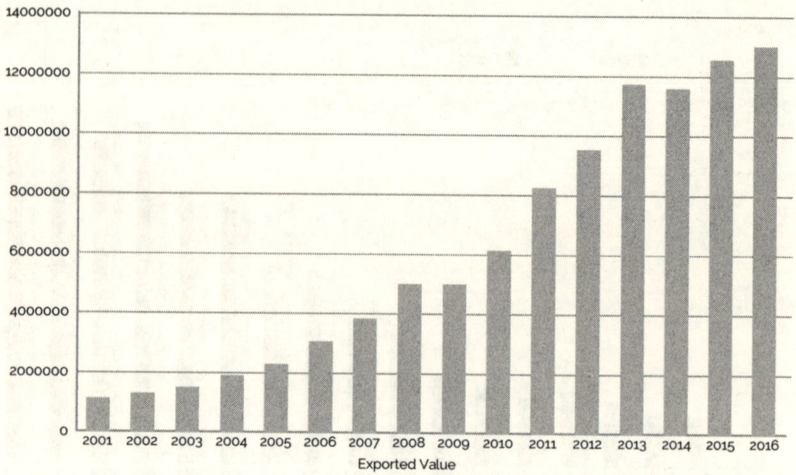

Graph 3: Exports of Pharmaceutical Products from India to the World
Source: International Trade Centre Database (000 $)

In terms of exports of formulations to the US, a leading pharmaceutical market, India is the top trade partner in terms of volume and fourth in terms of value. China, on the other hand, was seventh in terms of volume and eighteenth in terms of value.[8] India is host to the most number of the United States Food and Drug Administration (USFDA) approved plants outside the US.[9] In 2016, India accounted for 22 per cent, overall, of the United States Food and Drug Administration–approved plants across the globe.[10] China, on the other hand, had only half the number of the United States Food and Drug Administration–approved plants, as per 2014 data.[11]

Given the high number of the United States Food and Drug Administration–approved plants, international companies outsource their production to India to contain their costs. India is responsible for 60 per cent of global vaccine production, 30 per cent of UNICEF's annual supplies, 60 per cent of global supply of antiretroviral (ARV) drugs, and up to 80 per cent of annual UN purchases of vaccines.[12] Medicines are fourth among India's top ten export commodities, in terms of value, between 2014 and 2016, according to the *International Trade Statistics Yearbook* (2016).

China in India's Pharmaceutical Policy

It is not often discussed that the prices of medicines were brought under statutory control for the first time in India because of Chinese aggression, in 1962.[13] When it comes to bulk drugs, a looming war is not the only possible risk factor: many other things could go wrong. For example, experts have said that during the Beijing Olympics of 2008, when China closed many bulk drug production units to manage environmental pollution, a price rise of around 20 per cent followed in India.[14]

That Indian firms are depending on a single country for much of their import requirements should not take away from the fact that there is a thriving bulk drug manufacturing industry in India. Cipla, for example, manufactured the first Indian bulk drug way back in 1960.[15] As Graph 4 shows, Indian companies also enjoy being among the most cost competitive, internationally.[16] Chinese plants have unit conversion costs that are 60 per cent higher than Indian plants.

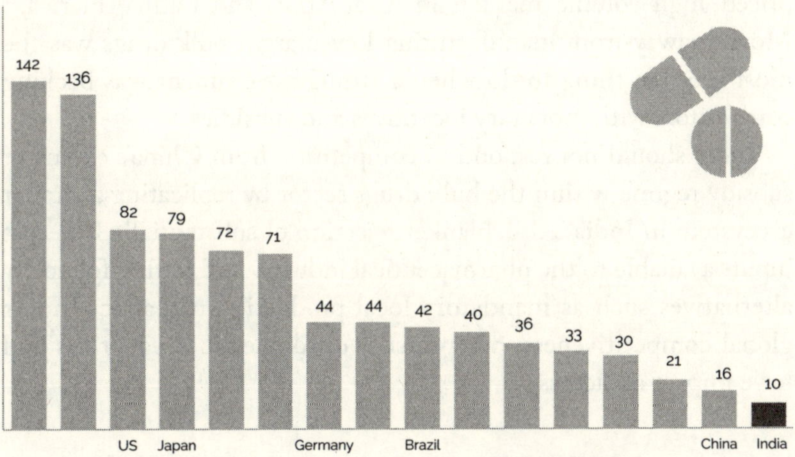

Graph 4: Unit conversion costs of the most competitive plants in countries (Average cost per tablet, in USD)

Source: FICCI

However, in the case of some commoditized bulk drugs, riding on economies of scale and strong government support, Chinese firms established price leadership. In the aftermath of India's trade liberalization, when industrial licensing was abolished, restrictions on imports (duty reduced from 120 per cent in 1990–91 to 7.5 per cent in 2007–8) were removed and the mandatory requirement that bulk drugs be locally produced was taken away, companies in India naturally moved away from producing bulk drugs, which required little innovation and offered only thin profit margins.[17] Due to lower electricity and labour costs, complemented with subsidies (tax holidays and low interest loans) from the government and better technology, Chinese firms were a natural choice for their low cost product. Instead of viewing Indian firms as hapless producers dependent disproportionally on a giant for their supply of bulk drugs, perhaps they need to be viewed as an agile industrial force, trying to maximize the benefit low costs offer at an overseas location.

Availability of low-cost Chinese bulk drugs worked for Indian firms that were exploring opportunities to shift to 'low-volume–high-priced' regulated markets, while retaining their traditional 'low-priced–high-volume' markets in Asia, Africa and Latin America.[18] Moving away from manufacturing low-margin bulk drugs was the most sensible thing to do when a strong government was backing competitors with monetary incentives and subsidies.

India should not respond to competition from China's extensive subsidy regime within the bulk drugs sector by replicating a similar ecosystem in India. Also, blanket rejection of substantially low-cost inputs available to the pharmaceutical industry and opting for costly alternatives such as mandatory local production can affect India's global competitiveness, put pressure on domestic drug prices and have impact on access.

Current Situation: Crisis or Evolution?

Diversifying risks is an important policy objective. However, a part of the transformation within the pharmaceutical sector needs to be viewed as a natural evolution of the Indian industry itself. A considerable amount of pharmaceutical production in India is due to the outsourcing of bulk drug production by multinational companies based in developed countries because it was a low-margin business requiring substantial investments in environmental controls.[19]

The Indian pharmaceutical industry acknowledges that the dependence is driven by cost alone – Chinese bulk drugs are almost 50–60 per cent cheaper than Indian products.[20] It does not make economic sense to produce them domestically if such a wide margin exists. Industry reports indicate that while difficult-to-manufacture bulk drugs give bargaining power to suppliers, producers of commoditized, low-margin bulk drugs do not have that power.[21] An export-oriented industry embracing its comparative advantage to produce formulations is a desirable outcome.

Given the fragile peace at the border, while reducing dependence on China for a substantial part of the bulk drugs supply may be required in the long run, import substitution using heavy state support and subsidies must be re-evaluated as a response strategy.

Indian pharmaceuticals are an outward-looking, export-oriented industry which should face the challenges of a globalized marketplace. As cost is the primary advantage that China has, developing a bulk drugs manufacturing base in India or elsewhere at relatively short notice need not be a major challenge for India as it is often made out to be, should such a need arise where cost is not a concern. It is to be kept in mind that the major Indian generic companies still produce bulk drugs in-house for their key products and have only outsourced commodified bulk drugs to China.[22] Also, just as China is a major seller of bulk drugs to India, India is a major market of Chinese products too. In such a situation of mutual dependence, any unilateral action will involve substantial costs on both trade partners, and will be therefore unlikely.

According to the UN's *International Trade Statistics Yearbook* (2017), for the year 2016, China was India's top partner for merchandise imports, accounting for 14.9 per cent of India's total imports. The next biggest partner was Saudi Arabia with just 6 per cent. Getting back to the telephone example at the beginning of this article, in about just two decades, China's share of mobile phone imports – at the heart of India's ongoing information revolution and digital inclusion initiatives – soared from 8 per cent to 71 per cent. Is anyone complaining?

There is indeed no room for complacency while dealing with China, but as a big market for Chinese goods, that should not prevent us from using China to our advantage.

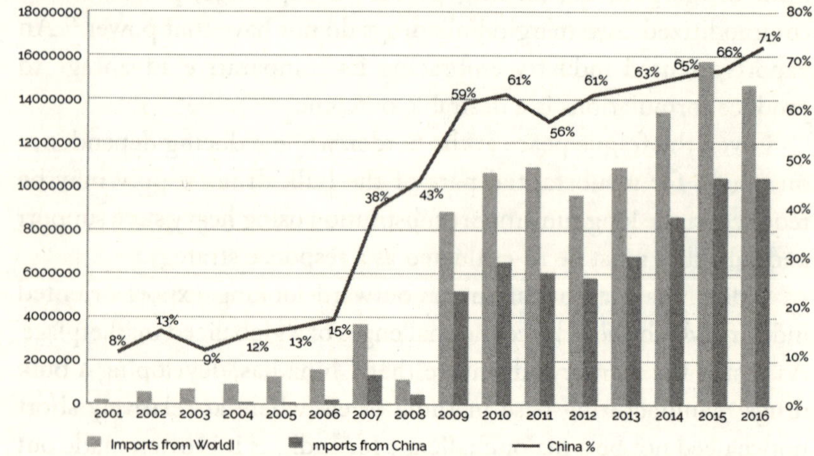

Graph 5: India's Dependency on China for Mobile Phones
Source: International Trade Centre Database

The Way Forward

Regional Comprehensive Economic Partnership (RCEP) negotiations in Hyderabad put the focus on access to medicines.[23]

Hyderabad, a major centre for bulk drug manufacturing in India, was in the news for the wrong reasons, linked to pharmaceutical pollution and the emergence of superbugs.[24] Apart from the industry, seeking comparative advantages in the production of formulations, Indian bulk drug manufacturing's decline was also a direct result of environmental law enforcement as well as the government's efforts after 2005 at ensuring better compliance with good manufacturing practices (GMP), affecting many small- and medium-sized firms.

The Katoch committee report on bulk drugs in 2015 admitted that bulk drugs manufacturing is one of the most polluting industries. Also, studies have shown that in India, making small and medium enterprises (SME) GMP-compatible will cost at least Rs 2 million per SME firm, a binding constraint for most such firms. In a bid to promote the 'Make in India' initiative, 2015 was declared as the year of bulk drugs; and the Katoch committee mooted mega bulk drug parks as an alternative to tap into economies of scale in the same year.[25] However, lack of financial assistance has prevented the initiative from taking off.[26]

The response from the Indian bulk drug manufacturers to such challenges remained predictable – they requested to increase import duty on Chinese goods, and asked the government to be more lenient towards pollution – both these obviously cannot offer a sustainable solution.[27] Perhaps what can be done is to work optimally within the global trade regime and harmonize import duties in such a way that Indian manufacturers take advantage of highly subsidized Chinese products while, at the same time, government revenue from imports support long-term risk diversification tactics including domestic manufacturing.

Any knee-jerk reaction may be unwarranted, and a wait-and-watch approach may have merits. Interestingly, the bulk drug manufacturing scene in China is going through a similar churn as its Indian counterparts, with a shift away from commoditized bulk drugs with low profit margins.[28] A 2017 World Health Organization (WHO) study states that, confronted with new environmental and regulatory restrictions, many Chinese bulk drug manufacturers are themselves considering moving production activities out of China.[29]

Given this complex situation, other options should be actively explored by India as well, along with encouragement to domestic manufacturing. Given India's role as a regional leader, the thriving pharmaceutical trade and friendly relations with Africa, perhaps a possibility is to diversify the 'China risk' by expanding the geography of bulk drug suppliers, by including and assisting other countries in Asia and Africa to develop production capacity. Until then, letting the Chinese subsidize bulk drug access to India and the world may not be a bad idea at all.

7

Harmonizing Ayush and Modern Medicine: Can India Learn from China?

OOMMEN C. KURIAN

It was estimated by the World Health Organization (WHO) that during the 1980s, 'in many countries, 80 per cent or more of the population living in rural areas [were] cared for by traditional practitioners and birth attendants'.[1] The decades that followed saw an unprecedented expansion of biomedicine/Western/modern medicine (allopathy), and the proportion of the population in rural areas of low- and middle-income countries cared for by traditional, complementary and alternative medicine (TCAM) came down significantly. Yet, in large countries like India and China, TCAM still wields considerable policy influence. [2]

In 2015, TCAM in China accounted for 16 per cent of total medical care, up from 14 per cent in 2011, as the *Economist* observes.[3] In India, TCAM accounts for a much lower proportion of overall medical care – data from the National Sample Survey in 2014 indicates that only 6.9 per cent of patients seeking outpatient care opted for TCAM.[4] In the case of hospitalized care, the proportion is less than 1 per cent. Both Indian and Chinese health systems privilege biomedicine over TCAM, but the latter is recognized by the state and receives sizeable state support.[5]

In addition, its low penetration within the Indian population has not prevented TCAM – AYUSH (covering ayurveda, yoga and naturopathy, unani, siddha, sowa rigpa and homoeopathy) as it is known in India – from getting a separate central ministry in India in 2014. The AYUSH ministry is responsible for policy formulation, development and implementation of programmes for the growth, development and propagation of TCAM medicine and treatment.[6]

The first National Health Policy of India (1983) had observed that planned efforts should be made to dovetail the functioning of both the modern medicine and TCAM practitioners and integrate services across different systems of medicine in the overall healthcare delivery system, especially with regard to preventive and public health objectives.[7] It also noted that well-considered steps need to be taken to move towards a meaningful, phased integration of TCAM and modern medicine systems.[8] However, at a functional level, such integration did not happen in India, culminating in a separate ministry for TCAM, thus formalizing the creation of a parallel structure in an already fund-starved sector.

The Chinese Experience

Indian and Chinese health systems have interesting parallels, as Milton Irwin Roemer (1991) observed. One of the first steps India took after Independence in 1947 was to develop, with foreign advice, its own plants for producing drugs.[9] Interestingly, China did the exact same thing after the social revolution in 1949. The policy influence of TCAM is another striking similarity. However, what China strived to achieve through its health policies over the decades was to integrate TCAM seamlessly into the overall healthcare delivery infrastructure.

Raffel (1984) shows that China's health policy has been unique in the developing world as it tried to organize its healthcare delivery around four basic principles:

1. Put prevention first
2. Combine Western and traditional medicine
3. Combine health with mass movements
4. Concentrate on rural areas[10]

Adhering to these tenets, China proceeded to find solutions to the most severe problem facing the health system: the shortage and disproportionate distribution of medical personnel. The Chinese strategy was to distribute scarce resources as widely as possible and to substitute less skilled labour for capital and skills that are more advanced. While a component of this Chinese approach, which considerably expanded access to healthcare featuring 'barefoot doctors' is still widely talked about, the equally important TCAM component is often overlooked.

In the Chinese case, the TCAM physician served as a complement to physicians trained in modern medicine.[11] Along with separate hospitals and clinics for TCAM (Figure 1), special wards within existing facilities were created, which helped increase healthcare utilization.

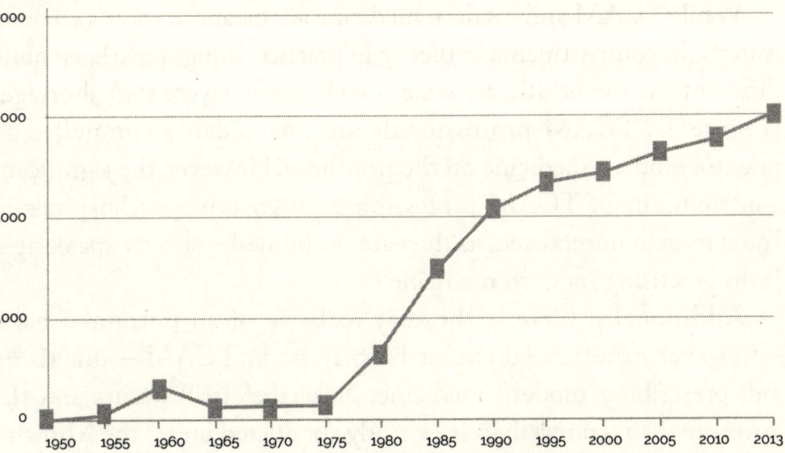

Figure 1: Development of TCAM Hospitals in China[12]

China's integration of TCAM into the national healthcare system was driven by the need to provide comprehensive healthcare services to the general population. Traditional medicine was also viewed as part of an imperial legacy to be replaced by a secular healthcare system where TCAM was harmonized with modern medicine.[13] This process of integration was guided by officials trained in modern medicine. They followed a science-based approach to the education of traditional Chinese medicine, placing an emphasis on research.

Indian Initiatives towards Integration

While co-location of TCAM facilities within government hospitals practising modern medicine is quite common in many Indian states, it was only as late as 2005 that India formally tried 'mainstreaming of AYUSH and revitalization of local health traditions' as part of the National Rural Health Mission (NRHM).[14] However, apart from giving them roles in the implementation of national health programmes, the TCAM and modern medicine systems have not been harmonized and the 'choice of treatment system' was left to the patient.[15]

While TCAM and modern medicine are meant to stay as separate watertight compartments in theory, in practice, things have been quite different. As the healthcare system reels under severe staff shortages (Figure 2), TCAM professionals are unavoidably compelled to practise modern medicine on the frontlines. However, the significant contributions of TCAM professionals in government hospitals in India remain unreported, as they are prohibited – strictly speaking – from practising modern medicine.[16]

Additionally, there is the very real risk of an untrained hand – however experienced she or he may be in TCAM – practising and prescribing modern medicine. Nevertheless, it occurs and the government acknowledges it. A study conducted under the Ministry of Health and Family Welfare (MoHFW) states: 'Where there is no other doctor, they (AYUSH doctors) practise both Allopathy and AYUSH. This is specially marked at the PHC level in most states.'[17]

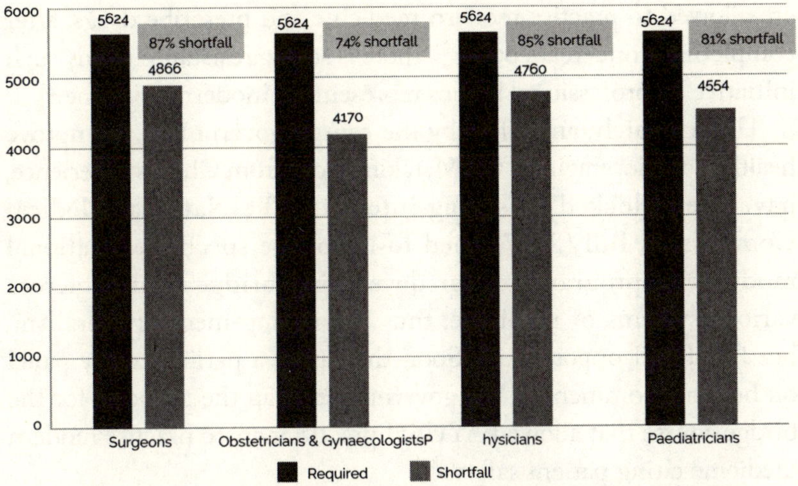

Figure 2: Doctor Shortages in Indian Public Hospitals: 2017

Source: Apurva Kumar, 'Rural Health Statistics 2017 explained in 10 charts', *Pubheal*, 24 December 2017, https://pubheal.wordpress.com/2017/12/24/rural-health-statistics-2017-explained-in-10-charts/

Government reports often acknowledge that in many hospitals, although the service is provided by a TCAM doctor, data is reported under the name of a doctor registered to practise modern medicine 'for legal reasons'.[18] Such 'invisibilization' of the significant contribution of TCAM professionals to the health system is deeply problematic and unethical. Modern medicine and TCAM, which represent professionalized and codified medical systems, need to be dovetailed, and the practice integrated in a way that will maximize access and clinical outcomes, keeping in mind national health goals.[19] This goal makes a scientific approach inevitable – the ongoing double-blind placebo-controlled clinical trial under the Central Council for Research in Ayurvedic Sciences (CCRAS) of an Ayurvedic cure for dengue is a very interesting development in this direction.[20]

Health, being a state subject, adds an extra layer of complexity to any national level initiative. Indeed, there are states like Maharashtra who have adopted a realistic approach where TCAM professionals are allowed to practise modern medicine and prescribe drugs, after completing a one-year course.[21] There is strong resistance to any such initiative by professional bodies representing modern medicine.[22]

Unfortunately, any effort by the central government to improve health access leveraging TCAM, taking a cue from China's experience, have been blocked by strong interests. The National Medical Commission Bill (2017) tried to introduce specific educational modules or programmes for developing bridge courses across various systems of medicine, thus promoting medical pluralism, but faced stiff opposition.[23] Soon thereafter, a parliamentary panel on health recommended the government scrap the proposal for the bridge course that allowed AYUSH practitioners to practise modern medicine citing patient safety.[24]

However, studies prove that for any policy initiative regarding patient safety, streamlining the system of modern medicine should be the first step. After all, a WHO study using the 2001 census data discovered in 2016 that in 2001, nearly one-third of the practitioners calling themselves 'allopathic doctors' in India were educated only till the secondary school level, and that 57.3 per cent of them did not have any medical qualification.[25] Meanwhile, in rural areas, only 18.8 per cent of 'allopathic doctors' had any medical qualification.[26]

Ayushman Bharat as the Way Forward

The National Family Health Survey has shown important indicators like full immunization coverage improving, albeit at a sluggish pace. It is, therefore, supremely important to have a health workforce that has a shared understanding of national health goals, a common approach and scientifically proven tools.[27] A fragmented system, with the possibility of different sections of the workforce working at cross-purposes, is a risk that needs addressing.

China successfully achieved universal health insurance (UHC) coverage in 2011, culminating in an effort widely known as 'the largest expansion of insurance coverage in human history'.[28] As India strives to reprise it and achieve UHC through the ambitious Ayushman Bharat initiative, lessons from China's TCAM approach – called 'interpenetrative pluralism' by scholars – may prove valuable.[29] As China has demonstrated, the integration of TCAM into the national healthcare system needs to be accompanied by an integrated approach to the training of health practitioners, and both need to be officially promoted for optimal impact.[30]

TCAM has the potential for a considerable role in the proposed Health and Wellness Centres (HWC) across the country in preventing and managing non-communicable diseases if and whenever such an integrated approach is taken. To further the harmonization of TCAM with modern medicine, adding TCAM procedures to the benefit package for the National Health Protection Mission (NHPM) will be imperative.

8

The Mystery of China's Shrinking Megacities

SAYLI UDAS-MANKIKAR

Many of Asia's megacities – like Yokohama, Jakarta and Mumbai – face the heat of uncontrolled rural-urban migration and exploding population, putting pressure on its infrastructure and environment. Several solutions have been discussed but the uncontrolled ever-increasing population only makes every move seem inadequate. China, however, has decided to tackle this differently, by taking some result-oriented, even if debatable, steps in redistributing its urban population, causing Shanghai and Beijing's population to plunge in 2017.

Beginning mid-November 2017, the municipal governments of Beijing and Shanghai, the two biggest megacities in the world, are on a demolition spree. They are trying to cap and redistribute city populations by bringing down illegal houses and unregistered commercial establishments in central areas to address the problem of *Chéngshì Bìng* (big city disease).

These waves of demolitions in the name of 'crackdown on illegal housing and safety' were kicked off following a fire at Xinjiancun in the crowded central Beijing district that killed nineteen people in November 2017.[1] In China, every person has a residency permit or a 'hukou' attached to his birthplace. The migrants are being stripped of their habitats and livelihoods overnight for lack of a 'hukou', which meant living without any social security and services in urban areas.

The action is swift and decisive – the migrants are put on short demolition notices or are forced to leave the city without any notice. The targets of such eviction are generally the once-unskilled migrants in their late fifties, who, along with their families, inhabited these cities at the hilt of globalization and economic reforms of the early 1990s. All of them are forced to return to their homes in rural China.

The Beijing local government has held job fairs for those who have lost their jobs in locations where factories and warehouses have been shut down. It has also aided workers returning to their hometown, by building subsidized rental housing. But ultimately, the migrants are required to fend for themselves, away from the cities that sustained them and their families. According to a *Reuters* report, Beijing would mow down at least 40 million square metres, or 15.44 square miles, of illegal structures, amounting roughly to an area twenty-eight times the size of London's Hyde Park, and shut down 500 manufacturing firms in 2018.[2] This will give way to modern, structured, public housing and commercial projects, to be occupied by residents with legal urban permits. It will 'ensure zero increase of such structures', acting mayor Chen Jining said in the Beijing annual work report in January 2018.

It was during my Mandarin class in 2017 that I came across the term 'Chéngshì Bìng'. When my teacher told me that the literal translation of it was 'big city illness', I really wondered what it meant. For us in India, it would probably translate into a health epidemic like the swine flu virus. But as it mostly is the case with China and its peculiar interpretations, the definition and understanding of the term loosely translates as a disease arising when a megacity (read: Beijing and Shanghai in the current context) becomes plagued with environmental pollution, traffic congestion and a shortage of public services, including education and medical care.

Officially, the government wants Beijing to cap its population at 23 million by 2020, while Shanghai will have to cap its population at 25 million by 2035[3]. China's National Bureau of Statistics (NBS) showed that the resident population of Beijing had swelled by 59 per cent in the past decade and that of Shanghai had increased by 50 per cent.[4]

The question that arises here is whether the approach adopted by the Chinese to trim their exploding cities is the right – and only – way ahead. Is this in line with the sustainable development goals (SDG) of having inclusive, sustainable, resilient and safe cities?

There are two opposing thoughts to this debate.

The first is the government version, which bats for a redistribution of the population for safety and security. The Beijing government launched a forty-day 'special operation' targeting structures with fire code and building safety violations post the fire at Xinjiancun in November 2017. A communique issued by the government in December 2017 claimed that such 'redistribution' was necessary to ensure 'the lives and safety of the people'. It refuted the argument that this operation was to drive out 'low-end population', calling it irresponsible and baseless. The communique explained that although the migrant population chooses these places to work and live in, they do not understand the dangers of living in such dense urban ghettoes.

Xu Lin, director of the China Centre of Urban Development, while talking to China.org.cn, justified this thought. He said that high-quality growth requires high-quality urbanization and many important issues – including disorderly expansion and inefficient use of urban space – need to be resolved.

The People's Republic of China's (PRC's) thirteenth five-year plan (2016–20)[5] makes it clear that it is not against migrants per se. It wants to replace the old lot with the upwardly mobile, aspirational and new generation workers. The government is now redefining who the new urban residency permits should be issued to in Beijing, Shanghai and other such megacities in China. It spells out its preferences to 'rural students moving up to the next level of education in an urban area, armed forces personnel settling in an urban area, people who have lived in an urban area for at least five years and have moved their families with them, and new generation migrant workers'. It also talks of linking professional and technical titles and skill levels with the granting of residency in large cities.

The 2018 China government work report supports this as well. It explains how redistribution of urban population will step up its efforts to supply public-rental housing in urban areas for eligible first-time migrant workers. It plans to build 5.8 million units in cities across China in 2018.

However, just about four years ago, China's National New-type Urbanization Plan (2014–20)[6] had no mention of capping the country's urban population as state policy. On the contrary, it focused on policies that would effectively trigger off the process of reverse migration. The plan noted that the 260 million migrant workers in the cities were putting increasingly unmanageable pressures on employment opportunities and healthcare.

Xu Xianping, the then vice-minister of the National Development and Reform Commission (NDRC), had stated how urbanization in China had reached a crucial stage. 'We must find a new way out,' he had said. The new way adopted by China, according to the plan, was to document and check official household registrations 'hukou' of permanent urban residents and those staying in cities with rural 'hukou'. Many of those not having permanent jobs and official 'hukou' slowly started moving out, but many clung on to city life, albeit without any social security.

But since then and especially after the incident of November 2017, this approach has changed – if you cannot manage the population, then you 'redistribute' (read: evict) it. Official figures given out by NBS shows that the approach is working. The population of Beijing dropped by 22,000 to 21.7 million from 2016 to 2017, a decline of 0.1 per cent. This came after a 59 per cent surge in Beijing's population between 2000 and 2016. Meanwhile, Shanghai's population dropped by 13,700 to 24.18 million.[7]

The other argument is against pushing those migrants out of cities who were harbingers of China's rapid progress through the 1990s. There is resentment against the way they are being abruptly stripped of their habitats and livelihoods for the lack of a 'hukou'.

Li Jianmin, professor of demographics at Nankai University in Tianjin, while talking to the *Financial Times*, argued that Beijing, like every city, needs people of all kinds. All humans are equal and should be respected. Driving people out of cities is not going to be effective in the long run and may cause social unrest.

While both Beijing and Shanghai aim at getting a young and upwardly mobile population, these dystopian urbanscapes have some problems. There will be an ageing population that needs help, but unfortunately, the cleaners, nannies, maids, drivers and people in smaller jobs are ousted, making living unaffordable. And for those who remain, hiring people for such jobs will come at a premium. The younger generation will pay higher rentals to stay in new-age condominiums, which will have to be replaced by the traditional terraced homes in the traditional 'hutongs' (courtyard residences). And finally, shrunken cities will have economic implications – residents will pay more for every service.

Could China have looked at this 'big city illness' differently or dealt with it in an equitable way? In contrast to China, Indian cities like Mumbai, which have a huge number of poor migrants living in slums, have adopted a policy of integration. This is a more humane approach and it supports the ecosystem of the city so that its social fabric is kept intact. But ultimately, there needs to be a realistic assessment, as in China, on how far a city can grow, how big it can get, and what is economically sustainable.

There are no tools to plan specifically for migration in urban planning. But, as a short-term measure, there could be a redistribution of resources and a cap on use of water and other essentials. An affordable housing plan can be worked out for rehousing migrants, as has been done in the Mumbai Development Plan. Creation of new cities and census towns too can lead to new urban areas in which to settle such populations.

In the long-term, new cities can adopt a 'decentralized urbanization' approach, where stronger linkages between urban and rural areas should be drawn up. The two areas can co-evolve, leading to the loss of traditional distinctions between them. Strong linkages which push equitable flow of resources can maximize economic and social benefits to people in the rural areas, thus keeping them away from cities.

China is a country in a hurry, and it has made its choice. It chose a different path, which is unconventional, to deal with its 'big city disease'. But the perils of an unequal society can create a bigger monster which it cannot ignore.

9

China Will Have to Hyphenate Itself with the Rule of Law

GAUTAM CHIKERMANE

The biggest problem when engaging with China is its unwillingness to deal with the world under the common and only currency that grants legitimacy: the rule of law. This works well politically – nobody is questioning the non-democratic nature of China's system, the lack of citizens' voices in its governance discourse, its clampdown on dissent, or even practices that in any democratic nation would be considered bad enough to vote governments out. Do what you want within your borders, the world seems to be saying.

Yet, when it comes to dealing with other nations, China's pretensions to glory through the creation of a new world order, whose sole goal is to stand on the economic carcasses of other nations, is slowly ending. The world is saying, 'Enough!' In strategic affairs, for instance, the looming presence of a bully smothering its neighbours, from aggression in the South China Sea and Bhutan, to embracing the world's terror-hub, Pakistan, to its West and supporting rogue nation North Korea to its northeast is finally being taken seriously enough to combat it. The revival of the 'Quad' is under way, a decade after it was first proposed, with the US, Japan, India and Australia joining hands, earlier this month, for a 'free and open Indo-Pacific' region.[1]

On the economic front, the government of Nepal seems to be abandoning the USD 2.5 billion project to build the Budhigandaki Hydroelectric project dam with the Chinese state company China Gezhouba Group, ostensibly due to the lack of an open tender process.[2] In other words, the absence of the rule of law. The alienation is not limited to only neutral nations like Nepal; even 'friends' are backing off. A week earlier, Pakistan had decided to pull out of a USD 14 billion deal to build the Diamer-Bhasha dam with China because it refused to accept the 'strict deal conditions'; it will now go ahead on its own. Such actions will increase as the reality of China's seemingly economic but strategically deadly One Belt, One Road (OBOR) initiative, now renamed the Belt and Road Initiative (BRI), begins to show its true strategic colours.

China's road to global dominance has been backed economically by the rest of the world. The greed of markets under the ideological rhetoric of ending communism got developed nations to accept China's economic mood swings, either in terms of foreign investment or market access. But three decades of what the West celebrated as China's 'economic reforms' has ended with what can only be termed politely as a 'socialist-market economy' that functions on the rule of whims, not the rule of law. Since the Chinese government is a major player in its economy – mirroring the Pakistan Army's role in that country – and its 1,50,000 state-owned enterprises (SOEs) account for about half its non-agricultural GDP, companies in other countries fight a power asymmetry in the market while dealing with them.

To get a sense of scale of China's SOEs, look at their place in global listings:

'Fortune's 2016 list of the world's 500 largest companies includes 103 Chinese firms (compared to 29 listed firms in 2007),' according to a 15 September 2017 report by the Congressional Research Service titled 'China's Economic Rise: History, Trends, Challenges, and Implications for the United States'.

> Of the 103 Chinese firms listed, Fortune identified 75 companies (73% of total) where the government owned 50% or more of the company. Together, these 75 firms in 2016 generated $7.2 trillion in revenues, had assets valued at $20.7 trillion, and employed 16.2 million workers. Of the 28 other Chinese firms on the Fortune 500 list, several appear to have financial links to the Chinese government.[3]

Essentially, the 'market' China works in has the power of its sovereign government fighting commercial companies of other nations.

What China has been doing, and continues to do, is in the best interests of the country and its people, it can be argued. 'The over-concentration of SOEs in the strategic market seems to have served specific government purposes to bolster the nation's economic growth,' write Xiao Geng, Xiuke Yang and Anna Janus.[4] But the absence of a rule-of-law-based economy means the seeping of political power of individuals who head senior positions in the Communist Party into economic power, creating inequalities and leading to what is known as 'credibility deficit'. Through a strange logic that it follows and ruthlessly implements, the development of a pluralistic society, a society where ideas and power are freely contested, is now further out of reach than it has been for decades.[5]

The absence of the rule of law in China has been a constant refrain. Beijing benefits from free global markets without making the necessary changes within, through a self-righteous take-all stance, which is seemingly reaching a flashpoint. According to a World Bank report:

> As the Chinese economy grows in complexity, not only must rules and regulations evolve to reflect changing reality and emerging priorities, but they should be fairly and effectively enforced.[6]

> If the enforcement of standards varies from sector to sector, region to region, entity to entity, and sometimes even person to person, then it will not only discourage innovation and lead to inefficient economic outcomes, it will also contribute to feelings of injustice.[7]

China's facade of 'social stability' – an elegant expression to silence or imprison dissent, particularly among Buddhist Tibetans and Muslim Uyghurs – too is wearing thin. True, this stability has lifted hundreds of millions of Chinese out of poverty in just a few decades; it has also placed China as a major global power. But now, it seems unable to manage its ambitions. By presuming that other countries owe it their sovereignty as much as their markets, China is standing on thin ice. The new world order it seeks to create and lead will not come. No democratic nation will allow it to happen. China may rave and rant but will finally be laughed out of the comity of civilized nations into an ideological and political isolation where such ideas belong: within its own borders and those hyphenated with it by the lack of the rule of law – notably, Pakistan and North Korea.

10

India, China and the Ironies of Maoism

NIRANJAN SAHOO

India's longest running internal insurgency, named after Chairman Mao Zedong, turned fifty in 2017.[1] Incidentally, 2017 also marked the completion of fifty years of Mao's infamous Cultural Revolution (1966–77). While Mao's ideological creation – the People's Republic of China (PRC) has gone through a massive makeover and transformation in its ideological and political orientation, closely resembling (on some levels even surpassing) any classical capitalist country of the West, his ideological progeny in India continue to maintain their unflinching faith in his strategy of 'political power flows from the barrel of the gun'. In a strange twist of ironies, Indian Maoists still hope to establish a proletariat state by 'overthrowing a semi-colonial bourgeoisie state'. While Chairman Mao has lost most of his lustre and appeal in his homeland, he remains 'Chairman' for most Maoists in India. In the irony of ironies, the Indian Maoists continue to say 'China's Chairman is our Chairman'.[2]

China's Long Shadow Over Indian Maoists

On 25 May 1967, poor peasants, mostly Santhal tribespeople with their lathis and bows, undertook a daring raid of *jotedars* or landlords and their paddy granaries in a Naxalbari village, situated in the Darjeeling district of West Bengal. This radical left-wing movement, ideologically inspired by Mao Zedong's revolutionary strategy, was openly endorsed by China's influential newspaper the *People's Daily* as: 'Spring thunder breaks over India'.

The Communist Party-run newspaper that devoted a full editorial page on the event declared:

> A peal of spring thunder has crashed over the land of India. Revolutionary peasants in the Darjeeling area have risen in rebellion under the leadership of a revolutionary group of the Indian Communist Party, a red area of rural revolutionary armed struggle has been established in India... The Chinese people joyfully applaud this revolutionary storm of the Indian peasants in the Darjeeling area as do all the Marxist-Leninists and revolutionary people of the world.[3]

It may puzzle the lay readers how an uprising of poor peasants surrounding a handful of villages in an eastern Indian state can make such an impact in Chinese circles. The Naxalbari rebellion, from where the name Naxalite (for Maoist) originated, was the culmination of a series of initiatives inspired by Mao's ideology and political thought. The Chinese Communist Revolution under Mao and its heroic overthrow of a nationalist government under Chiang Kai-Shek through an armed peasant rebellion in 1949 had left a deep impact on Indian communist leaders and revolutionaries. The success of the Chinese Revolution had its reverberations within the Communist Party of India (Marxist) [CPI(M)]. The CPI(M), which emerged as a new party in 1964 (after a major split in the original Communist Party of India or CPI), had many prominent leaders such as Charu

Majumdar and Kanu Sanyal, who wanted to drive the new party on the lines of Mao's ideology and strategy. The charismatic firebrand, Charu Majumdar, for instance, brought out his famous *Eight Documents* in 1965 that exhorted CPI(M) to endorse Mao's strategy of armed rebellion against the Indian state. So much so, that Kanu Sanyal took a five-member revolutionary team to China in 1968 for a two-and-a-half-month guerrilla warfare training programme. Of course, their radical and extremist ideological positioning led to a split in the CPI(M) with the formation of a radical left leaning party CPI Marxist–Leninist or CPI(M-L) in 1969.[4]

The CPI(M-L), easily known as Charu's faction (mainly led by Kanu Sanyal and Jangal Santhal), was instrumental in triggering the Naxalbari protests and its subsequent spread to wide swathes of areas in India. Charu Majumdar's assertion, that India's constitution was a mask for a semi-colonial system and should be overthrown by a peasant rebellion in the same way that the Chinese Communist Party (CCP) did in China, found support among landless peasants, dispossessed adivasis (tribals) and urban intellectuals and romantics. While the Naxalbari rebellion was put down by strong police action in a matter of weeks, its sparks had flown to many regions of the country.[5] Although Majumdar was easily nabbed by the police and he subsequently paid with his life in 1972 (allegedly by police torture), his ideological creation continues to wage the armed struggle against the Indian state.

The daring Maoist attack in Sukma in April 2017 that cost the lives of twenty-five soldiers belonging mainly to the paramilitary force, the Central Reserve Police Force (CRPF), is a reminder that the revolution is very much alive in India.

This brings one to ponder how an ideology that has long lost its appeal among the Chinese masses and often been demonized as 'catastrophic' and 'utopian' by the subsequent regimes in China and even among strong ideologues of the Communist Party, retains ideological appeal among Indian Maoists. Of course, it is open knowledge that Mao Zedong disliked Charu Majumdar and his revolutionary strategy.[6] On a number of occasions, the CCP derided Indian Maoists as 'revisionists', hell bent on replicating the Chinese model even if it clearly would not work in Indian conditions, India being a democracy. It is well known that during his own lifetime, Mao Zedong struggled with his own ideological prognosis and abandoned his earlier visceral dislike for capitalism by geopolitically embracing the United States in 1972. Thus, it is a puzzle why Indian Maoists continue to repose unwavering faith in Mao and his rusty ideology. As their movement turns fifty, the time is ripe for Maoists and their leadership to abandon Mao and embrace India's parliamentary democracy. They must take a leaf from the post-Mao Chinese leadership book and learn how 'real mass empowerment' can be achieved sans arms and rebellion.

11

Decoding China's New Threat from ISIS

KABIR TANEJA

On 1 March, 2017, for the first time, the so-called Islamic State (ISIS) released a video showcasing militants from the Uyghur ethnic minority from China's restive Xinjiang province in its ranks. The video proceeds to directly threaten Beijing with violence on behalf of ISIS before the Uyghur members of the terror group are shown executing an alleged informant.[1]

'Oh, you Chinese who do not understand what people say. We are the soldiers of the Caliphate, and we will come to you to clarify to you with the tongues of our weapons, to shed blood like rivers and avenging the oppressed,' the video narrates, according to loose translations corroborated by the SITE Intelligence Group, an American company that tracks the online activity of white supremacist and jihadist organizations.

The timing of the video's release seemed deliberate as it coincided with the time when China had been orchestrating a show of power in its Xinjiang province, where Uyghur Muslims were at loggerheads with the state over issues of religious freedom, ethnic autonomy and in some cases, secessionist Islamist ideologues wanting to set up a fundamentalist Islamic state in the region. As a result, Xinjiang has seen a host of knife attacks against its own people, and retaliatory policies by the Chinese government against Uyghur protestors that have reportedly killed hundreds over the past ten years.[2]

However, like most such extremist movements, the topography of jihadists in Xinjiang is not black and white in nature. The ISIS video points to a fresh threat to the region on China's western front, with returning ISIS fighters joining those already operating there, along with others who can be influenced via online propaganda to cause unrest under the branding of ISIS. While this video highlights ISIS's threat towards China, jihadism in the country has till date largely been led by the Turkestan Islamic Party (TIP, earlier known as the East-Turkestan Islamic Movement), which has been fighting the Chinese government for the formation of an independent nation of East Turkestan (or Uyghurstan). The TIP had hitherto been known as an affiliate of Al-Qaeda, receiving funds from Osama Bin Laden's groups to orchestrate operations in the Xinjiang province and, reportedly, even getting training from jihadists in both Afghanistan and Pakistan.[3]

However, in 2013, two years after the killing of Bin Laden in Pakistan, TIP announced its allegiance to ISIS's caliphate, joining other Uzbek jihadi groups such as the Islamic Movement of Uzbekistan (IMU) to carry on their activities. A year before, in 2012, Chinese Major General Yin Jiang had made the first reference of a possible Uyghur–Syria nexus, blaming groups belonging to the 'East Turkestan movement' for participating in the civil war in northern Syria, using smuggling routes via Southeast Asia and Turkey to get themselves to Syria.[4] Historically, Turkey has backed the East Turkestani movement and this support is still largely in place, with the country being a large host to pro-TIP leaders; Ankara is also slated to play a critical role in an attack in China, expected to be coordinated by ISIS. Some Chinese observers over the past years have compared Turkey's alleged harbouring of such TIP elements as analogous to the Taliban in Afghanistan, shielding Osama bin Laden for years.

In a 2013 interview, the Syrian Ambassador to China, Imad Moustapha, told China's *Global Times* newspaper that Damascus had intelligence suggesting that over thirty Uyghur jihadists had travelled from a Pakistani terror training camp to Syria via the porous Turkish border.[5] In 2015, *Al-Monitor* columnist Metin Gurcan highlighted that 1,500 jihadists from Central Asia, including Uyghurs, were fighting with ISIS as per intelligence sources. The same year, UAE based *Al Masdar News* announced the death of an Uyghur terrorist known as 'Abbas al-Turkistani' allegedly killed by the Syrian army in Hama province.[6] The Syrian government, as per Moustapha, is sharing all such instances and intelligence from the ground with China. In 2016, despite its previous views, TIP's emir, Abdul Haq al-Turkistani, denounced ISIS as 'illegitimate'. However, what remains debatable is the extent of the rift between TIP leaders over the emir's opinions that came six years after he was critically injured, reportedly in a drone strike in Pakistan's North Waziristan (it's important to note that TIP aligned with ISIS while Abdul Haq al-Turkistani was thought to be incapacitated).[7]

Despite the small number of Uyghurs joining ISIS or other groups in Syria's civil war, the implications of this for China in Xinjiang could be significant. The Uyghurs in Xinjiang are far from united in the causes supported by groups such as the TIP. While some demand a fundamentalist Islamist state, others are split between fighting for greater autonomy under the Chinese system, while some are even content to integrate with Beijing's stance on Xinjiang as they look to be part of the country's economic success story and move away from Xinjiang, which in itself is considered a threat by Beijing.[8]

Despite fractures within the Uyghur's historical fight for rights, the jihadists also have strong fault lines amongst themselves. The video released under the banner of ISIS also warned jihadists fighting with TIP, highlighting the conflicting schools of thought in TIP that are aligning with ISIS and those shunning it. Regardless of such differences, online propaganda along with returning fighters pose a threat to Xinjiang's complicated ethnic social fabric with further radicalization and now, some with war experience. It is possible that potential terror activities in China, not just in Xinjiang but in major coastal hubs as well, could take place under the flag of the so-called Islamic State. The Chinese government clearly seems to be gearing up for that eventuality, as is visible today through Beijing's heavy-handed control of Xinjiang and the Uyghur people via anti-religion camps and unprecedented surveillance.

12

China's Dark Secret Is Out, but the World Is Silent

KHALID SHAH

The Western press is abuzz with stories about the 'cultural cleansing' orchestrated by the Communist Party in the Xinjiang region of China.[1] While the horrific stories of China's re-education programme have uncovered the rampant assault on the identity and culture of the Uyghur Muslims, reactions from the Muslim world have been largely muted. The spiral of silence is not limited to the Muslim community, it spans across the world to democratic countries like India where the voices of supporters of human rights and freedom are also mute.

As per media reports, Uyghurs are detained in re-education camps where they are forced to eat pork and drink alcohol.[2] They are coerced to criticize and denounce their own ethnic group and belief system, coupled with indoctrination to accept the Communist Party culture. This process is rampant across the Xinjiang region where one million Uyghurs are detained in the camps, as per estimates of the United Nations.[3] The Chinese government is spending an immense amount of money on building new camps and security infrastructure in the region. In the eyes of party propagandists, these camps are similar to hospitals except that the treatments here are for 'ideological illnesses'.[4] The torture in these re-education camps has, in many cases, led to the death of detainees but so far there is no estimate of the death toll.

One news report quotes a party official saying: 'Ideological illnesses are the same as physical illnesses, in that they must be treated in time, and should never be ignored and allowed to become serious. Otherwise, later we will regret it, as it will be too late ... Being infected by religious extremism and violent terrorist ideology and not seeking treatment is like being infected by a disease that has not been treated in time, or like taking toxic drugs.'[5]

There is, in fact, a significant influence of religious extremism and radicalization in Xinjiang, but the Communist Party is holding the entire population of this ethnic minority hostage in the name of religious extremism.[6] China's reaction is out of proportion and has faced severe criticism from the UN and American officials.[7,8] What started as a campaign to eradicate extremist elements in the region has now become a widespread campaign to culturally integrate the Uyghurs.

Xinjiang, the largest province of China, covers an area of 16,60,000 square kilometres and has a population of around twenty-two million. Aksai Chin, a part of the Indian state of Jammu and Kashmir occupied by China, is part of the same region, and shares borders with Pakistan, Afghanistan and other Central Asian countries. Uyghurs are one of the fifty-five officially recognized minority groups in China and constitute 45 per cent of the Xinjiang population.[9]

While the ethnic minority is at the receiving end of the worst form of persecution, the world does not bat an eye.

China's all-weather friend, Pakistan, is feigning ignorance about the plight of the Uyghurs in China. Pakistanis have, in their self-proclamations, shown great zeal defending, supporting and protecting Muslims across the world. Be it the cause of Palestinians, the persecution of Rohingyas or any other issue regarding Muslims, Pakistan is always at the forefront. However, in the case of Uyghur

Muslims, their trumpet has lost its sound – not just the government of Pakistan but also the people of Pakistan, including the liberals and clerics, are on the same page. In an interview to the *Financial Times*, Pakistan Prime Minister Imran Khan said he 'doesn't know much' about the issue.[10] Commentators suggest that money flowing in from Beijing has bought Pakistan's silence on the Uyghurs.[11] Pakistan's silence has given a tacit approval to the persecution of the Uyghurs and has thus become a passive accomplice of China.[12]

On the other hand, the rest of the Muslim world except Turkey has also maintained a conspicuous silence, a hypocrisy quite similar to that of Pakistan. The Arab world, owing to vested interests, has seemingly ignored the fact that one million Muslims are being forced into camps to cleanse their belief in Islam. In February 2019, Turkey not only condemned the ill-treatment meted out to the Uyghur community but also put pressure on China to shut down the internment camps.[13] However, Turkey's condemnation didn't follow any action owing to China's strong reaction.[14]

This selective outrage is another indicator of how the champions of Islamic causes can betray an ethnic Muslim community for their own vested interests.[15] Many Islamists, who are known for decreeing against the persecution of Muslims, seem unfazed by the plight of the Uyghurs.[16]

Similarly, no one is outraged in India. China has in the past needled India on the Kashmir issue, but India could retaliate by raising the persecution of the Uyghurs at the diplomatic level. After the Doklam crisis and the subsequent diplomacy at Wuhan, New Delhi has avoided antagonizing Beijing. Therefore, it is very unlikely that the world's largest democracy will voice concerns on the issue.

In the past, champions of human rights and civil liberties in India have raised an empathetic cry in favour of the Rohingyas, and organized demonstrations in favour of the Palestinians, most recently on the issue of shifting the US Embassy in Jerusalem. The Left in India has advocated for many global causes and has always walked hand in hand with the Muslims of the country, to raise voices against the wrongful persecution of Muslims. Yet, both the Left and the Muslims in India are strangely silent on this issue.

China is setting a dangerous precedent in Xinjiang. It is imperative for the global Muslim community and human rights defenders to treat the Palestinians, Rohingyas and Uyghurs equally, and impose pressure on Beijing to stop its evil campaign in Xinjiang.

13

China's Strategy for the International Satcom Market

VIDYA SAGAR REDDY

China is systematically following a strategy to compete with the West in satellite launch and communication (satcom) services markets. This includes upstream and downstream activities. The upstream has been made possible with loans to key countries in the Global South, which are determined to launch their first telecommunications satellites. These countries in turn select Chinese state-owned space companies to manufacture and launch the satellites. Moreover, Chinese companies are gradually picking up stakes in companies that are operating these satellites, allowing them to embed themselves into regional satellite communications markets.

The following table shows the international satellite launch contracts China has fulfilled so far. The table also includes the cost of each satellite and the funding agency. China's Export-Import (Exim) Bank is the primary agency financing these satellite projects in the form of loans. China has covered South America, Africa, South Asia and Southeast Asia with these contracts. It may be noted that many of these countries are either part of China's Belt and Road Initiative (BRI), such as Pakistan and Laos, or aligned closely with China's domestic and international political priorities.

No.	Country	Satellite	Launch	In-Orbit Delivery	Satellite Bus	Cost	Funding
1	Nigeria	NigComSat-1	May-07	Jul-07	DFH-4	$300 million	China EXIM Bank
2	Venezuela	VeneSat-1 / Simon Bolivar	Oct-08	Dec-08	DFH-4	$241 million	China
3	Pakistan	PakSat-1R	Aug-11	Nov-11	DFH-4	$222 million	China EXIM Bank
4	Nigeria	NigComSat-1R	Dec-11	Mar-12	DFH-4	-	Insurance from NigComSat-1
5	Sri Lanka	SupremeSat-1 / ChinaSat 12 / Apstar-7B	Nov-12		SB4000	$100 million (leased transponders)	
6	Bolivia	Tupac Katari-1	Dec-13	Apr-16	DFH-4	$302 million	85% financed by China Development Bank
7	Laos	Laosat-1	Nov-15	Mar-16	DFH-4	$259 million	China EXIM Bank
8	Belarus	Belintersat-1	Jan-16	May-16	DFH-4 bus with Thales transponders	$280.9 million	China EXIM Bank
9	Algeria	Alcomsat-1	Dec-17	Apr-18	DFH-4		

These satellites are the first ever to be launched and therefore embolden the authoritarian regimes in most of these countries. For example, Venezuela's then president Hugo Chavez showcased VeneSat-1 as a political tool to advance the 'construction of socialism' and end 'media bombardment' by the United States.[1] Pakistan sees the advantage in contracting with China for its satellites, given the mutual rivalry with India and its own dilapidated space technology base. It intends to revive its space ambitions, which had led to the establishment of the Space and Upper Atmosphere Research Commission (SUPARCO) as a counter to India's space aspirations in the 1960s.

China also targeted Southeast Asian countries which help advance its regional geopolitical goals. Cambodia is one of China's primary allies, and has regularly forced ASEAN (Association of South East Asian Nations) to drop or withdraw anti-China rhetoric on the South China Sea in joint statements.[2] In return, China supported Hun Sen when the United States and the European Union opposed the dissolution of Cambodia's main opposition party.[3] Laos also took a similar stance and has refused to acknowledge the permanent court of arbitration verdict on the South China Sea dispute case launched by Philippines.[4]

In addition to geopolitical interests, the satellite contracts also advance China's commercial interests. For example, Nigeria has announced NigComSat-2&3 projects with funding from China's Exim bank.[5] The new loans will be granted by China in exchange for a stake in the Nigerian Communications Satellite Ltd (NigComSat), the company operating the NigComSat-1R. As a shareholder, China is set to benefit from the burgeoning African satcom market as well as business deals that NigComSat makes.

In the case of Sri Lanka, Chinese Exim bank is ready to fund SupremeSat-2. SupremeSat plans to become the largest private satellite operator in South Asia by making Sri Lanka the regional hub for such activities.[6] China is supporting this ambition by setting up a space academy to train Sri Lankan technicians under its mentorship and funding the academy through a USD 20 million joint venture with China Great Wall Industry Corporation (CGWIC). A major infusion of funds also occurred via a Chinese Forbes billionaire investing USD 30 million in SupremeSat.

Chinese companies command a 55 per cent share in the LaoSat-1 joint venture company. Pakistan too defines its satellite as commercial and is making plans for a follow-up satellite where the cost will be shared 50:50 between SUPARCO and CGWIC.

Other satellite contracts may not provide China such direct financial gains but can allow it to gain political influence in general, which could be directed towards resource acquisition. For example, Belarus is a major gateway for the Chinese Silk Road crossing into Western Europe. Bolivia is rich in lithium, the primary resource for manufacturing batteries. China is supporting its industries to commercialize this resource to enable its booming electric vehicle industry. The Supreme Group that holds SupremeSat has an agreement with Beijing Aerospace Great Wall Minerals Corporation, allowing the group's mines in Sri Lanka, Indonesia and Madagascar to be developed by China.[7]

China intends to connect many of these countries through the BRI. A 'Space Silk Road' is being outlined, which will include China's communication, remote sensing, weather and navigation services offered to BRI participants.[8] However, Fu Zhiheng, executive vice president of CGWIC, does not perceive BRI as the business driver for the company as there are other financial and technical constraints in the satellite launch process.[9] The bundling of satellite manufacturing, launch and ground support along with Chinese loans may have eased some of the domestic excess production challenges, though.

However, like other BRI infrastructure projects, developing countries need to generate enough revenue from the satellites to pay back the loan with interest or break even with ongoing expenditure on the projects. Many of these countries, except Belarus and Bolivia, are not in such a position at present, leading to fears of debt traps.

But the projects do allow China to meet its goal in the international satcom market. It has set a target of acquiring 10 per cent of the global satellite market, which is dominated by the Western companies, by 2020.[10] And to surmount the American restrictions on launching satellites with US components, it has developed an ITAR-free (International Traffic in Arms Regulations) satellite bus known as Dong Fang Hong 4 (DFH-4). This closes a critical option for the US which could otherwise restrict satellite components supply to pressure China or its customers, such as Venezuela.

Based on these projects, China even gained commercial satellite contracts in Southeast Asia. Thailand's commercial satellite operator Thaicom has contracted CGWIC for a high throughput satellite built on the DFH-4 bus. China even allowed Thaicom to sell bandwidth on its Thaicom-4/IPSTAR-1 to the mainland. However, Thaicom will have to become a shareholder in one of the Chinese companies that is part of the deal. Similar high-value contracts are also in place with Indonesian companies, which have long-established satcom businesses.

China is also becoming part of the downstream activities in certain countries such as Nigeria, Sri Lanka and Pakistan by buying stakes in the local companies managing the satellites. This gives China access to emerging markets dominated by Western satellite operators or local agencies such as the Indian Space Research Organization (ISRO).

The repeat contracts from some of these countries show that China's market is expanding. Moreover, these satellite contracts are not just standalone commercial opportunities but strategic initiatives strengthening China's BRI strategy. It remains to be seen whether the satellite projects could generate revenues to pay back the Chinese loans or if these countries risk falling into a debt trap, like the experience of those engaged with China in BRI-related projects.

14

Academia: A New Frontier in China's Foreign Policy

HARSH V. PANT, AKSHAY RANADE

As a rising power, China is increasingly aware of how its behaviour and actions are perceived on the global stage. While the perception of China's rise generates considerable apprehension, if not outright distrust, there is also a discernible trend whereby China is seen to be investing in its public diplomacy outreach with the agenda of projecting the image of a responsible global player. Public diplomacy is broadly defined as being aimed at creating a constituency favourable for advancing a country's national interest in a foreign country. It is a tool consciously used by states through various means to directly engage with the public and mould general opinion favourable for its national interest. One of the avenues which China seems to be using for this purpose is the academia. However, the way China has sought to use its increasing academic heft in pursuit of these goals is now inviting a lot of scrutiny and criticism.

There are growing concerns that China is actively using academic and cultural institutions as tools of its foreign policy, often to the detriment of local institutions. There are also reports of espionage as happened in the case when a 'pro-Beijing' professor was expelled from Singapore for being an 'agent' of a foreign power.[1] Singapore's ministry of home affairs alleged that the professor was engaged in activities like deliberately interacting with intelligence agencies of a foreign country to influence the Singapore government's policy and public opinion in a manner that was inimical to Singapore's interest. This unprecedented move by Singapore, of expelling an academician for alleged espionage, has brought to the fore the role of academia as a tool for furthering China's state objectives.

The most notable and arguably the most controversial of institutions in this regard are the Confucius Institutes (CI), which, according to Li Changchun, who was a Politburo member and head of propaganda for the Chinese Communist Party, are 'an important part of China's overseas propaganda set-up'.[2] Confucius Institutes and research centres located at colleges and universities across the globe aim to 'promote Chinese language and culture, support local Chinese teaching internationally and facilitate cultural exchanges'. First set up in 2004, the count of these institutes has risen dramatically by 2017 to around 500 with a total of 1.9 million people studying Chinese language and culture in these institutes and around 1,000 Confucius classrooms in 134 countries.[3] These institutes are largely funded by an agency of the Chinese government's ministry of education – the Office of Chinese Languages Council International also known as Hanban. These CIs became popular because of their generous funding, free course materials and even trained teachers and instructors provided by the Chinese government to expand the teaching and learning of Chinese language and culture.

However, these institutes have come under stringent criticism for their effect on host academic institutions as well as for compromising academic values such as freedom of opinion and for stifling an environment for critical thinking. These institutes tend to project a certain image of China which is devoid of its recent political history. References to Tiananmen Square, for instance, are deliberately eschewed as a matter of policy and even discussions of issues like human rights within China are consciously discouraged. In 2009, the North Carolina State University even declined an invitation to the Dalai Lama after the school's CI complained. This has sparked a debate within academic circles regarding the true nature of these institutes.[4] Some studies[5] conducted to examine the nature of these 'cultural centres' have raised major concerns regarding the transparency of these institutes and the adverse effects this is having on intellectual freedom. The American Association of University Professors (AAUP) has called these institutes 'an arm of the Chinese state' and that they 'advance a state agenda in the recruitment and control of academic staff, the choice of curriculum, and in the restriction of debate'.[6] The nature, role and the divide between the stated and perceived objectives of CIs is contested now to an extent that major universities, like the University of Chicago for instance, have closed the institutes on their campuses.[7]

The academia is being used by China as an instrument of 'state interest' and the political elite is not shy in mentioning it. Chinese President Xi Jinping has called for allegiance to the ruling Communist Party from the country's colleges and universities.[8] What should concern the rest of the world is the fact that these efforts are moving beyond Chinese borders and are affecting the functioning of academic institutions in other states. In 2017, Cambridge University Press (CUP) also decided to block online access in China to certain articles on subjects including the Tiananmen Square massacre, the Cultural Revolution and President Xi Jinping in the highly respected journal, the *China Quarterly*, at the request of Beijing. Although this decision was reversed after academics worldwide registered their complaints, the fact that the CUP gave in to such demands speaks volumes about the growing influence of Beijing even in matters related to academia.

Moreover, a section of the academia's role in acting as an 'asset' of the Chinese state in a foreign country to influence decisions favourable to Chinese interests is worrisome, as was underscored by the professor's case in Singapore. Liberal democratic spaces, like university campuses, are therefore becoming increasingly vulnerable to such tactics and the perceived assault on academic institutions continues to raise serious concerns.

Any effort at public diplomacy is essentially a political activity aimed at attaining a desired set of objectives and states pursue it in different ways. China's use of academia, when seen from this perspective, is not entirely novel. What is evident is that China has evolved its own means of effectively using academic institutions for furthering its political agenda and it has developed this model with discernible 'Chinese characteristics'. It involves tacit coercion, invalidation of contrarian opinion and censuring narratives perceived by political elites in China as detrimental to their interest. For the rest of the world, it is important to view this Chinese tactic for what it really is, in order to craft an effective response. Academic freedom and integrity are too important to be left unchallenged from the onslaught of the Chinese Communist Party.

Notes

Introduction

1 Jane Perlez and Mark Landler, 'Wooing Trump, Xi Jinping Seeks Great Power Status for China', *New York Times*, 6 November 2017, https://www.nytimes.com/2017/11/06/world/asia/trump-xi-jinping-visit-china.html
2 Xiang Bo, ' Backgrounder: Xi Jinping Thought on Socialism with Chinese Characteristics for a New Era', *Xinhua*, 17 March 2017, http://www.xinhuanet.com/english/2018-03/17/c_137046261.htm
3 'Full text of Xi Jinping's report at the 19th CPC National Congress', *Xinhua*, 3 November 2017, http://www.xinhuanet.com/english/special/2017-11/03/c_136725942.htm
4 Ibid.
5 Government of India, Ministry of External Affairs, 28 August 2017, https://www.mea.gov.in/press-releases.htm?dtl/28893/Press+Statement+on+Doklam+disengagement+understanding
6 Ankit Panda, 'Disengagement at Doklam: Why and How Did the India-China Standoff End?', *Diplomat*, 29 August 2017, https://thediplomat.

com/2017/08/disengagement-at-doklam-why-and-how-did-the-india-china-standoff-end/

7 Dipanjan Roy Choudhary, 'War is not a solution, border stand-off with China can be resolved through talks: Sushma Swaraj', *Economic Times*, 11 July 2018, https://economictimes.indiatimes.com/news/defence/war-is-not-a-solution-border-stand-off-with-china-can-be-resolved-through-talks-sushma-swaraj/articleshow/59901938.cms

PART 1: CHINA'S STRATEGIC POSTURE

1. In Search of China's Grand Strategy

1 C. Raja Mohan, 'Diplomacy for New India,' *Indian Express*, 22 March 2017, https://indianexpress.com/article/opinion/columns/diplomacy-for-new-india-china-narendra-modi-xi-jinping-4579619/

2 Hal Brands, *What Good Is Grand Strategy? Power and Purpose in American Statecraft from Harry S. Truman to George W. Bush*, Ithaca, NY: Cornell University Press, 2014, p. 3.

3 Zicheng Ye, *Inside China's Grand Strategy: The Perspective from the People's Republic*, Lexington, KY: University of Kentucky Press, 2011.

4 Ye, *Inside China"s Grand Strategy*, 137.

5 Ye, *Inside China"s Grand Strategy*, 174.

6 Ye, *Inside China"s Grand Strategy*, 79.

7 Abhijnan Rej, *Will Xi adopt Keynes? Post-2015 military spending and economic growth in China*, ORF Occasional Paper No. 85, New Delhi: *Observer Research Foundation*, 2016, https://www.orfonline.org/research/post-2015-military-spending-and-economic-growth-in-china/

8 Ye, *Inside China"s Grand Strategy*, 79.

9 Ye, *Inside China's Grand Strategy*, 113.

10 Ibid.

11 Colonels Qiao Liang and Wang Xiangsui, *Unrestricted Warfare: China's Master Plan to Destroy America*, New Delhi: Natraj Publishers, 2007

12 Michael Pillsbury, *The Hundred-Year Marathon: China's Secret Strategy to Replace America as the Global Superpower*, New York: Henry Holt and Company, 2015.

13 Robert Lawrence Kuhn, 'Xi Jinping's Chinese Dream,' *New York Times*, 4 June 2013, https://www.nytimes.com/2013/06/05/opinion/global/xi-jinpings-chinese-dream.html.
14 Wang Jisi, 'China's Search for a Grand Strategy', *Foreign Affairs*, March–April 2011, https://www.foreignaffairs.com/articles/china/2011-02-20/chinas-search-grand-strategy
15 Ibid.
16 Ibid.
17 Ibid.

2. China's Military Modernization and Its Implications

1 Ngo Minh Tri, 'China's A2/AD Challenge in the South China Sea: Securing the Air From the Ground', the *Diplomat*, 19 May 2017, https://thediplomat.com/2017/05/chinas-a2ad-challenge-in-the-south-china-sea-securing-the-air-from-the-ground/
2 Schell, Phillip Patton and Kristensen, Hans M., 'Chinese Nuclear Forces', *SIPRI Yearbook 2015: Armaments, Disarmament and International Security*, Oxford: Oxford University Press, 2015, p. 491.
3 'PRC State Council, China's Military Strategy in 2015, May 26, 2015', the *Jamestown Foundation*, May 2015, https://jamestown.org/wp-content/uploads/2016/07/China's-Military-Strategy-2015.pdf
4 Ibid.
5 Ibid.
6 O'Rourke, Ronald, 'China Naval Modernization: Implications for U.S. Navy Capabilities – Background and Issues for Congress', *Congressional Research Service (CRS)*, 1 August, 2018, Washington DC, https://fas.org/sgp/crs/row/RL33153.pdf
7 'PRC State Council, China's Military Strategy in 2015, May 26, 2015', *Jamestown Foundation*, May 2015.
8 Allen, Kenneth W., Blasko, Dennis J. and Corbett, Jr., John F., 'Updated – The PLA's New Organizational Structure: What Is Known, Unknown and Speculation, Parts 1 & 2', https://jamestown.org. February 2016 [accessed January/February 2017]; https://jamestown.org/wp-content/uploads/2016/02/Updated_The_PLA_s_New_Organizational_

Structure_-_What_is_Known__Unknown_and_Speculation_Parts_1_and_2.pdf
9 Ibid.

3. Can India Counter Emerging Chinese Capabilities like Stealth Aircraft?

1 Barrie, Douglas, International Institute for Strategic Studies, 02 February 2018, https://www.iiss.org/blogs/military-balance/2018/02/not-your-fathers-plaaf
2 Defence, Office of Secretary of, Military and Security Developments Involving the People's Republic of China 2016, Office of the Secretary of Defense, 2016.
3 Chan, Minnie, South China Morning Post, 19 October 2017, https://www.scmp.com/news/china/diplomacy-defence/article/2115968/xi-orders-massive-military-shake-meet-threats-worlds
4 Kokoshin, Andrei A., 2015 Military Reform in the People's Republic of China, Belfer Center for Science and International Affairs, 2016.
5 Joshi, Saurabh, StratPost, 30 October 2014, https://www.stratpost.com/iaf-fighter-strength-to-dip-further/
6 Bronk, Justin, 'Present and future challenges for the Indian Air Force', in Defence Primer 2017, by Sushant Singh and Pushan Das, *Observer Research Foundation*, 2017.
7 Gady, Franz-Stefan, the *Diplomat*, 02 October 2017, https://thediplomat.com/2017/10/chinas-first-5th-generation-fighter-jet-is-operational/

4. Sea Drones: Implications of the Great Underwater Wall of China

1 Barbara Starr and Ryan Browne, 'Pentagon Demands China Return US Underwater Drone', *CNN*, 17 December 2017, https://www.cnn.com/2016/12/16/politics/chinese-warship-underwater-drone-stolen/index.html
2 Missy Ryan and Dan Lamothe, 'Pentagon: Chinese Naval Ship Seized an Unmanned US Underwater Vehicle in South China Sea', *Washington Post*, 17 December 2016, https://www.washingtonpost.com/news/

checkpoint/wp/2016/12/16/defense-official-chinese-naval-ship-seized-an-unmanned-u-s-ocean-glider/?utm_term=.30a0b74c6cbc

3 'China Looks to Build Up Underwater Defences Following Seizure of US Drone', *South China Morning Post*, 1 January 2017, https://www.scmp.com/news/china/diplomacy-defence/article/2058156/china-looks-build-underwater-defences-following-seizure

4 Franz-Stefan Gady, 'China Scores Biggest Military Export Order for Killer Drones', the *Diplomat*, 2 March 2017, https://thediplomat.com/2017/03/china-scores-biggest-military-export-order-for-killer-drones/

5 Grant Turnbull, 'A New Era for Underwater Drones' Naval Technology', *Naval Technology*, 14 August 2013, http://www.naval-technology.com/features/feature-new-era-underwater-drones-unmanned-systems/

6 Jeffrey Lin and P.W. Singer, 'The Great Underwater Wall of Robots: Chinese Exhibit Shows Off Sea Drones,' *Popular Science*, 22 June 2016, http://www.popsci.com/great-underwater-wall-robots-chinese-exhibit-shows-off-sea-drones

7 Chase, Michael S., Gunness, Kristen A., Morris, Lyle J., Berkowitz, Samuel K. and Purser III, Benjamin S., 'Emerging Trends in China's Development of Unmanned Systems,' *Rand Report*, https://www.rand.org/content/dam/rand/pubs/research_reports/RR900/RR990/RAND_RR990.pdf

8 'PLA Navy Eyes China's Deep-Sea Underwater Glider After Successful Test Shows it Rivals US Vessels', *South China Morning Post*, 01 September 2017, https://www.scmp.com/news/china/article/2012137/pla-navy-eyes-chinas-deep-sea-underwater-glider-after-successful-test

9 Zachary Keck, 'China Tests New Unmanned Mini Sub', the *Diplomat*, 01 July 2014, https://thediplomat.com/2014/07/china-tests-new-unmanned-mini-sub/

10 Jeffrey Lin and P.W. Singer, 'These are China's New Underwater Drones', *Popular Science*, 22 June 2018, https://www.popsci.com/finding-qianlong-iii-chinas-new-underwater-drones

11 Abhijit Singh, 'Unmanned and Autonomous Vehicles and Future Maritime Operations in Littoral Asia', *ORF Special Report*, 28 July 2016, https://www.orfonline.org/research/unmanned-and-autonomous-vehicles-and-future-maritime-operations-in-littoral-asia/

12 Michael S. Chase, Kristen A. Gunness, Lyle J. Morris, Samuel K. Berkowitz and Benjamin S. Purser III, 'Emerging Trends in China's Development of Unmanned Systems', *Rand*, available at https://www.rand.org/content/dam/rand/pubs/research_reports/RR900/RR990/RAND_RR990.pdf

13 Zachary Keck, 'How the US Military Want to Unstealth Russian and Chinese Submarines', *National Interest*, 23 July 2017, https://nationalinterest.org/blog/the-buzz/how-the-us-military-wants-unstealth-russian-chinese-21618

14 Zachary Keck, 'America has a Plan to Find (and Kill) Russia and China's Most Deadly Submarines', *National Interest*, 15 August 2018, https://nationalinterest.org/blog/buzz/america-has-plan-find-and-kill-russia-and-chinas-most-deadly-submarines-28807

5. The Dragon Challenge: The Necessity for an Indian Space Deterrent Posture

1 Henry A. Kissinger, (ed.), *Problems of National Strategy: A Book of Readings*, New York, NY: Praeger, 1965, p. 4.

2 Richard K. Betts, 'Conventional Strategy: New Critics, Old Choices', *International Security*, Volume 7, Number 4, Spring 1983, p. 141.

3 Chandrashekhar, S., 'Space, War, and Deterrence: A Strategy for India', *Astropolitics*, Vol. 14, Nos. 2-3, 2016, p. 155, http://isssp.in/wp-content/uploads/2016/03/Space-War-and-Security-_A-Strategy-for-India.pdf

6. Should BRICS Rally Around China's Call for Cyber Sovereignty?

1 KPMG China, 'Overview of China's Cybersecurity Law', February 2017, last accessed 31 August 2018, https://assets.kpmg.com/content/dam/kpmg/cn/pdf/en/2017/02/overview-of-cybersecurity-law.pdf

2 'China releases first strategy on cyberspace cooperation', Xinhua, 01 March 2017, last accessed 31 August 2018, http://www.xinhuanet.com/english/2017-03/01/c_136094734.htm

3 NATO Cooperative Cyber Defence Centre of Excellence (CCDOE), '2015 UN GGE Report: Major Players Recommending Norms of

Behaviour, Highlighting Aspects of International Law', 31 August 2015, last accessed 31 August 2018, https://ccdcoe.org/2015-un-gge-report-major-players-recommending-norms-behaviour-highlighting-aspects-international-l-0.html

4 Katie Collins, 'UK surveillance law marks a "worse than scary" shift', *CNET*, 29 November 2016, last accessed 31 August 2018, https://www.cnet.com/news/snoopers-charter-investigatory-powers-bill-royal-assent-surveillance-uk/

5 'India Not Eager to Hop On to China's Cyber Sovereignty Bandwagon', *Indian Defence Update*, 8 March 2017, last accessed on 31 August 2018, http://defenceupdate.in/india-not-eager-to-hop-on-to-chinas-cyber-sovereignty-bandwagon/

6 Cheang Ming, 'China's Great Firewall is doubling up on VPN regulation', *CNBC*, 24 January 2017, last accessed 31 August 2018, https://www.cnbc.com/2017/01/24/chinas-great-firewall-is-doubling-up-on-vpn-regulation.html

7 Brian Fung, 'Computer security experts fear second wave of "biggest ransomware attack ever"', *Chicago Tribune*, 14 May 2017, last accessed 31 August 2018, http://www.chicagotribune.com/news/nationworld/ct-nsa-cyberattacks-20170513-story.html

7. Strategic Technology Might Disrupt India–China Status Quo

1 https://www.mea.gov.in/bilateral-documents.htm?dtl/27478/Agreed_Minutes_of_4th_IndiaChina_Strategic_Economic_Dialogue

8. China: A Threat to the Liberal Democratic Order?

1 Joseph S. Nye Jr., 'How Sharp Power Threatens Soft Power', *Foreign Affairs*, 24 January 2018, https://www.foreignaffairs.com/articles/china/2018-01-24/how-sharp-power-threatens-soft-power

2 Andrew J. Nathan, Andrew J., 'China's Challenge', *Journal of Democracy*, January 2015, https://www.journalofdemocracy.org/article/china%E2%80%99s-challenge

3 Thomas L. Friedman, *Hot, Flat, and Crowded: Why We Need a Green Revolution – and How It Can Renew America*, Picador: New York, 2008.

4 Robert Muggah and Taylor Owen, 'The global liberal democratic order might be down, but it's not out', *Globe and Mail*, 12 January 2018.

5 Christine Hackenesch, 'Not as bad as it seems: EU and US democracy promotion faces China in Africa', *Journal Democratization*, Vol. 22, Issue 3, 18 March 2015 <http://www.tandfonline.com/doi/full/10.1080/13510347.2014.1002476>

6 Ibid.

7 Maiko Ichihara, 'The Changing Role of Democracy in Asian Geopolitics', *Carnegie Endowment for International Peace*, 14 September 2017 https://carnegieendowment.org/files/RDN_Ichihara_FNL4WEB.PDF

8 'In South Asia, Chinese infrastructure brings debt and antagonism', *Economist*, 8 March 2018, https://www.economist.com/asia/2018/03/08/in-south-asia-chinese-infrastructure-brings-debt-and-antagonism

9 Sameer Arshad Khatlani, 'China's Rise has Consequences for Human Rights Beyond its Borders', *Indian Express*, 12 October 2017, https://indianexpress.com/article/opinion/chinas-rise-has-consequences-for-human-rights-beyond-its-borders-4885317/

10 For details, see Freedom in the world report, 'China: Taiwan Activist Jailed for Social Media Posts', *Freedom House*, 28 November 2017, https://freedomhouse.org/article/china-taiwan-activist-jailed-social-media-posts

9. China's Naval Power and National Prestige

1 David Tweed and Adrian Leung 'How China's Growing Naval Fleet Is Shaping Global Politics', *Bloomberg*, 1 June 2017, https://www.bloomberg.com/news/articles/2017-05-31/china-s-growing-naval-might-challenges-u-s-supremacy-in-asia [last accessed 7 January 2019]; 'East China Sea Tensions: Approaching A Slow Boil', *Asia Maritime Transparency Initiative,* 14 April 2016, https://amti.csis.org/east-china-sea-tensions/ [last accessed 7 April 2019]

2 Jesse Barker Gale and Andrew Shearer, 'The Quadrilateral Security Dialogue and the Maritime Silk Road Initiative', *The Center for Strategic and International Studies*, 2 April 2018 https://www.csis.org/analysis/quadrilateral-security-dialogue-and-maritime-silk-road-initiative/[last accessed 6 April 2019]

3 Bill Hayton, 'What does China really want in the South China Sea?', *Nikkei Asian Review*, 29 March 2017, https://asia.nikkei.com/Viewpoints/Bill-Hayton/What-does-China-really-want-in-the-South-China-Sea?n_cid=NARAN012 [last accessed 6 April 2019]

4 Jake Maxwell Watts, 'In China's Shadow, Communist Vietnam Links Arms With Old Enemy, the U.S.', *Wall Street Journal*, 2 March 2018, https://www.wsj.com/articles/in-chinas-shadow-communist-vietnam-links-arms-with-old-enemy-the-u-s-1519995603 [last accessed 6 April 2019]

5 Julian E. Barnes and Jeremy Page, 'U.S. Sends B-52s on Mission to Challenge Chinese Claims', *Wall Street Journal*, 27 November 2013, https://www.wsj.com/articles/us-flies-b52s-into-china8217s-new-air-defense-zone-1385483936/ [last accessed 6 April 2019]

6 'China's Military Strategy (2015)', *The State Council Information Office of the People's Republic of China*, May 2015, https://jamestown.org/wp-content/uploads/2016/07/China%E2%80%99s-Military-Strategy-2015.pdf [last accessed 5 April 2019]

7 Hannah Beech, 'Just Where Exactly Did China Get the South China Sea Nine-Dash Line From?' *Time*, 19 July 2016, http://time.com/4412191/nine-dash-line-9-south-china-sea/ [last accessed 5 April 2019]

8 'Playing Chicken in the East China Sea', *Asia Maritime Transparency Initiative*, 28 April 2017, https://amti.csis.org/playing-chicken-east-china-sea/ [last accessed 5 April 2019]

9 Ross, Robert, 'China's Naval Nationalism: Sources, Prospects, and the U.S. Response', *Quarterly Journal: International Security*, vol. 34. no. 2. (Fall 2009): 46-81.

10 Ibid

11 'China's New Spratly Island Defenses', *Asia Maritime Transparency Initiative*, 13 December 2016, https://amti.csis.org/chinas-new-spratly-island-defenses/ [last accessed 5 April 2019]; Tong, Linh, 'The Social Media 'War' Over the South China Sea', *The Diplomat*, 16 June 2016,

https://thediplomat.com/2016/07/the-social-media-war-over-the-south-china-sea/ [last accessed 5 April 2019]

12 'China condemns U.S. for South China Sea freedom of navigation operation', *Reuters*, 2 October 2018, https://uk.reuters.com/article/uk-usa-china-military/china-condemns-u-s-for-south-china-sea-freedom-of-navigation-operation-idUKKCN1MC04T/ [last accessed 5 April 2019]; Curtis Stone, 'US Navy's reckless operations in South China Sea will only hit a brick wall', *People's Daily Online*, 22 January 2018, http://en.people.cn/n3/2018/0122/c90000-9418218.html/ [last accessed 5 April 2019]

13 David Tweed, 'China Defense Spending Set to Rise 7.5% as Xi Builds Up Military', *Bloomberg*, 5 March 2019, https://www.bloomberg.com/news/articles/2019-03-05/china-s-military-spending-slows-as-economy-cools [last accessed 5 April 2019]; Ben Wescott, 'China's military is going from strength to strength under Xi Jinping', *CNN*, 5 March 2019, https://edition.cnn.com/2019/03/04/asia/china-military-xi-jinping-intl/index.html [last accessed 5 April 2019]

14 David Tweed and Adrian Leung, 'How China's Growing Naval Fleet Is Shaping Global Politics', *Bloomberg*, 1 June 2017, https://www.bloomberg.com/news/articles/2017-05-31/china-s-growing-naval-might-challenges-u-s-supremacy-in-asia [last accessed 7 January 2019]

10. From Silk Threads to Fiber Optics: The Rise of China's Digital Silk Road

1 'Vision and Actions on Jointly Building Silk Road Economic Belt and 21st Century Maritime Silk Road', National Development and Reform Commission (NDRC), Ministry of *Foreign Affairs*, and Ministry of Commerce, PRC, 28 March 2015, http://en.ndrc.gov.cn/newsrelease/201503/t20150330_669367.html

2 Central Government of the People's Republic of China, 'Outline of the Thirteenth Five-Year Plan for National Economic and Social Development of the People's Republic of China', *Xinhua News Agency*, 17 March 2016, http://www.gov.cn/xinwen/2016-03/17/content_5054992.htm

3 'Xi Jinping: To Build a 'Belt and Road' Space Information Corridor', *Networking Civil and Military Integration Magazine*, 11 July 2018, https://bit.ly/2UIFFnn
4 He Yini, 'Growth to be driven by powerful digital economy: Lu,' *China Daily*, 13 September 2015, http://www.chinadaily.com.cn/business/informationharbor/2015-09/13/content_21848853.htm
5 Hong Shen, 'Building a Digital Silk Road? Situating the Internet in China's Belt and Road Initiative', *International Journal of Communications*, Vol. 12, 2018, http://ijoc.org/index.php/ijoc/article/viewFile/8405/2386
6 R.J. Rapp, 'Cable Laying and Repair – Cable Ship Operations', *TE SubCom*, 23 October 2014, http://www.sargassoseacommission.org/storage/documents/Cable_Installation_and_Maintenance_-_TE_SubCom_Sargasso_Sea_Final1.pdf
7 Nadège Rolland, 'A Fiber Optic Silk Road', the *Diplomat*, 2 April 2015, https://thediplomat.com/2015/04/a-fiber-optic-silk-road/
8 Colby Smith, 'A digital silk road: BeiDou, China's rival to GPS goes global', *Economist*, 7 November 2017, http://www.theworldin.com/article/14433/edition2018digital-silk-road
9 Sarah Dai, 'China ramps up global coverage for domestic Beidou satellite navigation system as rival to GPS', *The South China Morning Post*, 28 December 2018, https://www.scmp.com/tech/big-tech/article/2179802/china-rolls-out-global-coverage-its-home-grown-beidou-satellite
10 Jordan Wilson, 'China's alternative to GPS and its implications for the United States', *US–China Economic and Security Review Commission*, 5 January 2017, https://bit.ly/2GbqyKR

PART 2: CHINA IN SOUTH ASIA

2. Friends with (Risky) Benefits

1 Michael D. Swaine, 'China and the AfPak Issue', *China Leadership Monitor*, Winter 2010, Issue 31, Hoover Institution, 2, http://carnegieendowment.org/files/CLM31MS.pdf
2 Andrew Small, 'China's Caution on Afghanistan-Pakistan', *Washington Quarterly*, July 2010, 33:3, p. 87,

https://csis-prod.s3.amazonaws.com/s3fs-public/legacy_files/files/publication/twq10julysmall.pdf

3 Lisa Curtis and Derek Scissors, 'The Limits of the Pakistan-China Alliance', *Reuters*, 20 January 2012, http://blogs.reuters.com/india-expertzone/2012/01/20/the-limits-of-the-pakistan-china-alliance/

4 PTI, 'Pak army chief on 1st visit to China, meets top leaders', *Times of India*, 16 March 2017, https://timesofindia.indiatimes.com/world/china/pak-army-chief-on-1st-visit-to-china-meets-top-leaders/articleshow/57674964.cms

3. China's Surreptitious Advance in Afghanistan: A Multi-Dimensional Move

1 Ben Blanchard, 'China formally opens first overseas military base in Djibouti', *Reuters*, 1 August 2017, https://www.reuters.com/article/us-china-djibouti/china-formally-opens-first-overseas-military-base-in-djibouti-idUSKBN1AH3E3 [accessed 7 October 2018].

2 Michael Martina, 'Afghan troops to train in China, ambassador says', *Reuters*, 6 September 2018, https://in.reuters.com/article/china-afghanistan/afghan-troops-to-train-in-china-ambassador-says-idINKCN1LM1N1> [accessed 7 October 2018].

3 Minnie Chan, 'China is helping Afghanistan set up mountain brigade to fight terrorism', *South China Morning Post*, 28 August 2018, https://www.scmp.com/news/china/diplomacy-defence/article/2161745/china-building-training-camp-afghanistan-fight [accessed 7 October 2018].

4 'Rivals for Authority in Tajikistan's Gorno-Badakhshan', *International Crisis Group*, 14 March 2018, https://www.crisisgroup.org/europe-central-asia/central-asia/tajikistan/b87-rivals-authority-tajikistans-gorno-badakhshan

5 'China and Pakistan decide to extend CPEC towards Afghanistan', the *Economic Times*, 10 September 2018, <https://economictimes.indiatimes.com/news/defence/china-and-pakistan-decide-to-extend-cpec-towards-afghanistan/articleshow/65754550.cms> [accessed 07 October 2018].

6 Chan, Minnie, 'China is helping Afghanistan set up mountain brigade to fight terrorism', *South China Morning Post*, 28 August 2018, <https://

www.scmp.com/news/china/diplomacy-defence/article/2161745/china-building-training-camp-afghanistan-fight> [accessed 07 October 2018].

7 Tanha, Gul Mohammad, 'China promises $90m in aid to Badakhshan', *Pajhwok Afghan News*, 10 September 2017, <https://www.pajhwok.com/en/2017/09/10/china-promises-90m-aid-badakhshan> [accessed 07 October 2018].

8 Patranobis, Sutirtho, 'Afghanistan disappointed by scale of China-India infrastructure project in country', *Hindustan Times*, 12 September 2018, <https://www.hindustantimes.com/world-news/afghanistan-says-disappointed-by-scale-of-china-india-infrastructure-project-in-country/story-KsTLZILbprFX48AcrIBRXP.html> (accessed 07 October 2018).

9 Putz, Catherine, 'Carefully, Kazakhstan Confronts China About Kazakhs in Xinjiang Re-Education Camps', the *Diplomat*, 14 June 2018, <https://thediplomat.com/2018/06/carefully-kazakhstan-confronts-china-about-kazakhs-in-xinjiang-re-education-camps/> [accessed 07 October 2018]

4. Decoding the China–Bangladesh Relationship

1 Alden, Robert 'China's First U.N. Veto Bars Bangladesh', the *New York Times*, 26 August 1972, <https://www.nytimes.com/1972/08/26/archives/chinas-first-un-veto-bars-bangladesh-soviet-union-and-india-are.html>

2 'China, Bangladesh lift ties to strategic partnership of cooperation', the *Global Times*, 15 October 2016, <http://www.globaltimes.cn/content/1011533.shtml>

3 Shamrat, Abu Sufian and Ali, Mohammed Kashem, 'China's Strategic Partnership with Bangladesh in 21st Century', the *South Asia Monitor*, 2 April 2018, <http://southasiajournal.net/chinas-strategic-partnership-with-bangladesh-in-21st-century/>

4 Chowdhury, Iftekhar Ahmed, 'Bangladesh-China: An Emerging Equation in Asian *Diplomat*ic Calculations', *ISAS Working Paper*, No. 105, National University of Singapore, 30 March 2010, <https://www.isas.nus.edu.sg/wp-content/uploads/media/isas_papers/ISAS_Working_Paper_105.pdf>

5 Observations made by a retired Bangladesh Air Force officer during an interaction with the author.

6 'Bangladesh China Trade and Economic Relations', *Embassy of Bangladesh Beijing* website access on 21 September 2017, <https://www.bdembassybeijing.org/bangladesh-china-trade-and-economic-relationship/>

7 Paul, Ruma and Blanchard, Ben, 'China to Give Bangladesh $24 Billion in Loans After India Gives $2 Billion', the *Wire*, 14 October 2016, <https://thewire.in/world/china-bangladesh-loan>

8 'Foreign secretary in Delhi: Bangladesh supports China's One-Belt-One Road', *Dhaka Tribune*, 7 October 2017, <https://www.dhakatribune.com/bangladesh/foreign-affairs/2017/10/07/foreign-secretary-bangladesh-supports-chinas-one-belt-one-road/>

9 'India Shouldn't Worry About China-Bangladesh Ties, says Sheikh Hasina', *NDTV.Com*, 21 February 2018, <https://www.ndtv.com/india-news/india-shouldnt-worry-about-china-bangladesh-ties-says-prime-minister-sheikh-hasina-1815352>

10 Shepard, Wade, 'Bangladesh's Deep Sea Port Problem', the *Diplomat*, 7 June 2016, <https://thediplomat.com/2016/06/bangladeshs-deep-sea-port-problem/>

5. India Faces the China Wall in Its NSG Drive

1 Rajagopalan, Rajeswari Pillai and Biswas, Arka, *Locating India Within the Global Non-Proliferation Architecture: Prospects, Challenges and Opportunities*, New Delhi: *Observer Research Foundation*, 2016.

2 Aneja, Atul and Haidar, Suhasini, 'India's bid to enter NSG not on Seoul conference agenda, says China', the *Hindu*, 20 June 2016, <https://www.thehindu.com/news/national/India%E2%80%99s-bid-to-enter-NSG-not-on-Seoul-conference-agenda-says-China/article14433939.ece>

3 Xingchun, Long, 'China no barrier to India's NSG membership', *Global Times*, 20 June 2016, <http://www.globaltimes.cn/content/989513.shtml>

4 'Delhi's NSG bid upset by rules, not Beijing,' *Global Times*, 28 June 2016, <http://www.globaltimes.cn/content/990889.shtml>

5 Roche, Elizabeth, 'NSG membership: India, China hold "pragmatic" talks', *Live Mint*, 13 September 2016, <https://www.livemint.com/Politics/9n7NEHaCMVqdQFMIBoqexJ/NSG-membership-India-

China-hold-pragmatic-talks.html>; 'India, China hold talks on NSG again', the *Tribune*, 31 October 2016, <https://www.tribuneindia.com/news/nation/india-china-hold-talks-on-nsg-again/317188.html>

6. Doklam Impasse: Why Confrontation with the PRC Matters

1 See Powell, Robert, 'Absolute and Relative Gains in International Relations Theory', *American Political Science Review*, 1991, Vol. 85, Issue 4, pp. 1304-1306.

2 Passi, Ritika. 'China's BRI forum: Pursuing Change from Within', Web Commentary, *Observer Research Foundation*, 3 May 2017, <https://www.orfonline.org/expert-speak/china-bri-forum-pursuing-change/>

3 Singh, Zorawar Daulet, 'Game of Chicken in High Himalayas', *The Hindu*, 13 July 2017, <https://www.thehindu.com/opinion/lead/game-of-chicken-in-the-high-himalayas/article19265421.ece>

4 Jacob, Jayanth, 'At the heart of Doklam Standoff is China's attempts to drive a wedge into Indo-Bhutan ties', 5 August 2017, <https://www.hindustantimes.com/india-news/analysis-at-the-heart-of-doklam-standoff-is-china-s-attempts-to-drive-wedge-into-indo-bhutan-ties/story-EZnbh5GoNhnIdMCtDX6yaJ.html>

5 Mercer, Jonathan, *Reputation and International Politics*, Ithaca: Cornell University Press, 1996.

6 Ibid.

7. The Sobering Arithmetic of a Two-Front War

1 Gurung, Shaurya Karanbir, 'India must be prepared for two-front war: Army chief General Bipin Rawat', *Economic Times*, 06 September 2017, <https://economictimes.indiatimes.com/news/defence/india-must-be-prepared-for-two-front-war-army-chief-bipin-rawat/articleshow/60396549.cms>

2 Chhina, Man Aman Singh, 'Two-front war not a good idea, says top general,' the *Indian Express*, 01 March 2018, <http://indianexpress.com/article/india/two-front-war-not-a-good-idea-says-top-general-5082346/>

3 Lendon, Brad, 'China boosts military spending 8% amidst ambitious modernization drive,' *CNN*, 06 March 2018, <https://edition.cnn.com/2018/03/04/asia/chinese-military-budget-intl/index.html>

4 'The Military Balance,' International Institute for Strategic Studies, accessed 16 March 2018, <https://www.iiss.org/en/publications/military-s-balance>

5 Sawhney, Pravin and Wahab, Ghazala, *Dragon on Our Doorstep: Managing China Through Military Power*, New Delhi: Aleph, 2017, p.p. 114-129.

6 Ladwig III, Walter C., 'Indian Military Modernization and Conventional Deterrence in South Asia', *Journal of Strategic Studies*, Vol. 38, No. 5, 2015, p.p. 729-72.

7 Mason, Shane, *Military Budgets in India and Pakistan: Trajectories, Priorities, Risks*, Washington DC: Stimson Center, 2016, Vol. 19, <https://www.stimson.org/sites/default/files/file-attachments/Military-Budgets-India-Pakistan-Trajectories-Priorities-Risks-Oct2016.pdf.pdf>

8 'Futuristic combat vehicle plan a game changer: Army', the *Hindu*, 15 November 2017, <http://www.thehindu.com/news/national/futuristic-combat-vehicle-plan-a-game-changer-army/article20460822.ece>

9 Kamphausen, Roy and Lai, David (editors), *The Chinese People's Liberation Army in 2025*, Carlisle Barracks, PA: US Army War College, 2015, <https://fas.org/nuke/guide/china/pla-2025.pdf>

10 Cordesman, Anthony H., (with the assistance of Joseph Kendall), *The PLA Rocket Force: Evolving Beyond the Second Artillery Corps (SAC) and Nuclear Dimension*, Washington, DC: Center for Strategic and International Studies, 11 October 2016, p. 3, <https://csis-prod.s3.amazonaws.com/s3fs-public/publication/161013_China_Missile_Forces_AHC.pdf>

11 Mohan, Vijay, '4 new mechanised battalions for Army', *Tribune*, 11 January 2017, <http://www.tribuneindia.com/news/nation/4-new-mechanised-battalions-for-army/349271.html>

12 Singh, Sushant, 'New report on IAF: it can't protect north-eastern and western frontiers simultaneously', the *Indian Express*, 28 March 2016, <http://indianexpress.com/article/explained/new-report-on-iaf-it-cant-protect-eastern-and-western-frontiers-simultaneously/>

8. The Future Trajectory of Sino–Indian Water Relations

1 Ministry of External Affairs, India, 'Starred Question No. 278 Hydrological Data of Brahmaputra and Satluj', *Lok Sabha*, 14 March 2018, <http://www.mea.gov.in/lok-sabha.htm?dtl/29613/question+no278+hydrological+data+of+brahmaputra+and+satluj+rivers>

2 Chen, Stephen, 'Chinese engineers plan 1,000km tunnel to make Xinjiang desert bloom', *South China Morning Post*, 29 October 2017, International Edition, <https://www.scmp.com/news/china/society/article/2116750/chinese-engineers-plan-1000km-tunnel-make-xinjiang-desert-bloom>

3 'PRESS RELEASE: 11th meeting of India-China Expert Level Mechanism (ELM) on Trans-border Rivers', *Embassy of India, Beijing*, 27 March 2018, <http://indianembassybeijing.in/trans-border-river.php>

4 'India-China Cooperation', *Ministry of Water Resources, River Development and Ganga Rejuvenation, International Cooperation, Government of India*, <http://mowr.gov.in/international-cooperation/bilateral-cooperation-with-neighbouring-countries/india-china-cooperation>

5 Samaranayake, Nilanthi, Limaye, Satu and Wuthnow, Joel, 'Water Resource Competition in the Brahmaputra River Basin', *Andrew S. Erickson*, Arlington, VA: CNA , 06 May 2016, <http://www.andrewerickson.com/2016/05/water-resource-competition-in-the-brahmaputra-river-basin-china-india-and-bangladesh/>

6 'Brief on India-China Trade and Economic Relations', *Embassy of India, Beijing*, 2016, <http://indianembassybeijing.in/economic-and-trade-relation.php>

7 Press Trust of India, 'India, China to resume military exercise; Antony to visit China', *India Today*, 04 September 2012, <https://www.indiatoday.in/india/north/story/india-china-to-resume-military-exercise-antony-to-visit-china-115162-2012-09-04>

8 Joshi, Manoj, 'Debsang Incursion: Decoding the Chinese Signal', *Observer Research Foundation*, Commentaries, 14 May 2013, <https://

www.orfonline.org/research/depsang-incursion-decoding-the-chinese-signal/>

9 'Memorandum of Understanding between the Ministry of Water Resources, the Republic of India and the Ministry of Water Resources, the People's Republic of China on Strengthening Cooperation on Trans-border Rivers', *Ministry of External Affairs, India*, Media Centre, 23 October 2013.

10 'India-China Cooperation', *Ministry of Water Resources River Development and Ganga Rejuvenation, International Cooperation, Government of India*, <http://mowr.gov.in/international-cooperation/bilateral-cooperation-with-neighbouring-countries/india-china-cooperation>

11 Kishor, Nanda M.S., 'Political Regimes and Water Sharing Disputes Between India and Bangladesh', *Himalayan and Central Asian Studies*, Vol. 19, Issue nos. 1-2, 2015, p.p. 197-210, <http://eprints.manipal.edu/146775/1/NK-Political%20regimes%20and%20water%20sharing%20disputes%20between%20India%20and%20Bangladesh.pdf>

12 Hill, Douglas, 'The Indus Basin: the potential for basin-wide management between India and Pakistan', *Imagining Industan – Overcoming Water Insecurity in the Indus Basin*, Switzerland: Springer International Publishing, 2017, p.p. 141-158, https://www.springer.com/in/book/9783319328430; Koh, Tommy and Duy, Phan Hao, 'The Asian way to settle disputes', *Asia-Pacific Journal of Ocean Law and Policy*, Vol. 1, Issue 1, 03 June 2016, p.p. 5-10, <https://brill.com/abstract/journals/apoc/1/1/article-p5_2.xml>

13 Freeman, Carla P., 'Dam diplomacy? China's new neighbourhood policy and Chinese dam-building companies', *Water International*, Vol. 42, Issue no. 2, 18 January 2017, p.p. 187-206, <https://www.tandfonline.com/doi/abs/10.1080/02508060.2017.1276040>

14 Biba, Sebastian, 'China's "old" and "new" Mekong River politics: the Lancang-Mekong Cooperation from a comparative benefit-sharing perspective,' *Water International*, Vol. 43(2), June 2018, p.p. 1-20.

15 Yasuda, Yumiko, et al, 'Transboundary Water Cooperation over the Brahmaputra River: Legal Political Economy Analysis of Current and Future Potential Cooperation', *The Hague Institute for Global Justice*, August 2017, p.p. 75-8, <http://www.thehagueinstituteforglobaljustice.org/wp-content/uploads/2017/08/WADI-Brahmaputra-basin-report-final_design.pdf>

16 Makhdoom, Atif Shan, Shah, Aisha Bashir and Sami, Kiran, 'Pakistan on the Roadway to Socio-Economic Development: A Comprehensive Study of China Pakistan Economic Corridor (CPEC)', the *Government-Annual Research Journal of Political Science*, Vol. 6(6), 2018.

17 Baruah, Darshana M., 'South China Sea: Beijing's "Salami-Slicing" Strategy', the *South China Sea Disputes: Flashpoints, Turning Points and Trajectories*, 21 March 2014, p.p. 255-8, <https://www.offiziere.ch/wp-content/uploads-001/2015/02/RSIS0542014.pdf>

18 Singh, Chhatrapati, 'Water Rights Principles of Water Resources Management', *Indian Law Institute, New Delhi*, 1991.

19 Chellaney, Brahma, 'Rising Powers, Rising Tensions: The Troubled China-India Relationship', *SAIS Review of International Affairs*, Vol. 32(2), 2012, p.p. 99-108.

9. 'Weather War': The Latest Addition to the Sino–India Conundrum?

1 Coonan, Clifford, 'How Beijing used rockets to keep opening ceremony dry', *Independent*, Sports section, UK edition, 11 August 2008, <https://www.independent.co.uk/sport/olympics/how-beijing-used-rockets-to-keep-opening-ceremony-dry-890294.html>

2 Dockrill, Peter, 'China is attempting the largest artificial rain experiment in history, over an area 3 times the size of Spain', *Business Insider*, 02 May 2018, <https://www.businessinsider.com/china-is-attempting-the-largest-artificial-rain-experiment-in-history-2018-5?IR=T>

3 Lovelle, Madeleine, 'Tibet: A Major Source of Asia's Rivers', *Future Directions*, 04 February 2016, <http://www.futuredirections.org.au/publication/tibet-a-major-source-of-asias-rivers/>

4 Ibid.

5 'Could Tibetan clouds save China from drought?' the *Economist*, Print edition, China, 05 April 2018, <https://www.economist.com/china/2018/04/05/could-tibetan-clouds-save-china-from-drought>

6 Hongqiao, Liu, 'China's bottled water industry eyes up the Tibetan plateau', the *Guardian*, 16 November 2015, <https://www.theguardian.com/sustainable-business/2015/nov/16/chinas-bottled-water-industry-eyes-up-the-tibetan-plateau>

7 Parashar, Utpal, 'Arunachal Pradesh, Assam on alert as China's Tsangpo river swells after heavy rainfall', *Hindustan Times*, 31 August 2018, <https://www.hindustantimes.com/india-news/arunachal-pradesh-on-alert-as-tsangpo-river-swells-after-heavy-rainfall-in-china/story-CWVgkCUK0krUt0GeejD1zK.html>

8 Purkayastha, Debasree, 'Understanding the Brahmaputra and the annual flooding in Assam', the *Hindu*, 27 November 2017, <https://www.thehindu.com/news/national/other-states/in-the-hands-of-the-brahmaputra-understanding-the-annual-flooding-in-assam/article20948196.ece>

9 Ibid.

10 Roy, Aparna, 'Don't rely on China for data on the Brahmaputra', *Hindustan Times*, 17 May 2018, <https://www.hindustantimes.com/analysis/don-t-rely-on-china-for-data-on-the-brahmaputra/story-2qOtRhfI1JM7hK70tOqjYN.html>

11 Ibid.

12 Prosser, Marc, 'China Plans to Bring Artificial Rain to Area Three Times the Size of Spain,' *Singularity Hub*, 24 April 2018, <https://singularityhub.com/2018/04/24/china-plans-to-bring-artificial-rain-to-area-three-times-the-size-of-spain/#sm.00000z8yisyra1dn2yji2y4ym8d56>

13 Schlanger, Zoë, 'China is engineering the biggest project yet to force rainfall,' *Quartz*, 30 March 2018, <https://qz.com/1241066/china-is-engineering-the-biggest-project-yet-to-force-rainfall/>

14 Wyoming Weather Modification Pilot Project, <http://www.ral.ucar.edu/projects/wyoming/faq.php>

15 Boyd, Olivia, 'Risky geoengineering a climate panacea?' *India Climate Dialogue*, 29 March 2016, <http://indiaclimatedialogue.net/2016/03/29/risky-geoengineering-climate-panacea/>

16 Lele, Ajey, 'China's Experiments with Weather Modification: A Cause for Concern', *Institute for Defence Studies and Analyses*, 12 October 2009, <https://idsa.in/idsastrategiccomments/ChinasExperimentswithWeatherModification_ALele_121009>

17 Pathak, Sriparna, 'Adding artificial rain to the Sino-Indian conundrum', *Asia Times*, 10 April 2018, <

18 Talukdar, Sreemoy, 'Tunnel or not, China is using water as a strategic weapon; India may stay indifferent at its own peril', *Firstpost*, 31 October

2017, <https://www.firstpost.com/india/tunnel-or-not-china-is-using-water-as-a-strategic-weapon-india-may-stay-indifferent-at-its-own-peril-4186087.html>

10. Indian Media and China: Changing Discourse

1 Haksar, P.N. in Guruswamy, Mohan and Singh, Zorawar Daulet, *India China Relations: The Border Issue and Beyond*, New Delhi: Viva Books, 2009, p. 115.
2 Ibid. p. 123.

PART 3: CHINA AND THE WORLD

1. The State of Play in Sino–Japanese Relations

1 Madoko Fukuda, 'Japan's Koizumi years, a time of lost opportunities', East Asia Forum, Canberra, 14 October 2015, http://www.eastasiaforum.org/2015/10/14/japans-koizumi-years-a-time-of-lost-opportunities/
2 'Japan-China Joint Press statement', *Ministry of Foreign Affairs, Japan*, Beijing, 8 October 2006, https://www.mofa.go.jp/region/asia-paci/china/joint0610.html
3 'Abe visits Yasukuni, angering Beijing and Seoul', *Japan Times*, 26 December 2013, https://www.japantimes.co.jp/news/2013/12/26/national/abes-surprise-visit-to-yasukuni-sparks-criticism/
4 See for example the Keynote address by Prime Minister Shinzo Abe at the Shangri La Dialogue, 'Peace and prosperity in Asia forevermore', *Ministry of Foreign Affairs, Japan*, 30 May 2014, https://www.mofa.go.jp/fp/nsp/page18e_000087.html
5 Policy speech by Prime Minister Shinzo Abe at the 196th session of the Diet, *Ministry of Foreign Affairs, Japan*, 22 January 2018, https://japan.kantei.go.jp/98_abe/statement/201801/_00002.html
6 'China-Japan hold 4th high-level economic dialogue', Xinhua Net, 16 April 2018, http://www.xinhuanet.com/english/2018-04/16/c_137115137.htm

7 Daisuke Nishimura and Naoyuki Fukuda, 'Chinese Premier seeks to reset bilateral ties in 1st visit to Japan', *Asahi Shimbun*, 8 May 2018, http://www.asahi.com/ajw/articles/AJ201805080045.html

2. Europe and China: Dependent but Ungrateful?

1 'Berlin calls for a One-Europe-Policy', German-Foreign-Policy.com, 9 November 2017, https://www.german-foreign-policy.com/en/news/detail/7382/

2 AFP, 'Mercedes Benz Owner Daimler issues second apology to China over Dalai Lama Post– China Media', Hong Kong Free Press (HKFP), 2 November 2018, https://www.hongkongfp.com/2018/02/08/mercedes-benz-owner-daimler-issues-second-apology-china-dalai-lama-post-china-media/

3 Thorsten Benner, et al, 'Authoritarian Advance: Responding to China's growing political influence in Europe', GPPi and Merics, 5 February 2018, http://www.gppi.net/publications/rising-powers/article/authoritarian-advance-responding-to-chinas-growing-political-influence-in-europe/

4 Yu Ning, 'Misguided Academics promote China-EU Confrontation', Global Times, 5 February 2018, http://www.globaltimes.cn/content/1088346.shtml

5 Matthias Müller and Nina Belz, 'Wie China seinen Einfluss in Europa ausbaut', *Neue Zeue Zt Zeitung*, 5 February 2018, https://www.nzz.ch/international/wie-china-seinen-einfluss-in-europa-ausbaut-ld.1354221

6 John Kampfner, 'Adults in the Room. My Battle with Europe's Deep Establishment by Yanis Varoufakis –Review', Guardian, 15 May 2017, https://www.theguardian.com/books/2017/may/15/adults-in-room-battle-europes-deep-establishment-yanis-varoufakis-review

7 'Juncker announced Strategy for successful Accession of Serbia and Montenegro to the EU', European Western Balkans, 14 September 2017, https://europeanwesternbalkans.com/2017/09/14/juncker-announced-strategy-successful-accession-serbia-montenegro-eu/

8 Zoltan Simon, 'Orban says he seeks to end Liberal Democracy in Hungary', *Bloomberg*, 28 July 2014, https://www.bloomberg.com/news/

articles/2014-07-28/orban-says-he-seeks-to-end-liberal-democracy-in-hungary

9 Francois Godement and Abigaël Vasselier, 'China at the gates: A new power audit of EU-China relations', European Council on Foreign Relations, 01 December 2017, https://www.ecfr.eu/publications/summary/china_eu_power_audit7242

10 'Chinesische Unternehmenskäufe in Europa, Eine Analyse von M&A Deals 2006-2017', Ernst and Young, July 2017, https://go.ey.com/2GyKlV5

11 François Godement, 'Dancing with the Bear: Macron in China', European Council on Foreign Relations, 12 January 2018, https://www.ecfr.eu/article/commentary_dancing_with_the_bear_macron_in_china

12 Volker Stanzel, 'Machtverschiedung in Ostasien. Chinas Welt und Europas Platz darin', OAG Notizen, June 2017, http://oag.jp/img/2017/06/1706_China_Europa.pdf

13 Charlotte Gao, 'Liu Xiaobos Death breathes Life into China-Norway Trade Talks', *Diplomat*, 28 August 2017, https://thediplomat.com/2017/08/liu-xiaobos-death-breathes-life-into-china-norway-trade-talks/

3. China's Rapid Growth in Africa: Lessons for India

1 Malancha Chakrabarty, 'Ethiopia-China Economic Relations: A Classic Win-Win Situation?' World Review of Political Economy, Vol 7, Issue 2 (Summer 2016): 226

2 Ibid.

3 Malancha Chakrabarty, 'Growth of Chinese trade and investment flows in DR Congo – blessing or curse?', *Review of African Political Economy*, Vol. 43, Issue 147, 2016: p. 116, http://bit.ly/2IN8wAo

4 'World Investment Report 2016', United Nations Conference on Trade and Development, 2016, https://unctad.org/en/pages/publicationwebflyer.aspx?publicationid=1555

5 Malancha Chakrabarty, 'Indian Investments in Africa: Scale, Trends, and Policy Recommendations', ORF Occasional Paper, 142, 7 February 2018, https://www.orfonline.org/research/indian-investments-in-africa-scale-trends-and-policy-recommendations/

4. Taiwan Faces PRC's Increased Pressure Tactics, More Countries Cut Ties with the Island

1 Elida Moreno and Philip Wen, 'Panama establishes ties with China, ditches Taiwan in win for Beijing', *Reuters*, 13 June 2017, https://www.reuters.com/article/us-panama-china/panama-establishes-ties-with-china-ditches-taiwan-in-win-for-beijing-idUSKBN194054

2 Ibid.

3 Yu-Shan Wu, 'Heading Towards Troubled Waters? The Impact of Taiwan's 2016 Elections on Cross-Strait Relations', *American Journal of Chinese Studies*, Vol. 23 (1), April 2016, p.p. 59—75.

5. Great Power Politics and the Tragedy of OBOR

1 Mukul Sanwal, 'China's One-Road-One Belt Initiative: A New Model of Global Governance', *Institute for Defence Studies and Analysis*, 29 September 2016, https://idsa.in/idsacomments/china-one-road-one-belt-initiative_msanwal_290916

2 Ibid.

3 'China's Belt and Road plan a bid to build new world order,' *Straits Times*, 20 May 2017, https://www.straitstimes.com/asia/chinas-belt-and-road-plan-a-bid-to-build-new-world-order

4 Katherine Morton, 'China's ambition in the South China Sea: is a legitimate maritime order possible?' *International Affairs*, Volume 92(4), 1 July 2016, https://doi.org/10.1111/1468-2346.12658

5 John J. Mearsheimer, *Tragedy of Great Power Politics*, New York: W.W. Norton and Company, 7 April 2014.

6 Ibid.

7 Ibid.

8 Ibid.

9 The Marshall Plan (European Recovery Program) was an American initiative to aid Western European economies rebuild after World War II by the United States. It gave over US$12 billion in economic assistance over a period of four years beginning on 03 April 1948. https://www.foreignaffairs.com/reviews/review-essay/2018-06-14/divide-and-invest

10 Ibid.
11 Ibid.
12 Ibid.
13 'The Geopolitics of the United States, Part 1: The Inevitable Empire', *Stratfor*, 4 July 2016, https://worldview.stratfor.com/article/geopolitics-united-states-part-1-inevitable-empire
14 'China is likely to set up military base in Pakistan: Pentagon', *Indian Express*, 07 June 2017, https://indianexpress.com/article/world/china-is-likely-to-set-up-military-base-in-pakistan-pentagon-4692850/
15 Ibid.
16 Ibid.
17 Damen Cook, 'China's Most Important South China Sea Military Base', *Diplomat*, 9 March 2017, https://thediplomat.com/2017/03/chinas-most-important-south-china-sea-military-base/
18 Ibid.
19 James Kynge, Chris Campbell, Amy Kazmin and Farhan Bokhari, 'Beijing's global power play: How China rules the waves', *Financial Times*, 12 January 2017, https://ig.ft.com/sites/china-ports/
20 Kyle Mizokami, 'Why the Chinese military is only a paper dragon', Week, 24 September 2014, http://theweek.com/articles/445300/why-chinese-military-only-paper-dragon
21 Kenneth Morgan, 'Symbiosis: Trade and the British Empire', BBC, 17 February 2011, http://www.bbc.co.uk/history/british/empire_seapower/trade_empire_01.shtml
22 Dave Majumdar, 'China's Aircraft Carrier: The Ultimate Weapon or Paper Tiger?' *National Interest*, 27 December 2016, https://nationalinterest.org/blog/the-buzz/chinas-aircraft-carrier-the-ultimate-weapon-or-paper-tiger-18866
23 Roberto Roccu, 'Gramsci in Cairo: Neoliberal Authoritarianism, Passive Revolution and Failed Hegemony in Egypt under Mubarak, 1991-2010', PhD diss., *London School of Economics and Political Science*, p. 45, https://core.ac.uk/download/pdf/5890874.pdf
24 Ibid.
25 Ibid.
26 Ibid.
27 Ibid.
28 Ibid.

29 Alex Merker, 'The Rise of Russia's Cold-Water Ports', the Compass, Vol. 1(4), Article 5, 2017, https://scholarworks.arcadia.edu/thecompass/vol1/iss4/5
30 Ibid.
31 'The Russian Quest for Warm Water Ports', *GlobalSecurity.org*, https://www.globalsecurity.org/military/world/russia/warm-water-port.htm
32 Ibid.
33 Lavina Lee, 'Reviving the Quad: Japan, India, the U.S., and Australia', *Real Clear Defense*, 16 February 2017, http://bit.ly/2ve21yN
34 Ibid.
35 'US revives two infrastructure projects in Asia to counter China's OBOR', *Times of India*, 24 May 2017, https://timesofindia.indiatimes.com/world/us/us-revives-two-infrastructure-projects-in-asia-to-counter-chinas-obor/articleshow/58821188.cms
36 Dipanjan Roy Chaudhury, 'Pushing back against China's One Belt One Road, India, Japan build strategic "Great Wall"', *Economic Times*, 16 May 2017, http://bit.ly/2ZrqtdG
37 Ibid.

6. One Belt, One Road, and Now, One Circle

1 The study, released earlier this year, cites insufficient transport volume to cover maintenance costs for the moment. The project has been put on hold, but Finland remains keen.
2 Tom Embury-Dennis, 'Container ship crosses Arctic route for first time in history due to melting sea ice, Independent, 18 September 2018, https://www.independent.co.uk/news/world/europe/maersk-container-ship-arctic-ocean-northern-sea-route-venta-global-warming-a8543431.html
3 'China's Arctic Policy', *State Council Information Office of the People's Republic of China*, 26 January 2018, http://english.gov.cn/archive/white_paper/2018/01/26/content_281476026660336.htm
4 'How much trade transits the South China Sea?' *CSIS China Power Project*, https://chinapower.csis.org/much-trade-transits-south-china-sea/

5 Carsten Ørts Hansen, Peter Grønsedt, Christian Graversen, and Christian Lindstrømand Hendriksen, 'Arctic Shipping – Commercial Opportunities and Challenges', *CBS Maritime*, January 2016, http://bit.ly/2W7727O

6 Virginia Marantidou, 'Shipping Finance: China's New Tool in Becoming a Global Maritime Power', *Jamestown Foundation*, China Brief, Issue 18(2), 13 February 2018, https://jamestown.org/program/shipping-finance-chinas-new-tool-becoming-global-maritime-power/

7 Ibid.

8 Liu Zhen, 'China reveals "Polar Silk Road" ambition in Arctic policy white paper', *South China Morning Post*, 26 January 2018, http://bit.ly/2UMtYwQ

9 'China's Arctic Policy', *State Council Information Office of the People's Republic of China*, 26 January 2018, http://english.gov.cn/archive/white_paper/2018/01/26/content_281476026660336.htm

10 Emily Feng, Alice Woodhouse and Richard Milne, 'China reveals Arctic ambitions with plan for "Polar Silk Road"', *Financial Times*, 26 January 2018, https://www.ft.com/content/c7bd5258-0293-11e8-9650-9c0ad2d7c5b5

11 Ryan Kilpatrick, 'China's Plan for the Arctic – And a Shipping Centre to Rival Singapore', *South China Morning Post*, 15 November 2016, https://www.scmp.com/week-asia/business/article/2046117/chinas-plan-arctic-and-shipping-centre-rival-singapore

12 The first shipment occurred in December 2016, marking the start of commercial operations.

13 Malte Humpert, 'Russia's Northern Sea Route sees record cargo volume in 2018', Arctic Today, 20 February 2019, https://www.arctictoday.com/russias-northern-sea-route-sees-record-cargo-volume-in-2018/

14 'First China-Finland train connection launched', *China Daily*, 11 November 2017, http://www.chinadaily.com.cn/world/2017-11/11/content_34404277.htm

15 Ma Chi, 'China's first home-built icebreaker named Snow Dragon 2', *Telegraph*, 09 October 2017, https://www.telegraph.co.uk/news/world/china-watch/technology/chinese-icebreaker/

16 *Bloomberg*, 'China mulls joining scheme to lay telecom cable across Arctic Circle', *South China Morning Post*, 14 December 2017, https://

www.scmp.com/news/china/diplomacy-defence/article/2124239/china-mulls-joining-scheme-lay-telecom-cable-across

17 AP, 'Alaska signs deal to advance gas pipeline with help from China', *Economic Times*, 9 November 2017, https://energy.economictimes.indiatimes.com/news/oil-and-gas/alaska-signs-deal-to-advance-gas-pipeline-with-help-from-china/61573019

18 'China's Arctic Policy', *State Council Information Office of the People's Republic of China*, 26 January 2018, http://english.gov.cn/archive/white_paper/2018/01/26/content_281476026660336.htm

19 Podcast: 'The Polar Silk Road: China's Arctic Ambitions', *Wilson Center*, 6 February 2018, https://www.wilsoncenter.org/event/the-polar-silk-road-chinas-arctic-ambitions

20 Menezes, Dwayne Ryan, 'World Economic Forum Launches Arctic Investment Protocol (January 2016)', *Polar Connection*, 17 May 2016, http://polarconnection.org/arctic-investment-protocol-december-2015/

21 Carsten Ørts Hansen, Peter Grønsedt, Christian Lindstrøm Graversen, and Christian Hendriksen, 'Arctic Shipping – Commercial Opportunities and Challenges', *CBS Maritime*, January 2016, http://bit.ly/2W7727O

7. What to Expect from China's New Development Cooperation Agency

1 Meibo Huang and Xiaohui Wei, 'The Chinese Foreign Aid Management System and its Reform', I*nstitutional Architecture and Development*; Edited by Elizabeth, 'Responses from Emerging Powers', *South African Institute of International Affairs*, Johannesburg, 2015, p.p. 101—14.

2 Axel Dreher, et al, 'Aid, China, and Growth: Evidence from a New Global Development Finance Dataset', *Aid Data*, Working Paper #46, Williamsburg, VA: Aid Data, 2017, https://www.aiddata.org/publications/aid-china-and-growth-evidence-from-a-new-global-development-finance-dataset accessed on 24 February 2018.

3 Lisa Cornish, 'Beijing's new partners: how China works with traditional donors', *Devex*, 11 August 2017, https://www.devex.com/news/beijing-s-new-partners-how-china-works-with-traditional-donors-90667 [accessed 15 March 2018].

4 Edited by Elizabeth Sidiropoulos, et al, 'Responses from Emerging Powers', *South African Institute of International Affairs*, Johannesburg, 2015, p.p. 101—14.

5 For a discussion of some of these challenges, see for instance: David Dollar, 'Is China's Development Finance a Challenge to the International Order?', *Asian Economic Policy Review* 13, Issue 2 (2018).

6 For international reactions to China's announcement of a development cooperation agency, see for instance: Alex Thier, Nilima Gulrajani, Barnaby Willitts-King, Annalisa Prizzon and Linda Calabrese, 'China's new development agency: five expert views', *Overseas Development Institute* (ODI), 14 March 2018, https://www.odi.org/comment/10624-china-s-new-development-agency-five-expert-views [accessed 15 March 2018]. Hannah Ryder, 'Opinion: China's foreign aid re-haul is finally here – or is it?', guest commentary, *CGTN*, 20 March 2018, https://news.cgtn.com/news/7845544e7a6b7a6333566d54/share_p.html?from=timeline [accessed 21 March 2018].

7 Marina Rudyak, 'Will China's new aid agency be effective?', *Lowy Institute*, 20 April 2018, https://www.lowyinstitute.org/the-interpreter/will-china-new-aid-agency-be-effective [accessed on 20 April 2018].

8. China Courts Latin America with Unrelenting Soft Power

1 Łukasz Fijałkowski, 'China's Soft Power' in Africa?', Journal of Contemporary African Studies, Vol. 29(2), 2011, p.p. 223–232, https://www.tandfonline.com/doi/abs/10.1080/02589001.2011.555197

2 Joshua Kurlantzick, 'China's Latin Leap Forward', World Policy Journal, Vol. 23(3),Fall 2006, p.p. 33—41, https://doi.org/10.1162/wopj.2006.23.3.33

3 Łukasz Fijałkowski, 'China's "soft power" in Africa?', *Journal of Contemporary African Studies*, Vol. 29(2), 5 April 2011, pp. 223–32, https://www.tandfonline.com/doi/abs/10.1080/02589001.2011.555197?src=recsys&journalCode=cjca20

4 Willy Lam, 'China's Encroachment on America's Backyard', *China Brief*, Volume 4(23), 24 November 2004, https://jamestown.org/program/chinas-encroachment-on-americas-backyard/

5 Binay Prasad, 'A Latin American Battle: China vs. Taiwan', *Diplomat,* 19 August 2017, https://thediplomat.com/2017/08/a-latin-american-battle-china-vs-taiwan/

6 Lei Yu, 'China's strategic partnership with Latin America: a fulcrum in China's rise', *International Affairs* 91(5),16 September 2015, p.p. 1047—86.

7 'Could China's "One Belt, One Road Initiative" Land in Latin America?' *Telesur*, 13 May 2017, https://www.telesurenglish.net/news/Asia-and-Latin-America-Strenthen-Economic-Ties-20170513-0003.html

8 Abdul Abiad, Margarita Debuque-Gonzales and Andrea Loren Sy, 'The Role and Impact of Infrastructure in Middle Income countries: Anything special', *ADB-Working Papers*, No. 518, August 2017, https://www.adb.org/sites/default/files/publication/359136/ewp-518.pdf; Joshua Aizenman, Barry Eichengreen and Donghyun Park, 'Overcoming the Middle-Income Challenge', *Emerging Markets Finance and Trade*, 54(6), 2018, p.p. 1205—1207, https://www.tandfonline.com/doi/abs/10.1080/1540496X.2018.1451052

9 R. Evan Ellis, 'Chinese Soft Power in Latin America: A Case Study,' *Joint Forces Quarterly*, 60, 1st quarter 2011, pp. 85-91, https://apps.dtic.mil/dtic/tr/fulltext/u2/a536568.pdf

10 'Global Image of the United States and China', *Pew Research Center,* Washington DC, 18 July 2013, http://www.pewglobal.org/2013/07/18/global-image-of-the-united-states-and-china/

11 Rebecca Ray and Kevin P. Gallagher, 'China-Latin America Economic Bulletin 2017 Edition', Boston University, https://www.bu.edu/pardeeschool/files/2014/11/Economic-Bulletin.16-17-Bulletin.Draft_.pdf

12 'China-Africa Research Initiative', *Johns Hopkins School of Advanced International Studies*, 2019, http://www.sais-cari.org/

13 Ketan Mehta, 'Balancing super rich, rich and poor Xi's big challenge', *ORF*, 21 November 2017, https://www.orfonline.org/research/balancing-super-rich-rich-and-poor-xis-big-challenge/

14 Justina Crabtree and Cheang Ming, 'Why soft power could be the real value of China's massive Belt and Road project', *CNBC*, 22 May 2017, https://www.cnbc.com/2017/05/22/one-belt-one-road-why-the-real-value-of-chinas-project-could-like-in-soft-power.html

9. Indonesia's 'Soft Balancing' Against China

1 Connelly, Aaron L., 'Indonesia's New North Natuna Sea: What's in a Name?' *Interpreter Lowy Institute*, 19 July 2017, https://www.lowyinstitute.org/the-interpreter/indonesia-s-new-north-natuna-sea-what-s-name> [accessed 10 April 2018].

2 The *Wire* Staff, 'Indonesia's Balancing Act: A Road with China, a Port with India', *Wire*, https://thewire.in/diplomacy/indonesia-china-india-modi-belt-and-road, [accessed 12 May 2018].

3 Ibid.

4 Tom Allard and Bernadette Christina Munthe, 'Asserting Sovereignty, Indonesia renames part of South China Sea', *Reuters,* 14 July 2017, https://www.reuters.com/article/us-indonesia-politics-map/asserting-sovereignty-indonesia-renames-part-of-south-china-sea-idUSKBN19Z0YQ [accessed 12 May 2018].

5 Aaron L. Connelly, 'Indonesia's New North Natuna Sea: What's in a Name?' *Interpreter Lowy Institute*, 19 July 2017, https://www.lowyinstitute.org/the-interpreter/indonesia-s-new-north-natuna-sea-what-s-name [accessed 10 April 2018].

6 'Joint Statement of the Foreign Ministers of ASEAN Member States and China on the Full and Effective Implementation of the Declaration of the Conduct of Parties in the South China Sea', *Foreign Ministry of the People's Republic of China*, https://www.fmprc.gov.cn/nanhai/eng/zcfg_1/t1384245.htm [accessed 12 May 2018]

7 The *Wire* Staff, 'Indonesia's Balancing Act: A Road with China, a Port with India', *Wire,* https://thewire.in/diplomacy/indonesia-china-india-modi-belt-and-road [accessed 12 May 2018].

8 Ibid.

9 Ankit Panda, 'Chinese Naval Exercise in Eastern Indian Ocean Sends Mixed Signals', *Diplomat*, 7 February 2017, https://thediplomat.com/2014/02/chinese-naval-exercise-in-eastern-indian-ocean-sends-mixed-signals/ [accessed 10 May 2018]

10 Sui Goh Noi, 'China keen to work with Indonesia on BRI', *Straits Times*, 10 February 2018, https://www.straitstimes.com/asia/east-asia/china-keen-to-work-with-indonesia-on-bri [accessed 8 May 2018]

11 'People's Republic of China and Indonesia Republic Joint Declaration', http://bit.ly/2PmyL21 [accessed 8 May 2018].

12 'The 6th Meeting on RI-RRT Politics and Security Dialogue Mechanism', *KEMLU* (Indonesian Ministry of *Foreign Affairs*), 24 August 2017, https://www.kemlu.go.id/en/berita/Pages/The-6th-Meeting-on-RI-RRT-Politics-and-Security-Dialogue-Mechanism.aspx [accessed 5 April 2018]. 'China and Indonesia Hold the Sixth Meeting of Dialogue Mechanism at Deputy Prime Minister Level', *FMPRC* (Foreign Ministry of the People's Republic of China), 22 August 2017, http://www.china-un.org/eng/zgyw/t1487070.htm [accessed 5 April 2018]

13 Xinhua (2018), 'China, Indonesia to further Comprehensive Strategic Partnership', *Xinhua Net*, 21 August 2017, http://www.xinhuanet.com/english/2017-08/21/c_136543808.htm [accessed 5 April 2018].

14 Dharma Siwage Negara, 'The Importance of One Belt One Road for Indonesia', *Asia News Network*, 29 May 2017, http://annx.asianews.network/content/opinion-importance-one-belt-one-road-indonesia-47002 [accessed 5 April 2018]

15 Indonesia has four Port Corporations.

16 'Dukung MEA, Pelindo 4 Tambah Direct Call ke Jepangdan Korea', *Poskota News*, 5 January 2016, (Supporting AEC, Pelindo 4 Add new Direct Calls to Japan), http://poskotanews.com/2016/01/05/dukung-mea-pelindo-4-tambah-direct-call-ke-jepang-dan-korea [Accessed 12 May 2018].

17 Ibid.

18 The *Wire* Staff, 'Indonesia's Balancing Act: A Road with China, a Port with India', *Wire*, https://thewire.in/diplomacy/indonesia-china-india-modi-belt-and-road [accessed 12 May 2018].

10. Rogue Nations: Assessing the China–Russia Relationship

1 Charles Clover, 'Russia resumes advanced weapons sales to China', *Financial Times*, 3 November 2018, https://www.ft.com/content/90b1ada2-a18e-11e6-86d5-4e36b35c3550

2 Tsvetana Paraskova, 'China is replacing Europe as Russia's No. 1 oil customer', *Business Insider*, 2 May 2018, https://www.businessinsider.com/china-is-replacing-europe-as-russias-no-1-oil-customer-2018-5?r=UK&IR=T

3 Henry Foy, Max Seddon and Lucy Hornby, 'Russia and China quietly build business bonds', *Financial Times*, 24 September 2017, https://www.ft.com/content/38f0ce22-9dd7-11e7-8cd4-932067fbf946

4 Nicole Gaouette, 'Russia, China use UN stage to push back on a US-led world order', *CNN*, 21 September 2017, https://edition.cnn.com/2017/09/21/politics/russia-china-us-unga-remarks/index.html

5 Ryan Browne, 'Trump's defense strategy sees China and Russia as biggest threats', *CNN*, 19 January 2018, https://edition.cnn.com/2018/01/19/politics/trump-defense-strategy-china-russia/index.html

6 Ivana Kottasová, 'Russia gets investment from China while sanctions keep U.S. off limits', *CNN*, 7 July 2017, https://money.cnn.com/2017/07/06/news/economy/russia-china-investment-deal-sanctions/index.html

7 Patrick Donahue and Ilya Arkhipov, 'Rapprochement with Russia is now a core policy objective for Germany', *Bloomberg*, 18 May 2018, https://www.bloomberg.com/news/articles/2018-05-17/trump-s-global-disruption-pushes-merkel-closer-to-putin-s-orbit

8 Paul Stronski and Nicole Ng, 'Cooperation and Competition: Russia and China in Central Asia, the Russian Far East and the Arctic', *Carnegie Endowment for International Peace*, 28 February 2018, http://carnegieendowment.org/2018/02/28/cooperation-and-competition-russia-and-china-in-central-asia-russian-far-east-and-arctic-pub-75673

9 'UN Security Council action on Crimea referendum blocked', UN News, 15 March 2014, <https://news.un.org/en/story/2014/03/464002-un-security-council-action-crimea-referendum-blocked>

10 'Minitrue: Crimea votes to join Russia', *China Digital Times*, 17 March 2014, https://chinadigitaltimes.net/2014/03/minitrue-crimea-votes-join-russia/

11 Alexander Gabuev, 'Friends with benefits? Russian-Chinese relations after the Ukraine crisis', *Carnegie Moscow Center*, 29 June 2016, https://carnegie.ru/2016/06/29/friends-with-benefits-russian-chinese-relations-after-ukraine-crisis-pub-63953

12 Ben Blanchard, 'China, Russia naval drill in South China Sea to begin Monday', *Reuters*, 11 September 2016, https://www.reuters.com/article/us-southchinasea-china-russia-idUSKCN11H051?
13 Rakesh Krishnan Simha, 'Russian Pacific Fleet's resurgence sets off alarm bells in Washington', *Russia Beyond*, 6 February 2017, https://www.rbth.com/blogs/continental_drift/2017/02/06/russian-pacific-fleets-resurgence-sets-off-alarm-bells-in-washington_696366
14 'Putin's plan in the South China Sea', *Oil Price*, 17 April 2017, https://oilprice.com/Geopolitics/International/Putins-Plan-In-The-South-China-Sea.html
15 'Russia, Vietnam ink military cooperation roadmap until 2020', *TASS*, 4 April 2018, http://tass.com/defense/997801
16 'Vietnam deemed one of *Gazprom*'s key partners in Southeast Asia', *Gazprom*, 10 November 2017, http://www.gazprom.com/press/news/2017/november/article379688/
17 James Kilner, 'Uzbekistan withdraws from Russia-led military alliance', *Telegraph*, 2 July 2012, https://www.telegraph.co.uk/news/worldnews/asia/uzbekistan/9369392/Uzbekistan-withdraws-from-Russia-lead-military-alliance.html
18 Edward Lemon and Joe Schottenfeld, 'Putin's ploy in Central Asia', *Foreign Affairs*, 14 January 2016, https://www.foreignaffairs.com/articles/china/2016-01-14/putins-ploys-central-asia
19 Paul Stronksi and Nicole Ng, Op cit.
20 Paul Stronski, 'China and Russia's uneasy partnership in Central Asia', *Carnegie Endowment for International Peace*, 29 March 2018, https://carnegieendowment.org/2018/03/29/china-and-russia-s-uneasy-partnership-in-central-asia-pub-75984
21 Gabuev, Op cit.

11. Contesting the Dragon: India and ASEAN Converge

1 Archis Mohan, 'Curbing China's hegemony: Modi invites ASEAN leaders for Republic Day', *Business Standard*, 8 January 2018, https://www.business-standard.com/article/politics/how-modi-curbing-china-influence-by-inviting-asean-leaders-on-republic-day-118010800538_1.html [accessed on 9 January 2018].

2 Ram Madhav, 'Uncharted Waters: In search for order in the Indo-Pacific', (opinion presented at the Raisina Dialogue, New Delhi, India, 16-18 January 2018)

3 Pragya Pandey, '2017 BRICS Summit: Post-Doklam, India, China Meet in Xiamen', *Diplomat*, 7 September 2017, https://thediplomat.com/2017/09/2017-brics-summit-post-doklam-india-china-meet-in-xiamen/ [accessed on 07 January 2018].

4 'India, China Have Established Mechanisms to Resolve Any Misunderstanding: MEA', *Wire*, 19 January 2018 https://thewire.in/diplomacy/india-china-have-established-mechanisms-to-resolve-any-misunderstanding-mea [accessed on 10 July 2018].

5 Sagar Kulkarni, 'Doklam not raised at Wuhan as issue was resolved', *Deccan Herald*, 1 August 2018, https://www.deccanherald.com/national/doklam-dispute-resolved-684893.html [accessed on 3 August 2018].

6 Col. Anil Bhat, 'China endangering 50 years of bullet-less border management', *Outlook India*, 16 July 2017, https://www.outlookindia.com/newsscroll/china-endangering-50-years-of-bulletless-border-management/1100769 [accessed on 15 July 2018].

7 Vinay Kaura, 'India's ASEAN overtures a calculated answer to China's unrestrained expansionism in the Asia-Pacific region', *Firstpost*, 26 Jan 2018,
https://www.firstpost.com/india/republic-day-2018-januray-26-indias-asean-overtures-calculated-answer-chinas-unrestrained-expansionism-india-pacific-region-4320601.html [accessed on 20 July 2018].

8 Max Fisher, 'The South China Sea: Explaining the Dispute', *New York Times*, 14 July 2016, https://www.nytimes.com/2016/07/15/world/asia/south-china-sea-dispute-arbitration-explained.html [accessed on 17 July 2018].

9 Jayanth Jacob, 'Countering China? Ahead of Modi-Trump meeting, emphasis on peace, stability in Indo-Pacific region', *Hindustan Times*, 12 November 2017, https://www.hindustantimes.com/india-news/countering-china-ahead-of-modi-trump-meeting-emphasis-on-peace-stability-in-indo-pacific/story-e8UikcHEiROUde3HsdwVqJ.html [accessed on 20 July 2018].

10 Premesha Saha, 'The Quad in the Indo-Pacific: Why ASEAN remains cautious', *Observer Research Foundation*, 26 February 2018, https://www.orfonline.org/research/asean-quad/ [accessed on 21 July 2018].

11 Dino Patti Djalal, 'Uncharted Water: In search for order in the Indo-Pacific', opinion presented at the Raisina Dialogue, New Delhi, India, 16-18 January 2018.

12. The BRI and Myanmar's China Debate

1 'State Counsellor participated in the Belt and Road Forum for International Cooperation held in Beijing', *Ministry of Information, Government of Myanmar*, 18 May 2017, http://www.moi.gov.mm/moi:eng/?q=announcement/14/11/2018/id-10676
2 'China proposes building China-Myanmar economic corridor to boost cooperation', *Xinhua*, 20 November 2017, http://www.xinhuanet.com/english/2017-11/20/c_136764453.htm
3 Nan Lwin, 'China, Myanmar Agree 15-Point MoU on Economic Corridor', the *Irrawaddy*, 6 July 2018, https://www.irrawaddy.com/news/burma/china-myanmar-agree-15-point-mou-economic-corridor.html
4 Thiha KoKo, 'Chinese to conduct feasibility study for two major highways', the *Myanmar Times*, 12 March 2018, https://www.mmtimes.com/news/chinese-conduct-feasibility-study-two-major-highways.html
5 Yuichi Nitta and Thurein Hla Htway, 'Myanmar will ask China to downsize project, minister says', *Nikkei Asian Review*, 4 July 2018, https://asia.nikkei.com/Politics/Myanmar-will-ask-China-to-downsize-project-minister-says
6 Jason Koutsoukis, 'China's $7.5 Billion Myanmar Port "Crazy," Suu Kyi Adviser Says', *Bloomberg*, 25 May 2018, https://www.bloomberg.com/news/articles/2018-05-25/china-s-7-5-billion-myanmar-port-crazy-suu-kyi-adviser-says
7 Ma, Josephine, '"There's no Chinese 'debt trap'," says Myanmar minister, as government pushes for joint port project to go ahead', *South China Morning Post*, 30 June 2018, https://www.scmp.com/news/china/diplomacy-defence/article/2153210/myanmar-minister-dismisses-chinese-debt-trap-fears-over
8 Yimou Lee and Thu Thu Aung, 'China to take 70 percent stake in strategic port in Myanmar –official', *Reuters*, 17 October 2017, https://www.reuters.com/article/china-silkroad-myanmar-port/china-

to-take-70-percent-stake-in-strategic-port-in-myanmar-official-idUSL4N1MS3UB

9 'New, Improved Deal on China-Backed Kyaukphyu SEZ Due Soon: Deputy Minister', *Irrawaddy*, 23 July 2018, https://www.irrawaddy.com/in-person/new-improved-deal-on-china-backed-kyaukphyu-sez-due-soon-deputy-minister.html

10 Ibid.

11 Debby Chan Sze Wan, 'China-Myanmar high-speed railway quietly back on track', *Myanmar Times*, 6 July 2018, https://www.mmtimes.com/news/china-myanmar-high-speed-railway-quietly-back-track.html

12 'China, Myanmar sign MoU on feasibility study of Muse-Mandalay railway', *Xinhua*, 23 October 2018, http://www.xinhuanet.com/english/2018-10/23/c_137550972.htm

13. Engaging Africa through Summits: The Chinese Experience

1 T. Deych, 'What does BRICS Mean for Africa?', *Athens: ATINER'S Conference Paper Series*, No: INL2016-2114, p.6., https://www.atiner.gr/papers/INL2016-2114.pdf

2 Ministry of Commerce, Peoples Republic of China, '*Statistics on China–Africa Bilateral Trade in 2017*', 26 January 2018, http://english.mofcom.gov.cn/article/statistic/lanmubb/AsiaAfrica/201803/20180302719613.shtml

3 Ibid.

4 China–Africa Cooperation Forum, '*Forum on China–Africa Cooperation – FOCAC*', September 2018, https://www.focac.org/chn/ltjj/ltjz/

5 Johanna Jansso, '*The Forum on China-Africa Cooperation (FOCAC)*', Center for Chinese Studies, University of Stellenbosch, p.2., http://www0.sun.ac.za/ccs/wp-content/uploads/2009/11/CCS-FOCAC-Briefing-Paper-August-2009.pdf

6 Lily Kuo, 'China's Xi Jinping pledges $60 billion to help Africa solve its problems its own way', *Quartz Africa*, 4 December 2015, https://qz.com/africa/565819/chinas-xi-jinping-pledges-60-billion-to-help-africa-solve-its-problems-its-own-way/

7 Sun Yun, 'What can we learn in 2018 from the $60 billion commitment?', *Brookings*, 30 January 2018, https://www.brookings.edu/blog/africa-in-focus/2018/01/30/foresight-africa-viewpoint-chinas-engagement-in-africa-what-can-we-learn-in-2018-from-the-60-billion-commitment/

8 'Xi says China to implement eight major initiatives with African countries', *Xinhua*, 3 September 2018, http://www.xinhuanet.com/english/2018-09/03/c_137441563.htm

14. Charting China's Approach to International Law

1 Malcom Shaw, 'International Law', *Encyclopaedia Britannica*, https://www.britannica.com/topic/international-law [accessed 11 May 2018].

2 Daniel Philpott, 'Sovereignty', *Stanford Encyclopedia of Philosophy*, 25 March 2016, https://plato.stanford.edu/entries/sovereignty/

3 The Editors of Encyclopaedia Britannica, 'Unequal Treaty', *Encyclopaedia Britannica*, https://www.britannica.com/event/Unequal-Treaty [accessed 11 May 2018].

4 Ian Black, 'Russia and China veto UN move to refer Syria to international criminal court', *Guardian*, 22 May 2014, World Section, International Edition, https://www.theguardian.com/world/2014/may/22/russia-china-veto-un-draft-resolution-refer-syria-international-criminal-court

5 Gianluigi Negro, 'Internet Sovereignty and China: Beyond the Wuzhen Summit', *Chinoiresie*, 13 November 2016, http://www.chinoiresie.info/internet-sovereignty-china-wuzhen-summit/

6 Tim Rühlig, 'How China Approaches International Law', *European Institute of Asian Studies*, May 2018, http://bit.ly/2IEbHeL

15. The Politics of the Redback: Chinese Economic Statecraft and Global Finance

1 William Shakespeare, *Henry IV, Part* 2, *Act III, Scene I*, http://shakespeare.mit.edu/2henryiv/full.html

2 'The Guardian view on the Asian Infrastructure Bank: the US should work with it, not oppose it', *Guardian*, 26 October 2014, https://www.theguardian.com/commentisfree/2014/oct/26/guardian-view-asian-infrastructure-bank-united-states-work-not-oppose [last accessed

10 November 2017]; James Reilly, *China's economic statecraft: turning wealth into power*, Lowy Institute for International Policy, November 2013, https://www.lowyinstitute.org/sites/default/files/reilly_chinas_economic_statecraft_web_0.pdf

3 James Reilly, *China's economic statecraft: turning wealth into power*, Lowy Institute for International Policy, https://www.lowyinstitute.org/sites/default/files/reilly_chinas_economic_statecraft_web_0.pdf

4 Zhou Xiaochuan, *Reform the International Monetary System*, BIS Review, Volume 41, March 2009, https://www.bis.org/review/r090402c.pdf

5 Meng Meng and Kevin Yao, 'China's FX reserves post surprise rise in March on more stable yuan', *Reuters*, 7 April 2016, https://www.reuters.com/article/us-china-economy-forexreserves/chinas-fx-reserves-post-surprise-rise-in-march-on-more-stable-yuan-idUSKCN0X41BE [last accessed 01 August 2018].

6 David Marsh, David, 'China SDR announcement enshrines move away from its dollar focus', *Market Watch*, 11 April 2016, https://www.marketwatch.com/story/china-sdr-announcement-enshrines-move-away-from-its-dollar-focus-2016-04-11 [last accessed 01 August 2018].

7 'Action plan on the Belt and Road Initiative', *State Council of the People's Republic of China*, 30 March 2015, http://english.gov.cn/archive/publications/2015/03/30/content_281475080249035.htm

8 Christine Lagarde, 'IMF Launches New SDR Basket Including Chinese Renminbi, Determines New Currency Amounts', *IMF Press Release*, 16/440, 30 September 2016, http://www.imf.org/en/News/Articles/2016/09/30/AM16-PR16440-IMF-Launches-New-SDR-Basket-Including-Chinese-Renminbi

9 'Special Drawing Right (SDR) Factsheet', *IMF*, 19 April 2018, https://www.imf.org/en/About/Factsheets/Sheets/2016/08/01/14/51/Special-Drawing-Right-SDR

10 'China's yuan joins elite club of IMF reserve currencies', *Reuters*, 1 October 2016, https://www.reuters.com/article/us-china-currency-imf-idUSKCN1212WC [last accessed 28 July 2018].

11 Saumya Vaishampayan, 'Donald Trump Charges China With Yuan Manipulation – Again', *Wall Street Journal*, 26 September 2016, https://www.wsj.com/articles/donald-trump-charges-china-with-yuan-manipulationagain-1474943701 [last accessed 28 July 2018].

12 Chris Brummer, 'Renminbi Internationalization and Systemic Risk', *Institute of International Economic Law*, Georgetown University Law Center, February 2017, https://www.law.georgetown.edu/iiel/wp-content/uploads/sites/8/2018/01/IIEL-China-Issue-Brief-Chris-Brummer-Accessible.pdf

13 Ibid; Craig Chan and Wee Choon Teo, 'RMB Internationalization: Prospects and Challenges', *Brink Asia*, 12 June 2018 https://www.brinknews.com/asia/rmb-internationalization-prospects-and-challenges/ [last accessed 28 July 2018]; Cindy Li, 'Banking on China through Currency Swap Agreements', *Federal Reserve Bank of San Francisco*, 23 October 2015, https://www.frbsf.org/banking/asia-program/pacific-exchange-blog/banking-on-china-renminbi-currency-swap-agreements/

14 R.A. Mundell, 'Capital Mobility and Stabilization Policy under Fixed and Flexible Exchange Rates', *Canadian Journal of Economics and Political Science*, Vol. 29, No. 4, November 1963, https://www.jstor.org/stable/139336?origin=crossref&seq=1#page_scan_tab_contents

15 Michael Pettis, 'Do Markets Determine the Value of the RMB?', *Carnegie Endowment for International Peace*, 18 August 2015, http://carnegieendowment.org/chinafinancialmarkets/61053

16 Jamil Anderlini, 'China defends new currency regime', *Financial Times*, 13 August 2015, https://www.ft.com/content/d42526ee-418c-11e5-b98b-87c7270955cf [last accessed 23 July 2018].

17 Karen Yeung, 'PBOC adjusts formula for yuan fixing, sparking rise in currency', *South China Morning Post*, 26 May 2017, http://www.scmp.com/business/article/2095829/pboc-plans-adjust-yuan-fixing-methodology-fed-interest-rate-rise-looms [last accessed 25 July 2018]; Maximilian Kärnfelt, 'China's tight capital controls fail to address underlying problems', *Financial Times*, 10 November 2017, https://www.ft.com/content/1d288888-c613-11e7-b2bb-322b2cb39656 [last accessed 25 July 2018].

18 Benjamin J. Cohen, 'Renminbi Internationalization: A Conflict of Statecrafts', *Chatham House*, March 2017, https://www.chathamhouse.org/sites/files/chathamhouse/publications/research/2017-03-20-renminbi-internationalization-statecraft-cohen.pdf

19 Michael Pettis, 'How China's 'Currency Manipulation' Enhances the Global Role of the US Dollar', *Foreign Policy*, 22 July 2016, https://

foreignpolicy.com/2016/07/22/chinas-currency-manipulation-actually-enhances-the-global-role-of-the-dollar-sdr-rmb-balance-of-payments/ [last accessed 20 July 2018].

20 Martin Feldstein, 'Quantitative Easing and the Renminbi', *Project Syndicate*, 26 November 2010, http://www.nber.org/feldstein/projectsyndicatenovember262010.pdf; Benjamin J. Cohen, 'The Demise of the Dollar?' Revue de la régulation [Online], Autumn 2015, http://journals.openedition.org/regulation/11501,

21 Bree Feng, 'Deal Set on China-Led Infrastructure Bank', *New York Times*, 24 October 2014, https://www.nytimes.com/2014/10/25/world/asia/china-signs-agreement-with-20-other-nations-to-establish-international-development-bank.html [last accessed 21 July 2018]; 'Brics nations to create $100bn development bank', *BBC*, 15 July 2014, https://www.bbc.com/news/business-28317555 [last accessed 28 July 2018].

22 'Why China is creating a new "World Bank" for Asia', *Economist*, 11 November 2014, https://www.economist.com/the-economist-explains/2014/11/11/why-china-is-creating-a-new-world-bank-for-asia [last accessed 20 July 2018]

23 Huileng Tan, 'China's currency is still nowhere near overtaking the dollar for global payments', *CNBC*, 2 February 2018, https://www.cnbc.com/2018/02/02/china-currency-yuan-the-rmb-isnt-near-overtaking-the-us-dollar.html [last accessed 25 July 2018]

24 'China pledges $174 billion for Belt and Road initiative, says open to everyone', *Straits Times*, 14 May 2017, https://www.straitstimes.com/asia/east-asia/free-trade-important-engine-for-development-says-xi-jinping-at-opening-of-one-belt [last accessed 21 July 2018]

25 Ibid.

26 Harold Trinkunas, 'Renminbi Diplomacy? The Limits of China's Influence on Latin America's Domestic Politics', *Brookings*, November 2016, https://www.brookings.edu/wp-content/uploads/2016/11/renminbi-diplomacy_harold-trinkunas.pdf

27 James Reilly, 'China's economic statecraft: turning wealth into power', *Lowy Institute for International Policy*, November 2013, https://www.lowyinstitute.org/sites/default/files/reilly_chinas_economic_statecraft_web_0.pdf

28 Ceri Parker, 'China's Xi Jinping defends globalization from the Davos stage', *World Economic Forum*, 17 January 2017, https://www.weforum.

org/agenda/2017/01/chinas-xi-jinping-defends-globalization-from-the-davos-stage/ [last accessed 25 July 2018].

29 'China FTA Network', *Ministry of Commerce, People's Republic of China*, http://fta.mofcom.gov.cn/english/

30 'China's Foreign Reserves Hold Steady in June as Trade War Loomed', *Bloomberg News*, 9 July 2018, https://www.bloomberg.com/news/articles/2018-07-09/china-s-foreign-reserves-increased-in-june-as-trade-war-loomed [last accessed 20 July 2018]; James Reilly, 'China's economic statecraft: turning wealth into power', *Lowy Institute for International Policy*, November 2013, https://www.lowyinstitute.org/sites/default/files/reilly_chinas_economic_statecraft_web_0.pdf

31 David Scutt, 'Here's how much currency is traded every day', *Business Insider Australia*, 2 September 2016, https://www.businessinsider.com/heres-how-much-currency-is-traded-every-day-2016-9?IR=T [last accessed 20 July 2018]

32 Chris Brummer, *Renminbi Internationalization and Systemic Risk*, Institute of International Economic Law, Georgetown University Law Center, February 2017, https://www.law.georgetown.edu/iiel/wp-content/uploads/sites/8/2018/01/IIEL-China-Issue-Brief-Chris-Brummer-Accessible.pdf; Shuli Ren, 'China's Panda Killers', *Bloomberg*, 1 November 2017, https://www.bloomberg.com/news/articles/2017-10-31/panda-bonds-are-collateral-damage-in-china-s-debt-hunt [last accessed 23 July 2018].

33 Dipanjan Roy Chaudhury, 'Not just land disputes, Beijing has been unilaterally changing maritime boundaries', *Economic Times*, 13 July 2018, https://economictimes.indiatimes.com/news/defence/not-just-land-disputes-beijing-has-been-unilaterally-changing-maritime-boundaries/articleshow/59762040.cms> [last accessed 20 July 2018].

34 Maria Abi-Habib, 'How China Got Sri Lanka to Cough Up a Port', the *New York Times*, 25 June 2018, https://www.nytimes.com/2018/06/25/world/asia/china-sri-lanka-port.html [last accessed 21 July 2018].

35 Molly Elgin-Cossart and Melanie Hart, *China's New International Financing Institutions*, Center for American Progress, 22 September 2015, https://www.americanprogress.org/issues/security/reports/2015/09/22/121668/chinas-new-international-financing-institutions/; Ibid.

36 Enda Curran, 'Why Weaker Yuan Risks Making Trade War a Currency War', *Bloomberg*, 24 July 2018, https://www.bloomberg.com/news/articles/2018-07-24/why-weaker-yuan-risks-making-trade-war-a-currency-war-quicktake [last accessed 31 July 2018].
37 David Dollar and Samantha Gross, 'China's currency displacing the dollar in global oil trade? Don't count on it', *Brookings*, 19 April 2018, https://www.brookings.edu/blog/order-from-chaos/2018/04/19/chinas-currency-displacing-the-dollar-in-global-oil-trade-dont-count-on-it/
38 Ibid.
39 'What is cryptocurrency, how does it work and why do we use it?' *Telegraph*, 17 August 2018, https://www.telegraph.co.uk/technology/0/cryptocurrency/ [last accessed 25 August 2018].
40 Benjamin J. Cohen, *Renminbi Internationalization: A Conflict of Statecrafts*, Chatham House, March 2017, https://www.chathamhouse.org/sites/files/chathamhouse/publications/research/2017-03-20-renminbi-internationalization-statecraft-cohen.pdf; Michael Pettis, 'How China's "Currency Manipulation" Enhances the Global Role of the U.S. Dollar', *Foreign Policy*, 22 July 2016, https://foreignpolicy.com/2016/07/22/chinas-currency-manipulation-actually-enhances-the-global-role-of-the-dollar-sdr-rmb-balance-of-payments/ [last accessed 20 July 2018].

PART 4: CHINA'S ECONOMY, SOCIETY AND CULTURE

2. China's Protectionist Tendencies Will Continue

1 Gregory C. Chow, 'Economic Reform and Growth in China', *Annals of Economics and Finance*, Vol. 5 (1), 2004, p. 132, http://www.aeconf.com/Articles/May2004/aef050107.pdf
2 Thomas Rumbaugh and Nicolas Blancher, 'China: International Trade and WTO Accession', *IMF Working Paper*, WP/04/36, March 2004, https://www.imf.org/external/pubs/ft/wp/2004/wp0436.pdf
3 World Trade Organization, Tariff Profile: China, retrieved from http://stat.wto.org/TariffProfiles/CN_e.htm

4 US Government Accountability Office, 'World Trade Organization: Analysis of China's Commitments to Other Members', *GAO-03-4*, October 2002, https://www.gao.gov/assets/240/236049.pdf
5 Charles Wallace, 'China's Abusive Trade Practices Likely to Focus Trump's Wrath', *Forbes*, 8 February 2017, https://www.forbes.com/sites/charleswallace1/2017/02/08/chinas-abusive-trade-practices-likely-to-focus-trumps-wrath/#4175d11a6fdc
6 Stephen J. Ezell, Adams B. Nager and Robert D. Atkinson, 'Contributors and Detractors: Ranking Countries' Impact on Global Innovation', *Information Technology and Innovation Foundation (ITIF)*, 1 January 2016, http://www2.itif.org/2016-contributors-and-detractors.pdf
7 Ibid.
8 Author's calculation using World Development Indicators (2019) database. https://databank.worldbank.org/data/source/world-development-indicators#> [accessed 08 April 2019].

3. Pollution-Free Progress? Ambient Air Quality in India and China

1 John Ross, 'Why Are China and India Growing So Fast? State Investment', *HuffPost*, 29 August 2016, https://www.huffingtonpost.com/john_ross-/china-india-growth_b_11655472.html [accessed on 20 July 2018].
2 Peng Yin, et al, 'Particulate air pollution and mortality in 38 of China's largest cities: time series analysis', *BMJ*, 356:j667, 14 March 2017, https://www.bmj.com/content/356/bmj.j667
3 'Ambient Air Pollution: A global assessment of exposure and burden of disease', *World Health Organization*, 2016, http://apps.who.int/iris/bitstream/handle/10665/250141/9789241511353-eng.pdf?sequence=1&isAllowed=y [accessed on 20 July 2018].
4 'WHO | Ambient Air Pollution: A Global Assessment of Exposure and Burden of Disease,' *WHO*, http://www.who.int/phe/publications/air-pollution-global-assessment/en/ [accessed 08 August 2018].
5 Geeta Anand, 'India's Air Pollution Rivals China's as World's Deadliest', *New York Times*, sec. Asia Pacific, 14 February 2017, https://www.

nytimes.com/2017/02/14/world/asia/indias-air-pollution-rivals-china-as-worlds-deadliest.html

6 Ibid.

7 Edward Wong, 'Opinion | Life in a Toxic Country,' *New York Times*, 3 August 2013, https://www.nytimes.com/2013/08/04/sunday-review/life-in-a-toxic-country.html [accessed 08 August 2018].

8 'Air Pollution in Delhi An Analysis', *Central Pollution Control Board* (CPCB), New Delhi, India: Government of India, 2016.

9 'How China is (Surprise!) Winning its War on Air Pollution', https://www.huffingtonpost.in/entry/china-air-pollution-2014_us_568e592ce4b0a2b6fb6ecb73 [accessed 08 August 2018].

10 'State of Global Air 2017: A Special Report on Global Exposure to Air Pollution and its Disease Burden', *IHME*, Boston, MA: Health Effects Institute, 2017.

11 Joanne Lu, 'Pressure Mounts on India to Tackle Air Pollution That Now Rivals China's', *Humanosphere*, 15 February 2017, http://www.humanosphere.org/global-health/2017/02/pressure-mounts-india-tackle-air-pollution-now-rivals-chinas/ [accessed 08 August 2018].

12 J. Lelieveld, et al, 'The Contribution of Outdoor Air Pollution Sources to Premature Mortality on a Global Scale', *Nature* 525, 17 September 2015, p.p. 367-71, https://www.nature.com/articles/nature15371

13 World Health Organization. 'Ambient air pollution: A global assessment of exposure and burden of disease' (2016), https://apps.who.int/iris/handle/10665/250141, [accessed on 9 April 2019], 40.

14 Jennifer Burney and V. Ramanathan, 'Recent Climate and Air Pollution Impacts on Indian Agriculture', *Proceedings of the National Academy of Sciences*, 111(46), 18 November 2014, p. 16319-24 https://doi.org/10.1073/pnas.1317275111

15 Stephen Chen, 'Agriculture Feels the Choke as China Smog Starts to Foster Disastrous Conditions', *South China Morning Post*, 25 February 2014, https://www.scmp.com/news/china/article/1434700/china-smog-threatens-agriculture-nuclear-fallout-conditions-warn [accessed 08 August 2018].

16 Aamir Manzoor, 'Air Pollution Threatens Delhi's Wildlife Havens,' *Pioneer*, 9 May 2014, https://www.dailypioneer.com/city/air-pollution-threatens-delhis-wildlife-havens.html [accessed 8 August 2018].

17 'State of Global Air 2017: A special report on global exposure to air pollution and its disease burden', *HEI*, p. 7, https://www.stateofglobalair.org/sites/default/files/SOGA2017_report.pdf

18 Op cit.

19 Stephen Chen, 'What Exactly is Causing China's Toxic Smog?' *South China Morning Post*, 21 December 2016, https://www.scmp.com/news/china/policies-politics/article/2056366/what-exactly-causing-chinas-toxic-smog [accessed 08 August 2018].

20 Neha Madaan, 'Biomass Burning a Major Source of Pollution in India,' *Times of India*, 10 November 2014, https://timesofindia.indiatimes.com/home/environment/pollution/Biomass-burning-a-major-source-of-pollution-in-India/articleshow/45093405.cms [accessed 08 August 2018].

21 D.G. Kaskaoutis, 'Effects of Crop Residue Burning on Aerosol Properties, Plume Characteristics, and Long-Range Transport over Northern India', *Journal of Geophysical Research: Atmospheres*, 119(9), 14 April 2014, p.p. 5424–44, https://doi.org/10.1002/2013JD021357

22 Ajanta Chakraborty, 'CSE Welcomes National Action Plan to Curb Antimicrobial Resistance; Lauds Move to Set up Authority', *Times of India*, Kolkata News, 24 April 2017, <https://timesofindia.indiatimes.com/city/kolkata/cse-welcomes-national-action-plan-to-curb-antimicrobial-resistance-lauds-move-to-set-up-authority/articleshow/58345672.cms> [accessed 08 August 2018].

23 Sara Hsu, 'Is China's Pollution Accelerating Climate Change?', *Forbes*, 8 September 2016, <https://www.forbes.com/sites/sarahsu/2016/09/08/is-chinas-pollution-accelerating-climate-change/#7e3b34f437ef>

24 Wayne Ma, 'China's Air Pollution Problem: Whose Responsibility?', *WSJ* (blog), 30 January 2013, <https://blogs.wsj.com/chinarealtime/2013/01/30/chinas-air-pollution-problem-whose-responsibility/>

25 Ma Tianjie, 'China's Environment in 2015: A Year in Review', 23 December 2015, <https://www.chinadialogue.net/article/show/single/en/8497--China-s-environment-in-2-15-a-year-in-review> [accessed 08 August 2018].

26 Op cit.

27 Hefeng Zhang, et al, 'Air Pollution and Control Action in Beijing', *Preventing Smog Crises*, 112(2), 20 January 2016, p.p. 1519-27, https://doi.org/10.1016/j.jclepro.2015.04.092

28 Haoran Liu, et al, 'A Paradox for Air Pollution Controlling in China Revealed by "APEC Blue" and "Parade Blue"', *Scientific Reports*, 6, 29 September 2016, p. 34408.

29 'China looks at plans to ban petrol and diesel cars', *BBC News*, 10 September 2017, sec. Business, https://www.bbc.co.uk/news/business-41218243

30 Beth Gardiner, 'China's Surprising Solutions to Air Pollution', *National Geographic*, 5 May 2017, https://news.nationalgeographic.com/2017/05/china-air-pollution-solutions-environment-tangshan/ [accessed 08 August 2018].

31 Government of India, 'Ministry of Environment, Forest and Climate Change', various orders available at http://www.moef.nic.in/environmental_standards [accessed 08 August 2018].

32 'The Ministry of Road Transport & Highways,' 27 December 2016, http://pib.nic.in/newsite/PrintRelease.aspx?relid=155892 [accessed 08 August 2018].

33 'Delhi Car Rationing Starts Again,' *BBC News*, 15 April 2016, https://www.bbc.co.uk/news/world-asia-india-3605162> [accessed 08 August 2018].

34 Editors Parmod Kumar, Surender Kumar and Laxmi Joshi, 'Policies for Restricting the Agriculture Residue Burning in Punjab,' *Springer Link*, Socioeconomic and Environmental Implications of Agricultural Residue Burning, New Delhi: Springer India, 2015, p.p. 117-31, https://doi.org/10.1007/978-81-322-2014-5_>

35 'National Clean Air Programme (NCAP) – India', *Centre for Pollution Control Board*, 29 December 2015, http://envfor.nic.in/sites/default/files/NCAP%20with%20annex-ilovepdf-compressed.pdf

36 'Delhi Air Pollution: CSE Reports Upto 30,000 Deaths Annually,' *NDTV Food*, 12 July 2017, https://food.ndtv.com/health/delhi-air-pollution-cse-reports-upto-30-000-deaths-annually-1255463 [accessed 08 August 2018].

37 Navneet Anand, 'Graded Response to Tackle Air Pollution', *Pioneer*, 7 December 2016, https://www.dailypioneer.com/columnists/oped/

graded-response-to-tackle-air-pollution.html [accessed 08 August 2018].

38 Chandra Shekhar, 'Delhi's Air Pollution Puzzle', *Mint*, 5 September 2017, https://www.livemint.com/Opinion/gxdnb5FqKXkE1mQd9LYP2N/Delhis-air-pollution-puzzle.html [accessed 08 August 2018].

39 Ibid.

40 Priyanka Mittal, 'Supreme Court lifts order banning sale of firecrackers in Delhi-NCR', *Mint*, 12 September 2017, https://www.livemint.com/Industry/KnyY6oKnSHPZPY52RXEY9K/Supreme-Court-lifts-order-banning-sale-of-firecrackers-in-De.html

41 'Supreme Court lifts ban on sale of fire crackers, favours graded approach', *Moneycontrol*, 12 September 2017, https://www.moneycontrol.com/news/india/supreme-court-lifts-ban-on-sale-of-fire-crackers-favours-graded-approach-2386021.html [accessed 08 August 2018].

42 'BRICS Leaders Xiamen Declaration: Full Text,' *Times of India*, 4 September 2017, https://timesofindia.indiatimes.com/india/brics-leaders-xiamen-declaration-full-text/articleshow/60359120.cms [accessed 08 August 2018].

43 *Integrated Solutions for Multifaceted Challenges: Role of Technology*, n.d., Amitabh Kant, CEO, NITI Aayog and Prof. Pratap Bhanu Mehta, VC, Ashoka University in conversation with Dr Samir Saran, Vice President, ORF, https://www.youtube.com/watch?v=-CJnGMldmZU

44 Benjamin Haas, 'Beijing creates anti-smog police to tackle air polluters', *Guardian*, 9 January 2017, https://www.theguardian.com/world/2017/jan/09/beijing-creates-anti-smog-police-to-tackle-air-polluters

45 Sowmiya Ashok, 'Despite real-time monitoring, no data on Gurgaon's air quality for 10 days', *Indian Express*, 23 June 2017, https://indianexpress.com/article/cities/delhi/despite-real-time-monitoring-no-data-on-gurgaons-air-quality-for-10-days-4717816/

46 'China, India can join hands to tackle urban pollution: Official', *Business Today*, 22 June 2016, https://www.businesstoday.in/current/world/china-india-can-join-hands-to-tackle-urban-pollution/story/234061.html

4. China's Innovation Boom: Lessons for India

1 Shira Ovide, 'Who's the Tech Copycat Now?' *Bloomberg Businessweek*, 26 June 2017, https://www.bloomberg.com/news/articles/2017-06-26/former-tech-copycat-china-turns-tables-on-innovation

2 Ibid.
3 Ibid.
4 Ojasvi Goel and Yash Bajaj, 'Breaking Free of the Digital Dragon: Responding to China's Growing Control over India's ICT', *Observer Research Foundation*, 22 September 2017, http://www.orfonline.org/research/breaking-free-digital-dragon-responding-china-growing-control-india-ict/
5 Edward Jung, 'China's Internet Boom', *MIT Technology Review*, 21 June 2016, https://www.technologyreview.com/s/601686/chinas-internet-boom/
6 Ibid.
7 Ibid.
8 Shin-Horng Chen and Pei-Chang Wen, 'The Evolution of China's Mobile Phone Industry and Good-Enough Innovation', *Chung-Hua Institution for Economic Research*, April 2013, http://www.cier.edu.tw/public/Data/2013-1.pdf
9 Ibid.
10 Ibid.
11 Ibid.
12 'Number of internet users in China from 2015 to 2022 (in millions)', *Statista*, https://www.statista.com/statistics/278417/number-of-internet-users-in-china/
13 Dominique Patton, ed. Mark Potter, 'China's Spending on R&D Rises to 2.07 Per cent of GDP', *Reuters*, 21 November 2016, https://www.reuters.com/article/us-china-r-d/chinas-spending-on-rd-rises-to-2-07-per cent-of-gdp-idUSKBN13G1NG
14 Alex Gray, 'These Countries Have the Most Doctoral Graduates', *World Economic Forum*, 27 February 2017, https://www.weforum.org/agenda/2017/02/countries-with-most-doctoral-graduates/
15 'Top Engineering in the World', *US News Education*, 2015, https://www.usnews.com/education/best-global-universities/engineering
16 T.V. Padma, 'India's Science Test', *Nature*, Vol. 521, 14 May 2015, https://www.nature.com/polopoly_fs/1.17518!/menu/main/topColumns/topLeftColumn/pdf/521144a.pdf
17 Ibid.
18 Ibid.
19 Ibid.
20 Ibid.

5. Transition to a Low-Carbon Economy: China's Influence on Outcomes

1 International Energy Agency, 'World Energy Outlook 2017', *IEA*, 2017, Paris, https://www.iea.org/weo2017/

2 Kate Gordon and Anders Hove, 'How China Wastes Its Renewable Energy', *Wall Street Journal Blogs*, 13 September 2016, https://blogs.wsj.com/experts/2016/09/13/how-china-wastes-its-renewable-energy/

3 Michael Forsythe, 'China Aims to Spend at Least $360 Billion on Renewable Energy by 2020', *New York Times*, 5 January 2017, https://www.nytimes.com/2017/01/05/world/asia/china-renewable-energy-investment.html

4 Jiang Kejun and Jonathan Woetzel, 'How China is leading the renewable energy revolution', *World Economic Forum*, 29 August 2017, https://www.weforum.org/agenda/2017/08/how-china-is-leading-the-renewable-energy-revolution

5 Ibid.

6 'Global Trends in Renewable Energy Investment 2017', *Frankfurt School of Finance and Management*, April 2017, https://www.researchgate.net/publication/318987792_Global_Trends_in_Renewable_Energy_Investment_2017

7 'China Set to Dominate US in Global Renewables Boom', *Institute of Energy Economics and Financial Analysis (IEEFA)*, 6 January 2017, http://ieefa.org/ieefa-report-china-set-dominate-%E2%80%A8global-renewable-energy-boom-expands-lead-u-s/

8 Ibid.

9 Adam Minter, 'China Wants to Power the World', *Bloomberg Opinion*, 4 April 2016, https://www.bloomberg.com/view/articles/2016-04-03/china-s-state-grid-wants-to-power-the-whole-world

10 Michael Slezak, 'China cementing global dominance of renewable energy and technology', *Guardian*, 6 January 2017, https://www.theguardian.com/environment/2017/jan/06/china-cementing-global-dominance-of-renewable-energy-and-technology

11 Akshat Rathi, 'Chinese companies account for 90 per cent of the production of lithium', *Quartz*, 30 May 2018, https://qz.com/1292202/china-now-effectively-controls-half-the-worlds-lithium-production/

12 Julia Ebner, 'Europe's rare earth dependence on China: Future perspectives', *EIAS* Briefing Paper, December 2014, http://www.eias.org/wp-content/uploads/2016/02/EIAS_Briefing_Paper_2014-7_Ebner.pdf

13 Takuma Yatsui, 'China's Energy Policy and Related Issues towards 2020', *Mitsui Global Strategic Studies Institute Monthly Report*, April 2017, https://www.mitsui.com/mgssi/en/report/detail/__icsFiles/afieldfile/2017/07/19/170406c_yatsui_e_1.pdf

14 Yimin Liu, Yong Yang and Erica Klampfl, 'Energy Challenges the Automobile Industry Faces in China', *International Association of Energy Economics*, Quarter 2010, https://www.iaee.org/en/publications/newsletterdl.aspx?id=97

15 'Renewable Energy and Jobs: Annual Review 2016', *International Renewable Energy Agency* (IRENA), https://www.irena.org/publications/2016/May/Renewable-Energy-and-Jobs--Annual-Review-2016

16 Angus Maddison, 'Chinese Economic Performance in the Long Run', *OECD Development Centre*, Second Edition Revised and Updated 960-2030 ad, 2007, http://piketty.pse.ens.fr/files/Maddison07.pdf

17 'Statistical Review of World Energy', *British Petroleum*, 2017, https://www.bp.com/content/dam/bp-country/de_ch/PDF/bp-statistical-review-of-world-energy-2017-full-report.pd>

18 Ibid.

19 Joe Myers, 'China's working-age population will fall 23 per cent by 2050', *World Economic Forum*, (WEF, 25 July 2016), https://www.weforum.org/agenda/2016/07/china-working-ageing-population/

20 International Monetary Fund, 'People's Republic of China: Selected Issues', *IMF Country Report*, Vol. 17(248), August 2017, https://www.imf.org/en/Publications/CR/Issues/2017/08/15/People-s-Republic-of-China-Selected-Issues-45171

21 Robert C. Allen, 'Energy Transitions in History: Shift to Coal', *RCC Perspectives*, No. 2, Global Cases of Continuity and Change, 2013, p.p. 11–16, http://www.environmentandsociety.org/perspectives/2013/2/article/energy-transitions-history-shift-coal

22 Ibid.

23 Fridolin Krausmann, 'The Social metabolism of European Industrialisation: Changes in the Relation of Energy and Land Use from the 18th to the 20th century', *RCC Perspectives*, No. 2, Energy

Transitions in History: Global Cases of Continuity and Change, 2013, p.p. 31–36, http://www.environmentandsociety.org/sites/default/files/seiten_aus_2013_i2_web-4_0.pdf

24 Rossana Galli, 'The Relationship Between Energy Intensity and Income Levels: Forecasting Long Term Energy Demand in Asian Emerging Countries', *Energy Journal*, 19(4), October 1998, pp. 85–106, https://www.researchgate.net/publication/227363514_The_Relationship_Between_Energy_Intensity_and_Income_Levels_Forecasting_Long_Term_Energy_Demand_in_Asian_Emerging_Countries

25 Bin Liu, 'China's Solar Industry at Crossroads', https://www.chinadialogue.net/article/show/single/en/10775-China-s-solar-industry-is-at-a-crossroads, August 2018

26 BNEF, Conference Presentation at Energy and Mobility Transitions, 4 February 2019, San Francisco

27 Indra Overland, The Geopolitics of Renewable Energy: Debunking Four Emerging Myths, 2019 Volume 49, pp 36-40, April

28 Goksin Kavlak, James McNerney, Jessika E. Trancik, 'Evaluating the causes of cost reduction in photovoltaic module Energy Policy, 2018, 123 (C): 700-710, Elsevier

6. China as India's Main Bulk Drugs Supplier: Helplessness or Cautious Evolution?

1 'Baba Ramdev gets trolled for his tweet on boycotting Chinese products; here's why', *Indian Express*, 27 October 2016, https://indianexpress.com/article/trending/trending-in-india/baba-ramdev-gets-trolled-for-his-tweet-on-boycotting-chinese-products-heres-why-3105304/ [Accessed on 22 July 2017].

2 Definition: Bulk drugs or active pharmaceutical ingredients (API) are the basic chemicals and ingredients necessary to produce medicines. When active ingredients are put into dosage forms, they become formulations ready for use by patients. (Source: Joseph, Reji K., *Pharmaceutical industry and public policy in post-reform India*, New Delhi: Routledge, 2016.)

3 Naga G. Sridhar, 'Centre looks to trim drug input imports from China', *Hindu Business Line*, 3 August 2017, https://www.thehindubusinessline.com/economy/centre-looks-to-trim-drug-input-imports-from-china/article22085538.ece1 [Accessed on 7 August 2017].

4 Op cit.
5 Ibid.
6 Ibid.
7 'List of importing markets for a product exported by India', *Trademap.org*, https://www.trademap.org/Country_SelProductCountry_TS.aspx?nvpm=1|699||||30|||2|1|1|2|2|1|2|1|1 [Accessed on 22 July 2018].
8 United Nations, *Comtrade Database*, https://comtrade.un.org/data/ [Accessed on 22 July 2017].
9 Ari Altstedter, 'Why India's generic-drug industry has a long way to go to gain US FDA's trust', *Mint*, 24 January, 2017, https://www.livemint.com/Industry/cK6JIaYhi07KyYmDb3w9QP/Why-Indias-genericdrug-industry-has-a-long-way-to-go-to-ga.html [Accessed on 22 July 2017].
10 'Sector Report: Pharmaceuticals', *India Brand Equity Foundation*, June 2017, https://www.ibef.org/download/Pharmaceutical-June-2017.pdf [Accessed on 22 July 2017].
11 'Realizing "Make in India" – Journey to become the most preferred manufacturer of high quality affordable medicines', Federation of Indian Chambers of Commerce and Industry, 2015, http://ficci.in/spdocument/20712/Final-Realizing-Make-in-India-Vision.pdf [Accessed on 22 July 2017].
12 Ibid.
13 'Task Force to Explore Options other than Price Control for Achieving the Objective of Making Available Life-saving Drugs at Reasonable Prices', *Department of Chemicals and Petrochemicals, Government of India*, 2005, http://pharmaceuticals.gov.in/sites/default/files/Dr.%20Pronab%20Sen%20Committee%20Report1_0.pdf [Accessed on 22 July 2017].
14 Soma Das, 'India relies on China for 90 per cent of drug raw materials', *Economic Times*, 29 October 2014, http://economictimes.indiatimes.com/articleshow/44965918.cms?utm_source=contentofinterest&utm_medium=text&utm_campaign=cppst [Accessed on 4 July 2017].
15 Op cit.
16 Op cit.
17 Jan-Ulrich Rothacher, 'The ambivalent influence of the domestic industries on India's meandering foreign economic policies', *India Review*, 15 (1), 12 February 2016, pp. 61–97.
18 Op cit.

19 'Indian policies to promote local production of pharmaceutical products and protect public health', *World Health Organization*, 2017, licence-CC BY-NC-SA 3.0 IGO, https://www.who.int/phi/publications/2081India020517.pdf
20 Op cit.
21 Op cit.
22 Op cit.
23 Rohit Malpani, 'Trading away health', the *Hindu*, 23 July 2017, https://www.thehindu.com/sci-tech/health/trading-away-health/article19333287.ece [Accessed on 2 August 2017].
24 Christoph Lübbert, Christian Baars, Anil Dayakar, Norman Lippmann, Arne C. Rodloff, Martina Kinzig and Fritz Sörgel, 'Environmental pollution with antimicrobial agents from bulk drug manufacturing industries in Hyderabad, South India, is associated with dissemination of extended-spectrum beta-lactamase and carbapenemase-producing pathogens', *Infection*, 45(4), 2017, pp. 479–91.
25 Jacob Shine, 'Chinese scare looms over India's bulk drug industry', *Mint*, 3 November 2015, <https://www.livemint.com/Industry/L8C3Zb8G80FsCxu97IVj1K/Chinese-scare-looms-over-Indias-bulk-drug-industry.html> [Accessed on 22 July 2017].
26 Deepak Patel, 'Bulk drug parks: Still waiting for financial backing', *Indian Express*, 7 June 2017, https://indianexpress.com/article/business/bulk-drug-parks-still-waiting-for-financial-backing-ajit-doval-china-4692287/ [Accessed on 22 July 2017].
27 *IDMA Bulletin*, 2017, XLVIII (07), https://idma-assn.org/pdf/55th-annual-day-report.pdf [Accessed on 22 July 2017].
28 Op cit.
29 Ibid.

7. Harmonizing Ayush and Modern Medicine: Can India Learn from China?

1 Gerard Bodeker, 'Lessons on integration from the developing world's experience: Traditional medicine', *British Medical Journal*, 322(7279), 2001, p.p. 164–7.
2 Felix Cheung, 'Made in China', *Nature*, 480(22), 2011, pp. S82–3.

3 'Why China's traditional medicine boom is dangerous', *Economist*, 1 September 2017, https://www.economist.com/china/2017/09/01/why-chinas-traditional-medicine-boom-is-dangerous [accessed on 02 January 2018].
4 Shalini Rudra, Aakshi Kalra, Abhishek Kumar and William Joe, 'Utilization of alternative systems of medicine as health care services in India: Evidence on AYUSH care from NSS 2014', *PloS One*, 12(5), 4 May 2017, 0176916.
5 Sarah Cant and Ursula Sharma, 'A New Medical Pluralism: Complementary Medicine, Doctors, Patients and the State', London: Routledge, 2004.
6 Ministry of AYUSH website, *Government of India*, http://ayush.gov.in/about-us/about-the-ministry [Accessed on 02 January 2018].
7 'Ministry of AYUSH Annual Report 2016-17', *Ministry of AYUSH,* New Delhi: Government of India, http://ayush.gov.in/sites/default/files/ANNUAL%20R%20EPORT%202016-17%20ENGLISH.pdf [Accessed on 02 January 2018].
8 Ibid.
9 Milton I. Roemer, *National Health Systems of the World*, New York: Oxford University Press, 1993.
10 Ed. Marshall W. Raffel, , *Comparative Health Systems: Descriptive Analyses of Fourteen National Health Systems*, London: Pennsylvania State University Press, 1984.
11 Ibid.
12 Wang, Liang, Suo, Sizhuo, Li, Jian, Hu, Yuanjia, Li, Peng, Wang, Yitao and Hu, Hao, 'An Investigation into Traditional Chinese Medicine Hospitals in China: Development Trend and Medical Service Innovation', *International Journal of Health Policy and Management*, 6(1), January 2017, p. 19.
13 Ed. Marshall W. Raffel, , *Comparative Health Systems: Descriptive Analyses of Fourteen National Health Systems*, London: Pennsylvania State University Press, 1984.
14 Janmejaya Samal, 'Role of AYUSH Workforce, Therapeutics, and Principles in Health Care Delivery with Special Reference to National Rural Health Mission', *Ayu*, 36(1), January–March 2015, p. 5.
15 Ibid.
16 'Report of Committee on empowering of AYUSH,' *Government of India*, New Delhi: Ministry of Health and Family Welfare, 2012.

17 Ibid.

18 Ibid.

19 Sandra Albert and John Porter, 'Is "mainstreaming AYUSH" the right policy for Meghalaya, northeast India?' *BMC Complementary and Alternative Medicine*, Vol. 15(1), 18 August 2015, p. 288.

20 Press Trust of India, 'Ayurvedic dengue cure: Indian scientists create first of its kind drug to treat the disease', *Hindustan Times*, 17 April 2018, https://www.hindustantimes.com/health/ayurvedic-dengue-cure-indian-scientists-create-first-of-its-kind-drug-to-treat-the-disease/story-7JE1Qj4u0ptwbTLg6gOh9K.html> [Accessed on 03 August 2018].

21 'Maharashtra Govt Issues Notification Allowing Homeopaths To Continue Practicing Allopathy, Leaves IMA Fuming', *Huffington Post India*, 5 October 2017, <https://www.huffingtonpost.in/2017/10/05/maharashtra-govt-issues-notification-allowing-homeopaths-to-continue-practicing-allopathy-leaves-ima-fuming_a_23233328/> [Accessed on 02 January 2018].

22 Ibid.

23 'Bill Introduced in Lok Sabha Seeks to Allow Ayurveda, Homeopathy Doctors to Practice Allopathy', the *Wire*, 1 January 2018, https://thewire.in/health/bill-introduced-in-lok-sabha-allowing-ayurveda-homeopathy-doctors-to-practice-allopathy [Accessed on 02 January 2018].

24 Saubhadra Chatterji, 'No "crosspathy": House panel to oppose bridge course on allopathy for AYUSH practitioners', *Hindustan Times*, 23 February 2018, https://www.hindustantimes.com/india-news/no-crosspathy-house-panel-to-oppose-bridge-course-on-allopathy-for-ayush-practitioners/story-ZdL3iADGtUMAb0D2mr54BN.html [Accessed on 25 February 2018].

25 Dharminder Nagar, 'Integration of AYUSH Doctors into Modern Medicine Has Both Benefits and Fallouts', *Economic Times*, 11 January 2017, https://health.economictimes.indiatimes.com/news/industry/integration-of-ayush-doctors-into-modern-medicine-has-both-benefits-and-fallouts/56478296 [Accessed on 02 January 2018].

26 Ibid.

27 Shalini Rudra, 'Immunisation coverage: India far away from meeting targets', *Health Express*, ORF Expert Speak, 1 April 2017, https://www.

orfonline.org/expert-speak/immunisation-coverage-india-far-away-from-meeting-targets/ [Accessed on 02 January 2018].

28 Hao Yu, 'Universal health insurance coverage for 1.3 billion people: What accounts for China's success?' *Health policy*, Vol. 119(9), 2015, pp. 1145–52.

29 Jae-Mahn Shim, , 'Three plural medical systems in East Asia: interpenetrative pluralism in China, exclusionary pluralism in Korea and subjugatory pluralism in Japan', *Health Policy and Planning*, Vol. 33(3), 01 April 2018, p.p. 401–10.

30 'Legal Status of Traditional Medicine and Complementary/Alternative Medicine:
A Worldwide Review', *World Health Organization*, PAHO, 2001, http://www1.paho.org/spanish/ad/ths/ev/PM-WHOTraditional_medicines_legal_status.pdf [Accessed on 02 January 2018].

8. The Mystery of China's Shrinking Megacities

1 Philip Wen, Yawen Chen, 'Backlash as Beijing fire safety blitz forces exodus of city's underclass', *Reuters*, 28 November 2017, https://uk.reuters.com/article/uk-china-fire/backlash-as-beijing-fire-safety-blitz-forces-exodus-of-citys-underclass-idUKKBN1DS08E

2 Elias Glenn, 'Beijing to demolish 15 square miles of illegal structures', *Reuters*, 24 January 2018, https://uk.reuters.com/article/uk-china-migrants/beijing-to-demolish-15-square-miles-of-illegal-structures-idUKKBN1FD0RG

3 Du Juan, 'Beijing drop in population first for 17 yrs', *China Daily*, 22 January 2018, http://global.chinadaily.com.cn/a/201801/22/WS5a6526d1a3106e7dcc1359c4.html

4 Helen Roxburg, 'China's radical plan to limit the populations of Beijing and Shanghai', *Guardian*, 19 March 2018, https://www.theguardian.com/cities/2018/mar/19/plan-big-city-disease-populations-fall-beijing-shanghai

5 Compilation and Translation Bureau, Central Committee of the Communist Party of China, 'The 13th Five-Year Plan for Economic and Social Development of the People's Republic of China', 2016–20, http://en.ndrc.gov.cn/newsrelease/201612/P020161207645765233498.pdf

6 Xinhua, 'China's urbanization plan 2014–20', *China Daily*, 18 March 2014, http://www.chinadaily.com.cn/business/2014-03/18/content_17355936.htm
7 'Beijing, Shanghai record first population decline in 40 years', 24 January 2018, *The Straits Times*, https://www.straitstimes.com/asia/east-asia/beijing-shanghai-record-first-population-decline-in-40-years

9. China Will Have to Hyphenate Itself with the Rule of Law

1 Ankit Panda, 'US, Japan, India, and Australia Holding Working-Level Quadrilateral Meeting on Regional Cooperation', *Diplomat,* 13 November 2017.
2 Peter Guy, 'Nepal and Pakistan pulling the plug on Belt and Road plans, casts spotlight on public tender issues', *South China Morning Post,* 20 November 2017.
3 Wayne M. Morrison, 'China Economic Rise: History, Trends, Challenges, and Implications for the United States', *Congressional Research Service,* 15 September, 2017, https://fas.org/sgp/crs/row/RL33534.pdf
4 Xiao Geng, Xiuke Yang and Anna Janus, 'State-owned enterprises in China: Reform Dynamics and Impacts', Ross Garnaut, Ligang Song and Wing Thye Woo (eds.), *China's New Place in a World in Crisis*, Canberra: Australian National University Press, 2009, pp. 155–78.
5 Susan Trevaskes, 'China's party-led rule-of-law regime', *East Asia Forum,* 2 October 2017.
6 'China 2030: Building a Modern, Harmonious, and Creative Society', *World Bank and the Development Research Center of the State Council, the People's Republic of China*, Washington DC: World Bank, 2013.
7 Ibid.

10. India, China and the Ironies of Maoism

1 However, some experts trace the origins of the Indian Maoist movement to the Telangana movement (1946–51) when Indian Communists, inspired by Chairman Mao's 'people's war', took up armed struggle in

rural Telangana to free peasants from feudal rule. Led by the Communist Party of India (CPI), the agrarian uprising was initially organized around simple demands related to the eviction of peasants from their land. When met with the combined repression by landlords and the Nizam's administrative machinery, it quickly expanded into a movement for overthrow of Nizam's rule. The movement then went underground, and the Communists found refuge in the thick forests of northern Andhra. It was during this period that the revolutionaries began working with the tribals, laying the foundation for the subsequent focus of the Maoists on tribal deprivation. Venugopal, N., *Understanding Maoists: Note on Participant observation in Andhra Pradesh*, Kolkata: Setu Prakashani Publications, 2014; also Balagopal, K., 'Maoist Movement in Andhra Pradesh', *Economic and Political Weekly*, 22 July 2006.

2 Rabindra Ray, *The Naxalites and their Ideology*, Delhi: Oxford University Press, 1992.

3 For an interesting perspective on this, see Arun Mukherjee's blog, https://www.cse.iitk.ac.in/users/amit/books/mukherjee-2007-maoist-spring-thunder.html

4 For more, read Sudeep Chakravarti, *Red Sun, Travels in Naxalite Country*, New Delhi: Penguin, 26 November 2008.

5 With Kanu Sanyal and other leaders, Charu Mazumdar formed the All India Coordination Committee of Communist Revolutionaries (AICCCR) in 1967. This forum which rejected the parliamentary path (election) and opted for violent rebellion led to a formal split in the mother party (CPI) in 1969. Consequently, on 22 April 1969 (coinciding with Lenin's birthday), the Communist Party of India (Marxist-Leninist) was formed by AICCCR with Charu Majumdar as Secretary of the Central Organizing Committee. It must be mentioned that Charu Mazumdar and Kanu Sanyal were vital to the formation of Communist Party of India, Marxist-Leninist [CPI(M-L)] in April 1969, and the basic objective of the party was spelt out in its resolution adopted at the first party congress in 1970 that 'India's liberation would be achieved by a People's War, which would involve creating small bases of armed struggle all over the country by waging guerrilla warfare'. See Sumanta Banerjee, *India's Simmering Revolution*, New Delhi: Select Book Syndicate, 1980.

6 Sudeep Chakravarti, '"Naxal" Mao: Method over the man', *Mint*, 20 April 2017. https://www.livemint.com/Opinion/q6NEKYKLJM0iGoBlKXd9bO/Naxal-Mao-Method-over-the-man.html

11. Decoding China's New Threat from ISIS

1 Lucy Hornby, 'Isis Uyghurs threaten "rivers of blood" in China', *Financial Times*, 2 March 2017, https://www.ft.com/content/ddeb5872-ff1f-11e6-96f8-3700c5664d30
2 Teddy Ng, 'Eight killed in Xinjiang knife attack: police shoot three attackers', *South China Morning Post*, 15 February 2017, https://www.scmp.com/news/china/society/article/2070868/eight-killed-xinjiang-knife-attack
3 Colin P. Clarke and Paul Rexton Kan, 'Uyghur Foreign Fighters: An Underexamined Jihadist Challenge', *International Centre for Counter-Terrorism – The Hague*, November 2017, p. 3, https://icct.nl/wp-content/uploads/2017/11/ClarkeKan-Uyghur-Foreign-Fighters-An-Underexamined-Jihadist-Challenge-Nov-2017-1.pdf
4 Ben Blanchard, 'Syria says up to 5,000 Chinese Uyghurs fighting in militant groups', *Reuters*, 11 May 2017, https://www.reuters.com/article/uk-mideast-crisis-syria-china/syria-says-up-to-5000-chinese-Uyghurs-fighting-in-militant-groups-idUSKBN1840UP
5 Lin Meilian, 'Xinjiang terrorists finding training, support in Syria, Turkey', *Global Times*, 1 July 2013, http://www.globaltimes.cn/content/792959.shtml
6 Leith Aboufadel, 'Uyghur Terrorist Killed by the Syrian Army in Northwest Hama', *Al Masdar News*, 26 October 2015, https://www.almasdarnews.com/article/uyghur-terrorist-killed-by-the-syrian-army-in-northwest-hama/
7 Thomas Joscelyn and Bill Roggio, 'Turkistan Islamic Party criticizes the Islamic State's "illegitimate" caliphate', *Long War Journal*, 11 June 2016, https://www.longwarjournal.org/archives/2016/06/turkistan-islamic-party-leader-remains-loyal-to-al-qaeda-criticizes-islamic-states-illegitimate-caliphate.php

8 Nodirbek Soliev, 'How serious is the Islamic State threat to China?' *Diplomat*, 14 March 2017, https://thediplomat.com/2017/03/how-serious-is-the-islamic-state-threat-to-china/

12. China's Dark Secret Is Out, but the World Is Silent

1 'Opinion: China's Repugnant Campaign to Destroy a Minority People', *Washington Post*, 20 May 2018, https://www.washingtonpost.com/opinions/chinas-repugnant-campaign-to-destroy-a-minority-people/2018/05/20/9fe061b4-5ac0-11e8-b656-a5f8c2a9295d_story.html?noredirect=on&utm_term=.9e816d9f6d58 [Accessed 09 October 2018].

2 Gerry Shih and Dake Kang, 'Muslims Forced to Drink Alcohol and Eat Pork in China's "re-education" Camps, Former Inmate Claims', *Independent*, 18 May 2018, https://www.independent.co.uk/news/world/asia/china-re-education-muslims-ramadan-xinjiang-eat-pork-alcohol-communist-xi-jinping-a8357966.html [Accessed 09 October 2018].

3 'UN calls on China to free 1 million Uyghurs from alleged re-education camps', *ABC News*, 31 August 2018, http://www.abc.net.au/news/2018-08-31/un-calls-on-china-to-free-Uyghurs-from-re-education-camps/10185962 [Accessed 09 October 2018].

4 Nathan Vanderklippe, 'Beijing is spending its way to "an experiment of what is possible" to police Xinjiang's Uyghurs', *Globe and Mail*, 8 March 2018, https://www.theglobeandmail.com/news/world/beijing-increases-presence-over-xinjiangs-uyghurs/article38256591/ [Accessed 09 October 2018].

5 RFA Staff, 'Xinjiang Political "Re-Education Camps" Treat Uyghurs "Infected by Religious Extremism": CCP Youth League', *Radio Free Asia*, 8 August 2018, https://www.rfa.org/english/news/uyghur/infected-08082018173807.html [Accessed 09 October 2018].

6 Nathan Vanderklippe, '"It is about Xi as the Leader of the World": Former Detainees Recount Abuse in Chinese Re-education Centres', *Globe and Mail*, 3 July 2018, https://www.theglobeandmail.com/world/article-former-detainees-recount-abuse-in-chinese-re-education-centres/ [Accessed 09 October 2018].

7 David Brunnstrom and Philip Wen, 'Group of U.S. Lawmakers Urges China Sanctions over Xinjiang Abuses', *Reuters*, 30 August 2018, https://www.reuters.com/article/us-usa-china-rights/group-of-u-s-lawmakers-urges-china-sanctions-over-xinjiang-abuses-idUSKCN1LE2MK [Accessed 09 October 2018].

8 Stephanie Nebehay, 'U.N. calls on China to free Uyghurs from alleged re-education camps', *Reuters*, 30 August 2018, https://www.reuters.com/article/us-china-rights-un/u-n-calls-on-china-to-free-Uyghurs-from-re-education-camps-idUSKCN1LF1D6 [Accessed 09 October 2018].

9 'Xinjiang Profile – Full Overview', *BBC News*, 17 November 2016 https://www.bbc.com/news/world-asia-pacific-16913494 [Accessed 09 October 2018].

10 Ben Westcott, 'Imran Khan Dodges Questions on Chinese Muslim Detentions', *CNN*, 29 March 2019.

11 Alexandra Ma, 'Pakistan Abruptly Stopped Calling out China's Mass Oppression of Muslims. Critics Say Beijing Bought Its Silence', *Business Insider*, 13 January 2019, https://www.businessinsider.in/Pakistan-abruptly-stopped-calling-out-Chinas-mass-oppression-of-Muslims-Critics-say-Beijing-bought-its-silence/articleshow/67511387.cms [accessed 11 April 2019].

12 Jyoti Malhotra and Simrin Sirur, 'Friend China is torturing Muslims, but Islamic Republic Pakistan is quiet. Here's why', *The Print*, 3 September 2018, https://theprint.in/governance/friend-china-is-torturing-muslims-but-islamic-republic-pakistan-is-quiet-heres-why/110477/ [accessed 9 October 2018].

13 Al Jazeera, '"Shame for Humanity': Turkey Urges China to Close Uyghur Camps', Al Jazeera, February 2019.

14 Gerry Shih, 'After Years of Silence, Turkey Rebukes China for Mass Detention of Muslim Uyghurs', *Washington Post*, February 2019.

15 Ben Farmer, Sophia Yan and Umar Farooq, '"We Owe China, What Can We Do?" Why Muslim Countries Stay Silent over China's Mass Detention of Uyghurs', *Telegraph*, 19 January 2019.

16 Alexandra Ma, 'Why the Muslim world isn't saying anything about China's repression and "cultural cleansing" of its downtrodden Muslim minority', *Business Insider*, 27 August 2018, https://www.businessinsider.in/Why-the-Muslim-world-isnt-saying-anything-about-Chinas-

repression-and-cultural-cleansing-of-its-downtrodden-Muslim-minority/articleshow/65559376.cms

13. China's Strategy for the International Satcom Market

1 Nikolas Kozloff, 'Hugo Chávez's geopolitical rivalry reaching soaring new heights', *Huffington Post*, 14 June 2010, https://www.huffingtonpost.com/nikolas-kozloff/hugo-chvezs-geopolitical_b_609870.html
2 Ananth Baliga and Vong Sokheng, 'Cambodia again blocks ASEAN statement on South China Sea', the *Phnom Penh Post*, 25 July 2016, https://www.phnompenhpost.com/national/cambodia-again-blocks-asean-statement-south-china-sea
3 Darren Touch, 'What Does Chinese Investment Mean for Cambodia?' *Diplomat*, 2 February 2018, https://thediplomat.com/2018/02/what-does-chinese-investment-mean-for-cambodia/
4 Nandini Krishnamoorthy, 'Laos backs China over South China Sea dispute, rejects Hague ruling', *International Business Times*, 15 July 2016, https://www.ibtimes.co.uk/laos-backs-china-over-south-china-sea-dispute-rejects-hague-ruling-1570737
5 'FG, CGWIC sign NigComSat 2 and 3 Framework Agreement', *NigComSat*, 29 March 2016, http://nigcomsat.gov.ng/news.php
6 Jason Rainbow, 'Making Sri Lanka a global space player', *Satellite Finance*, 13 March 2015, https://drive.google.com/file/d/0BzsiAYWJ3hPMVjZFZGJ3dXFaNjQ/view
7 Charundi Panagoda, 'It's ChinaSat-12 with a Lankan payload', *Sunday Times*, 2 December 2012, http://www.sundaytimes.lk/121202/news/its-chinasat-12-with-a-lankan-payload-23100.html
8 Malcolm Davis, 'The coming of China's Space Silk Road', *Strategist*, Australian Strategic Policy Institute, 11 August 2017, https://www.aspistrategist.org.au/coming-chinas-space-silk-road/
9 Caleb Henry, 'Back-to-back commercial satellite wins leave China Great Wall hungry for more', *Space News*, 22 August 2017, http://spacenews.com/back-to-back-commercial-satellite-wins-leave-china-great-wall-hungry-for-more/
10 Andrew Jones, 'China expects 10 per cent global satellite market share by 2020', *GB Times*, 1 June 2016, https://gbtimes.com/china-expects-10-per cent-global-satellite-market-share-2020

14. Academia: A New Frontier in China's Foreign Policy

1. Leslie Shaffer, 'Pro-Beijing professor expelled from Singapore for being "agent" of foreign power', *CNBC*, 7 August 2017, https://www.cnbc.com/2017/08/07/pro-beijing-professor-expelled-from-singapore-for-being-agent-of-foreign-power.html
2. 'A message from Confucius', *Economist*, 22 October 2009, https://www.economist.com/special-report/2009/10/22/a-message-from-confucius
3. '500 Confucius institutes worldwide', *Global Times*, 4 December 2015, http://www.globaltimes.cn/content/956498.shtml
4. Matteo Mecacci, et al, 'The Debate over Confucius Institutes in the United States', *Foreign Policy*, 11 July 2014, https://foreignpolicy.com/2014/07/11/the-debate-over-confucius-institutes-in-the-united-states/
5. Rachelle Peterson, 'Outsourced to China: Confucius institutes and Soft Power in American Higher Education', *National Association of Scholars (NAS)*, April 2017, https://www.nas.org/images/documents/confucius_institutes/NAS_confuciusInstitutes.pdf
6. 'On Partnerships with Foreign Governments: The Case of Confucius Institutes', *American Association of University Professors (AAUP)*, June 2014, https://www.aaup.org/file/Confucius_Institutes_0.pdf
7. Peter Foster, 'China Soft Power set back as US universities shut second Confucius Institute in a week', *Telegraph*, 1 October 2014, https://www.telegraph.co.uk/news/worldnews/northamerica/usa/11133921/China-soft-power-set-back-as-US-universities-shut-second-Confucius-Institute-in-a-week.html
8. Michael Martina, 'China's Xi calls for universities' allegiance to the Communist Party', *Reuters*, 9 December 2016, https://www.reuters.com/article/us-china-education/chinas-xi-calls-for-universities-allegiance-to-the-communist-party-idUSKBN13Y0B5

Index

A Note on the Contributors

Vidya Sagar Reddy Avuthu is a research analyst at Jane's by IHS Markit. Previously, he was an associate fellow in the Nuclear and Space Policy Initiative of Observer Research Foundation.

Meghna Bal is a lawyer and a technology policy researcher based in New Delhi. She has previously been with Observer Research Foundation, New Delhi.

Joyeeta Bhattacharjee is a senior fellow with ORF's Neighbourhood Regional Studies Initiative. She specializes in India's neighbourhood policy, Bangladesh's domestic politics and foreign policy, border management, conflict and conflict resolution in India's northeast.

Preety Bhogal is a graduate student in the Department of Economics at Kansas State University, United States. Prior to this, she was working with the Observer Research Foundation as a junior fellow. Her research interests lie in the areas of international trade, WTO, behavioural economics and agriculture.

Arka Biswas is associate fellow, Observer Research Foundation. He has previously served as the intelligence specialist at Pinkerton's Global Risk Group, South Asia Visiting Fellow at Stimson Center and Research Associate at Vivekananda International Foundation.

Kartik Bommakanti is an associate fellow in the Strategic Studies Programme at the ORF, New Delhi. He is a specialist on space military issues and strategic coercion.

Malancha Chakrabarty works as a fellow at the Observer Research Foundation, New Delhi. She researches on India's economic relations with African countries. Her doctoral research focused on the economic impact of China on Africa.

Rakhahari Chatterji is currently advisor, ORF, Kolkata and was formerly a professor in political science and dean of the Faculty of Arts, Calcutta University.

Anasua Basu Ray Chaudhury is a senior fellow with ORF's Neighbourhood Initiative. She specializes in South Asia, energy politics, forced migration and women in conflict zones.

Gautam Chikermane is vice-president at Observer Research Foundation. His areas of research focus on economic policies of India and the G20 nations. Earlier, he has held leadership positions at some of India's top newspapers. His last book was *70 Policies That Shaped India* (Observer Research Foundation, 2018).

Pushan Das is an associate fellow and programme coordinator working at ORF. He tracks and analyses developments in Indian foreign and security policies. He is currently working on issues related to Indian military modernization.

Kanak Gokarn is a former research assistant at ORF. Her research interests include Russian foreign policy, India–Russia relations and matters related to energy. She is currently pursuing her master's in international energy from Sciences Po in Paris.

Gayathri Iyer is a researcher for the Strategic Studies programme at the Observer Research Foundation, New Delhi, tracking maritime policy, ocean governance and international maritime trade. She has worked at the legal department for Multilateral Diplomacy Programme with UNITAR, UNOG and has trained as a remote participation moderator for multilateral diplomacy and dialogue at the ITU in Geneva.

Manoj Joshi is a distinguished fellow with the Observer Research Foundation. He has an abiding interest on national security issues and currently his research is focused on China.

K.V. Kesavan, a noted Indian scholar in Japanese studies, is a distinguished fellow at Observer Research Foundation, New Delhi. He was on the faculty of the Center for East Asian Studies, Jawaharlal Nehru University, for over thirty years. In 2011, the Emperor of Japan conferred on him the Order of the Rising Sun for his contribution to Japanese studies in India.

Keshav Kelkar was a programme coordinator and research fellow for China at Observer Research Foundation. Keshav holds a master's in Asia Pacific Policy Studies from the University of British Columbia and a master's in China Studies (Economics and Management) from Peking University.

Oommen C. Kurian focuses on the political economy of health care as well as nutrition policy in India, while tracking the national implementation of the Sustainable Development Goals. He is currently a fellow at ORF, where he leads the Health Initiative.

Ashok Malik is press secretary to the President of India. At the time he wrote the original piece, he was distinguished fellow at Observer Research Foundation, New Delhi. The essay, 'India, China and The BRI' reflects his personal views.

Ketan Mehta is a research assistant with ORF's Strategic Studies programme. His current research is focused on the foreign policies of emerging powers.

Maya Mirchandani is a broadcast journalist with vast reporting experience on Indian foreign policy. She now teaches media studies at Ashoka University and is a senior fellow at Observer Research Foundation.

Abhishek Mishra is a research assistant with ORF's Strategic Studies Programme. His primary research interest includes India and Africa's maritime cooperation in the Indian Ocean Region.

Sylvia Mishra is a 2019 India-US Fellow at New America. Her research is focused on Asian security, India–US relations and South Asian nuclear dynamics. She has been a Scoville fellow at the Nuclear Threat Initiative, visiting fellow at Center for Non-proliferation Studies and a nuclear scholar at the Center for Strategic and International Studies.

Sonali Mittra was a programme director at Observer Research Foundation, New Delhi. She has also worked as an academy senior fellow at Chatham House, London.

Tuneer Mukherjee is a researcher of Asian Security Studies and is currently researching naval modernization in South Asia. Mukherjee has previously been a junior fellow with Observer Research Foundation's Maritime Policy Initiative, and a researcher with the Asia Maritime Transparency Initiative at the Center for Strategic and International Studies, Washington D.C.

Shubhangi Pandey is a junior fellow with the Strategic Studies Programme at Observer Research Foundation. Her research focuses on Afghanistan, particularly exploring internal political dynamics, developments related to terrorism, and the role of non-state militant actors in the region, including the security dynamics of South Asia.

Harsh V. Pant is director, Studies and head of the Strategic Studies Programme at Observer Research Foundation, New Delhi. He holds a joint appointment with the Department of Defence Studies and King's India Institute as professor of International Relations at King's College London. His current research is focused on Asian security issues.

Ritika Passi is an associate fellow and project editor at ORF. She looks at regional connectivity initiatives across Eurasia and the emerging Indo-Pacific, and follows developments related to Indian foreign policy and global governance.

Sebastian Paulo is a freelance researcher focusing on international development cooperation, global governance and India's role as a global development partner. He has worked for various think tanks, including Observer Research Foundation, the German Development Institute, and the OECD Development Centre.

Britta Petersen is a senior fellow at Observer Research Foundation (ORF). She mainly works on India–Europe relations as well as Afghanistan and Pakistan. Previously she was South Asia correspondent for *Financial Times Deutschland* (FTD) based in Kabul and country director for Pakistan of the Heinrich Böll Foundation (HBS).

Lydia Powell is senior fellow at Observer Research Foundation and works primarily on energy policy in India. Her most recent work includes a chapter on energy politics in India for *Oxford Handbook on Energy Politics* and a chapter on China and India and climate change negotiations for *Routledge Handbook on China-India Relations*.

Akshay Ranade is an assistant professor at MIT School of Government, Pune. Prior to that he was associated with ORF's Strategic Studies Programme in New Delhi.

Abhijnan Rej is a New Delhi-based analyst. His current research focuses on Indian foreign and defence policies and international security. Rej's research and analysis has appeared in *The Washington Quarterly*, *War on the Rocks*, *The Interpreter*, *The National Interest* (online), *Global Policy* (online), *Wired* (online), *Journal of Physics A* and *Contemporary Mathematics*.

Aparna Roy is an associate fellow working with Observer Research Foundation's Climate Change and Development Initiative. Her current research explores the impact of and vulnerability to climate change with potential for adaptation.

Shalini Rudra is associated with the Tata Trusts under the 'India Nutrition Initiative' based in New Delhi. She is part of the Data Analytics Team that engages in analysis of large-scale survey data, programmatic and official data on health and nutrition to inform stakeholders. Previously, Shalini worked as an associate fellow for the health initiative of the Observer Research Foundation, Delhi.

Premesha Saha is an associate fellow with ORF's Strategic Studies Programme. Her research focuses on Southeast Asia, East Asia and the South Pacific – spanning the Eastern Indian Ocean. Her other research interests include: Indonesia's maritime strategy, the emerging dynamics of the Indo-Pacific region, India and Southeast Asia, India's Act East Policy, Asia-Pacific multilateralism.

Niranjan Sahoo is a senior fellow at Observer Research Foundation. He anchors studies and programmes on governance, democracy, electoral reforms, conflict and insurgency and human rights.

Khalid Shah is an associate fellow at Observer Research Foundation. His work focuses on the Kashmir conflict, insurgencies and violent extremism.

Kriti Shah is a junior fellow at Observer Research Foundation. Her research focuses on the internal and external political dynamics in Afghanistan and Pakistan.

Priyanka Shah is a public health professional focusing on women's health issues. She currently works with Population Foundation of India (PFI), as part of their family-planning advocacy team. Prior to joining PFI, Priyanka was a researcher in the health initiative at Observer Research Foundation.

Mihir Swarup Sharma was trained as an economist and political scientist in Delhi and in Boston. From 2008, he edited and wrote a column for the opinion pages of *Indian Express* and *Business Standard*, both based in New Delhi, and has won a Shriram Sanlam Award for financial journalism. He is also the India columnist for Bloomberg View.

Madhulika Srikumar is an associate fellow and programme coordinator with ORF's Cyber Security and Internet Governance Initiative. Previously she worked with the Internet & Jurisdiction Project, Centre for Communication Governance.

Arun Sukumar heads ORF's cyber security and internet governance initiative and is the co-chair of CyFy: The India Conference on Cyber Security and Internet Governance. He is a member of the World Economic Forum's Global Future Council on the Digital Economy and Society.

Kabir Taneja is an associate fellow with ORF's Strategic Studies Programme. His research focuses on India's relations with West Asia, specifically looking at the domestic political dynamics, terrorism, non-state militant actors and the general security paradigm of the region.

Aarshi Tirkey is a research assistant with ORF's Strategic Studies Programme. Her research focuses on international law – its relevance and application to Indian foreign policy, such as security, trade, bilateral relations and multilateral engagements.

Sayli Udas-Mankikar is a senior fellow with Observer Research Foundation, working on issues of urban governance. An award-winning journalist, Sayli has been studying the civic, infrastructure and political landscape of India for over fifteen years.

H.H.S. Viswanathan is a distinguished fellow at Observer Research Foundation New Delhi from 2010. Earlier, he was an Indian diplomat and has served in many countries and at the Indian Ministry of External Affairs.

K. Yhome is senior fellow at Observer Research Foundation (ORF), New Delhi. His research interests cover the emerging geopolitical dynamics in South Asia and Southeast Asia. His most recent research has focused on sub-regionalism, India's neighbourhood policy and political developments in Myanmar.

Acknowledgements

As India's rise continues to shape the global economic and political architecture, its most important foreign policy priority will be to manage its relationship with China. China impinges on India's growth story in ways that are often not well understood in India and abroad.

At Observer Research Foundation (ORF), we have sought to engage China as a subject in a multidimensional way. This volume bears testimony to some of the interesting ways in which researchers at ORF have dealt with the subject over the last few years.

I would like to thank Sunjoy Joshi, chairman, ORF and Samir Saran, president, ORF for engendering an institutional environment where young scholars can work freely with the seniors without the stultifying hierarchies that often cripple research organizations, and for making me a part of this dynamic entity. This volume would not have been possible without the enthusiastic participation of ORF researchers who managed to find time for this endeavour. Some of the authors are no longer with ORF but patiently dealt with all the editorial queries.

Special thanks to Kartik Bommakanti, associate fellow, ORF for managing ORF's monthly series, China Chronicles, from where some of the material is drawn for this volume. Thanks also to Chetan Khanna and Rahil Shaikh in ORF's digital team for helping with the images used in this volume. Finally, I would like to thank Krishan Chopra of HarperCollins India for commissioning this volume, and I'm grateful for the support I received from Arcopol Chaudhuri, Usha Surampudi and Suzanne Hughe for editing this rather complex manuscript.

We present this volume hoping that it would ignite a serious debate on the impact of China on India and the rest of the world.